The Process of Interpersonal Communication

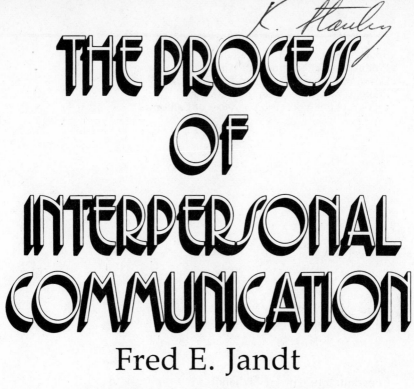

THE PROCESS OF INTERPERSONAL COMMUNICATION

Fred E. Jandt

State University College at Brockport

Canfield Press San Francisco
A Department of Harper & Row, Publishers, Inc.
New York Hagerstown London

Sponsoring Editor: Ann K. Ludwig
Production Editor: Jonathan W. Baker
Cover and Interior Designer: Jon Goodchild
Photographic Researcher: Kay Y James
Typographer: Typesetting Services of California

Library of Congress Cataloging in Publication Data

Jandt, Fred E.
   The process of interpersonal communication
   Includes index
   1.   Interpersonal communication   2.   Self-
actualization (Psychology)   3.   Socialization.
I.   Title
HM132.J35   301.11   76-366
ISBN 0-06-38-4253-X

76 77 78 10 9 8 7 6 5 4 3 2 1

Contents

Small-Group Communication and Interpersonal Conflict 139

Cross-Cultural Communication 183

7

PREFACE

¶ Why was this book written? After years of studying interpersonal communication, as both a graduate student and as a college professor, I feel I have something to say about interpersonal communication which has not been said in any other textbook. Too many of the textbooks on interpersonal communication emphasize or encourage classroom demonstrations and games and fail to help the student understand the underlying theories which make the games meaningful and which make it possible for the student to generalize and apply what is learned in the classroom situations outside the classroom. A most important point to understand about the theory of interpersonal communication is its connection with the socialization process—that interpersonal communication process through which we become who we are.

While the entire text is rooted in that belief about socialization and related theories, the importance of skills development has not been abandoned. As the general objective, the text provides a means for interpersonal communication skills development within the integrated framework. This book is designed, then, for a community college, college, or university one-quarter or one-semester introductory course in speech communication which partially or totally focuses on interpersonal communication and for which no prerequisites are required.

The book includes the topics of perception, consciousness, verbal and nonverbal communication, socialization, self-concept, interpersonal attraction, small group communication, interpersonal conflict, and cross-cultural and subcultural communication. These topics are further developed in *Adapted Readings*—selected from various sources. Some of these topics are new to interpersonal communication textbooks and are included because they naturally develop out of the underlying theory of interpersonal communication presented here. The theories discussed in the book suggest that the topics covered reflect something about the author as well—above all else a real concern for the student. I have tried to avoid writing just for my colleagues.

At times it seems impossible to discuss interpersonal communication without also discussing personal values. For example, research may indicate that in some groups the use of profanity serves definite purposes in interpersonal communication and that by understanding communication in subcultures, one may become more sensitive to communication patterns elsewhere. My emphasis in treating a wide variety of communication topics is on examination, however, not advocacy.

As the author I have chosen to organize these topics into chapters. However, as the chapters are relatively independent, this ordering of chapters may easily be adjusted according to need. For example, in a course which focuses on small group skills, Chapter 5 may be used first.

This book is intended to be foremost a learning instrument that can be used easily by the student. To facilitate this, the book has several special features: Each chapter begins with a statement of *General Objectives* to guide the reader. *Probe Questions* are used to help readers evaluate, confirm, or change their stance on the issues. *Adapted readings, figures,* and *photographs* have been carefully selected to illustrate important concepts in each chapter. A concise *Summary* concludes the chapters and helps put the chapters into perspective. The *Glossary Index* contains bold face page numbers indicating where the term definition is located. Finally, a rather complete *Instructor's Manual* prepared by Allan D. Frank and myself is available. For each chapter, the *Instructor's Manual* specifies cognitive and affective behavioral objectives, suggests learning experiences, class discussions and essay test questions, and multiple-choice questions.

Finally, I wonder if you, the students, have ever thought about the process that goes into the production of a textbook. As a student I assumed that because something was in a textbook it was somehow right and that authors were somehow important people. As I became involved in editing and writing, however, I learned that the production of a textbook, particularly an introductory textbook, involves the hard work of many people. The final product goes much beyond the author's early, formulative, ideas. It is my hope that you, the student, will find this book interesting and useful to you inside and outside of the classroom and that you, the instructor, will find the book a respectable theoretical statement and a useful guide for classroom learning.

The following people served as reviewers: Francine Busalacchi, College of Marin; Gerald Miller, Michigan State University; Daniel S. Prentice, California State University, Hayward; and Joan E. Shields, Miama-Dade Community College, South. The copyeditor was Barbara Rose. Other professional assistance I want to single out for personal thanks are: A.L.; D.H.; M.M.; V.M.; N.O.; and P.P. There is one irony which struck me about writing a book on interpersonal communication. Communication involves people; writing is a solitary activity. My family and some important friends have helped me deal with what I hope to be a temporary seclusion—C.B.; A.F.; D.J.; K.M.; and E. and J.W.—and some friends and good times I will never forget helped too—P.C.; A.D.; R.K.; M.M.; and M.S. To all of these I acknowledge my debt.

Fred E. Jandt

Photographic Credits

Chapter

1

After reading Chapter 1, you should be able to:

⁋ Develop your own definition of interpersonal communication.

⁋ Identify and define the interpersonal influences that have shaped the unique person that is you.

⁋ Identify those interpersonal encounters that make you uncomfortable and the ways in which you think you might be able to change.

⁋ Develop, with your instructor, personal objectives for your course in interpersonal communication.

INTRODUCTION

¶ In authoring this textbook, I have necessarily made some assumptions about you, the reader. I assume that you are a student in a college course that may be titled something like "Interpersonal Communication"—or some variation of those words—which is offered by a department of speech, or that you are in a course with a different sort of title but one in which your instructor wishes to focus on interpersonal communication for part of the term. Interpersonal communication is what this book is about, and as such, I feel it is useful to begin the book with a definition of that phrase.

Defining Interpersonal Communication

Historically, the traditional concern of those academicians who today are known as speech communication scholars has been the study of *persuasion,* or how one induces others to behave according to one's desires. This basic concern with the persuasive function of communication led to a preoccupation with the teaching of *public speaking;* that is, the performance and analysis of prepared speeches delivered to an audience. The ability to speak effectively in public is of definite value to many people, and public speaking may constitute a course, or segments of courses, available to you in your curriculum. Believing, though, that public speaking represents only a

What makes this an interpersonal communication situation?

small percentage of a person's communicative behavior, many speech communication theorists attempted to devise courses that they felt to be more relevant to people's daily communication needs. Two important trends have emerged from such attempts to achieve relevancy:

The first, *the communication theory approach*, adapted the theories and research techniques from the field of social psychology to the study of all forms of human communicative behavior. The most notable of these efforts was the book *The Process of Communication* by David K. Berlo, published in 1960. These adaptations have been applied to the traditional content of speech communication to make students more aware of the utility of studying and analyzing communication from a scientific perspective and better able to apply what they had learned to contemporary needs.

It has been said that all of us in our culture view ourselves as having the power to affect others and to affect the world around us. In other words, we think of ourselves as having the power to act upon our environment—from being responsible for who we are and what we do to being able to cut down and utilize a forest for our own purposes. Similarly, the communication theory approach and persuasion and public speaking focus on a communicator's attempts to manipulate the behavior of the receiver of the communication; that is, to change the behavior of others in one's environment. But in this context, the teaching of public speaking and the study of communication theory must necessarily be more a reflection of the way one views the world than they are a revelation of a universal process of human communication. Thus, the communication theory approach may be criticized in that it represents a culture-bound world view, as do persuasion and public speaking.

A recent text by Gerald R. Miller, perhaps the most influential figure among communication scholars, and Mark Steinberg, a graduate student at Michigan State University, applies the communication theory approach to interpersonal communication. They begin by explaining that when we communicate, we make predictions about the effects, or outcomes, of our communicative behavior on the basis of *cultural* information (that is, on the basis of what we know about the norms and values of our receiver's cultural group), on the basis of *sociological* information (that is, on the basis of what we know about the social group to which our receiver belongs), or on the basis of *psychological* information (or unique information about our receiver). According to Miller and Steinberg, communication based primarily on cultural and sociological predictions is *noninterpersonal*, since interpersonal communication involves predictions based primarily on the psychological level. But they argue that the basic function of all communication is to control the environment so as to realize physical, economic, or social rewards from it.[1]

The second attempt to achieve relevancy was *the small group communication approach*. Some educators began to recognize and act upon the fact that most of our communicative behavior is *not* formal, as is public speaking or broadcasting, but is very informal and personal and takes place with one, two, or a very few people we recognize and know. Thus, the defining characteristics of small group communication—and later of interpersonal communication—are an informal setting and a small number of people.

Let's review some typical definitions of interpersonal communication. In 1968, Dean C. Barnlund defined it as *the study of two or more people in face-to-face encounters sustaining focused interaction through reciprocal exchange of verbal and nonverbal cues*.[2] Let's look more closely at each of the two key phrases in Barnlund's definition: *Two or more people in face-to-face encounters*—note that Barnlund is explicitly excluding from his definition communication with oneself and communication directed to a large group of people. *Sustaining focused interaction through reciprocal exchange of . . . cues*—here Barnlund is explicitly requiring that each communicator be aware of the *intentionality* of the communication and that each communicator be capable of *understanding* the meaning of the communication (by virtue of a shared code). Note that this key phrase does not really help to *define* interpersonal communication as an awareness of the intentionality of the communication, and, too, a shared code can readily apply to any communication transaction.

Patton and Giffin, the authors of a widely used interpersonal

Does the presence of media define this as a public speaking situation?

communication text, wrote: "As opposed to one-way communication, interpersonal communication requires constant adaptation and spontaneous adjustment to the other person."[3] And, for another definition, William D. Brooks wrote: "Interpersonal communication refers to that communication in which persons are engaged directly with each other in the overt transmission and reception of messages. It does not refer to communication situations in which the sender of a message cannot communicate *directly with an individual as a person,* with each aware of the other as a unique person."[4]

At this point I suggest you review your daily encounters and characterize those which you consider to be interpersonal communication experiences, using one of the definitions presented thus far. I can guess that your list demonstrates the extent and importance of interpersonal communication in your life.

The Content of Interpersonal Communication

Invariably, students wonder about how the contents of a textbook are selected. In writing this book, I first had to consider two of the established methods used to supply information about the function and purpose of interpersonal communication. The first of these methods has its roots in humanistic psychology, or that branch of psychology that seeks to promote personal growth toward the goal of self-actualization (the realization of one's full potential). Through a selective reading of such psycholgists as Abraham Maslow, Carl Rogers, Rollo May, William Schutz, and others, speech communication theorists and educators came to view the study of interpersonal communication primarily from a therapeutic perspective. Their focus was on the communicative relationship that takes place between a trained therapist, psychoanalyst, or counselor and a client, or patient. But this method alone is insufficient in that the humanistic psychologists themselves never intended to present a theory of interpersonal communication. There is the question, too, whether speech communication educators are abandoning their own unique specialties by dealing so exclusively with the therapeutic encounter. Thus, although this textbook does not abandon this method, I have not designed it to serve as a basis for classroom therapy.

The second method used to define the function and purpose of interpersonal communication focuses on our attempts to control our environment through the process of communication. This method also concerns itself with the development of self-concept, in that our self-identity is a direct consequence of whether we succeed or fail at gaining such control. Gerald R. Miller wrote that although persuasion will continue as a focus for speech communication research and teaching, "students of communication must realize that human discourse serves other vital functions, functions that can only be labeled 'persuasive' if the term is defined in its most general, unrestricted—and therefore useless—sense. One such function is the development of self-concept and the subsequent conditioning of mental health."[5] In a book written after that statement, Miller used different words and changed his intent: "The development of self-identity is not primarily a function of communication, but rather a consequence of the outcomes of a person's communicative efforts to achieve environmental control."[6] Others, such as Cushman and Florence, have argued that interpersonal communication has as its principal goal the coordination of human activity in regard to the development, presentation, and validation of individual self-concepts.[7]

Thus, after considering the above methods, I have chosen a related but somewhat different position. This textbook proposes that the study of interpersonal communication should be about how each of us became the unique person we are as a result of interpersonal contacts. Interpersonal communication will be viewed here as the continuing process by which all of us acquire an awareness both of the attributes we hold in common with all other humans and of the attributes that distinguish us as unique individuals. For example, in this textbook you will find that the study of the socialization

Should the size of the audience affect this speaker's behaviors?

process is a central issue and that deviance is also included because interpersonal communication is central both to our individuality and to our degree of conformity.

The material that constitutes the development of this perspective is presented in seven chapters, including the present, introductory chapter. Adapted and abridged readings have been included to support and to expand on the important concepts. In none of these chapters, however, are there presented facts that you must learn to recite per se. As in all scientific disciplines, some of the ideas that today are cited as "facts" may already have been, or may soon be, proven incorrect. Instead, each of these chapters is intended to offer some ideas, which you may accept or reject, that will hopefully lead you to formulate some ideas of your own. Additionally, at certain points throughout the text you will find "probe questions" to aid you in applying these facts to your everyday life. In doing so, you will undoubtedly make use of many of your own past experiences.

Interpersonal Communication Skills

All of us have certain skills, many of which we take for granted. And one of those skills is our ability to communicate with others. No matter how successful one already is, however, there is still the opportunity for improvement. Therefore, it is useful to examine the nature of these skills so that we may become even better. Bochner and Kelly have described five interpersonal communication skills: (1) *empathic communication,* or the process whereby we form accurate impressions of other people and their communication by analyzing the content and tone of their messages so that we can correctly perceive and accept their feelings and thoughts; (2) *descriptiveness,* or the ability to make concrete, specific, and descriptive statements rather than to give vague, abstract, and evaluative messages; (3) *owning one's own feelings and thoughts* by indicating through our messages that we take responsibility for our own feelings and thoughts rather than blaming others for the way we feel; (4) *self-disclosure,* or the willingness to discuss our personal feelings; and (5) *behavioral flexibility,* or the ability to relate in new ways when necessary. [8]

It is inevitable that all of us have at least some interpersonal encounters in our normal, day-to-day interactions that make us uncomfortable and for which we desire to become more skilled. To that end, I have selected content for this volume that should enable the student to become better able to identify those interpersonal encounters that cause difficulty, such as interactions with academic advisers, persons of the opposite sex, parents, siblings, and so on, and better able to select and develop the appropriate skills for making those encounters less difficult.

The speech communication scholar James C. McCroskey has been using one method of improving communication skills by alleviating apprehension about the encounter. This method, a technique developed by behavior therapists, is called *systematic desensitization.* [9] The technique involves getting a person to associate relaxation, rather than anxiety, with a feared object or event through a gradual, step-by-step process. Joseph Wolpe describes three basic steps in systematic desensitization: training in deep muscle relaxation, construction of a list of anxiety-producing situations arranged in a hierarchy from least threatening to most threatening, and the juxtapositioning of relaxation and anxiety-evoking stimuli taken from the hierarchy. [10] The hierarchy used by McCroskey is shown in Figure 1.1. Although this particular list was developed to apply to public speaking, it can be used as a model by which you can identify some of the interpersonal encounters that make you uncomfortable.

The method McCroskey describes consists of seven one-hour sessions. During the first session, the trainer explains the procedures of systematic desensitization and plays a tape recording of instructions for attaining deep muscular relaxation. The remaining six sessions are devoted to replaying the relaxation tape until everyone reports being relaxed. After playing the tape, the trainer reads the hierarchy of items describing anxiety-producing situations. Whenever anyone begins to feel anxious he raises his right index finger and the trainer then issues instructions to the group to mentally erase the image created by that item and concentrate on relaxation. After a brief pause, the trainer again presents the same item

Below is a hierarchy of anxiety-producing stimuli designed for college students. The number in parentheses at the left indicates the degree of anxiety (on a 0.0 to 8.0 scale) associated with this stimulus for a representative sample of students.

(.3) You are talking with your best friend.

(.9) You are talking to a sales clerk in a department store.

(1.2) You are answering the telephone and do not know who is calling.

(1.7) You are talking to a member of another race.

(2.4) You are talking to a policeman in a restaurant.

(2.7) You are talking with a minister.

(3.2) You are about to talk with your academic adviser.

(3.9) You are trying to make conversation with your date whom you have not dated previously.

(4.2) You are trying to make a point at a bull session, and you notice that everyone is looking at you.

(4.5) Each person in a group discussion has given his opinion and it is your turn next.

(5.3) You are going in for an interview with a potential employer.

(5.7) You are scheduled to give a presentation in a panel discussion.

(6.1) You are to give a speech in class today.

(6.4) You are getting up to give a speech on a topic that the previous speaker just covered thoroughly.

(6.7) Your instructor has just called on you to give an impromptu speech.

(7.0) You are about to give your speech and you find that you have lost your notes.

(7.1) It is the night before an important speech and you are not yet prepared.

(7.1) You have been asked to give a speech on a local television show.

FIGURE 1.1 This hierarchy was developed through Thurstone scaling techniques by James McCroskey for use in a program for treatment of students suffering from high apprehension about communicating with others.

until everyone reports feeling relaxed. Systematic desensitization has been found to be an effective method of helping people to overcome communication apprehension. This method can easily be used in a variety of settings, including the classroom.

At Pennsylvania State University, communication specialists Gerald M. Phillips and Nancy J. Metzger have been using a similar method to work with reticent speakers—those of us who cannot communicate sufficiently to achieve our goals in relationships with other people.[11] In this method, rather than creating a hierarchy of threatening situations, each person makes a list of personal goals, such as "I want to be able to invite a particular person to the movies with me." Everyone's list is then arranged in a hierarchy from least to most difficult, and then each person practices achieving each of his or her goals in role-playing situations before attempting to achieve that goal in the real world. Phillips and Metzger reported that about 70 percent of the people they worked with achieved their goals.

Objectives for Studying Interpersonal Communication

Now might be a good time for you to develop, with the help of your instructor, some personal objectives for your course in interpersonal communication. In the first adapted reading which you will find at the end of this section, Allan D. Frank, a specialist in speech communication education, discusses possible outcomes from a course in interpersonal communication. It will be useful to refer to his list when developing your own goals or objectives.

Finally, regardless of the ways in which you and your instructor utilize this textbook, it is my hope that you will take the opportunity to observe your own and your classmates' communicative behavior in the classroom. For in a course such as the one you are taking, everyone must be willing to verbalize, in the classroom setting, observations about others' communicative behavior and to accept the feedback as a means for improving one's skills. This process of giving and receiving feedback serves the dual purpose of not only enabling you to find out objectively how you are being perceived, but also of helping you to become more accepting of yourself and of others. You will discover that no one among us is perfect, and that by exposing our strengths and weaknesses in an atmosphere of openness and acceptance, we all become better able to become the person we want to be.

Although some of the material presented in this first chapter is usually reserved for the instructor's manual, I feel you, the student,

How would you read the feedback being given to the speaker by the woman on the right?

Establishing Personal Goals

How can the study of interpersonal communication help you? This reading suggests personal goals one might achieve through a better understanding of communication and its relationship to the development of a positive self-concept.

People are often strangers to themselves. They do not understand their own feelings, behavior, and motivations.

The self-images people carry around in their heads are usually a blend of fact, fancy, and error. And, often, people develop a self-concept—or a way of viewing oneself—that is inaccurate. Young people are especially prone to forming inaccurate and unsatisfying self-concepts because they have a strong desire to avoid disapproval. When a person speaks, his total speaking behavior prints out a version of "This is me." Each time he speaks his speech behavior reveals the kind of person he is trying to be. The listener responds: "I understand"; "I like you"; or "No, that is not you—examine the facts."

Adolescents tend to be preoccupied with such questions as "Who am I?" and "What kind of person *should* I be?" Because adolescence is a time of self-searching and of finding emotional self-expression, the young person's thoughts and feelings are often confused. A useful tool for satisfactorily resolving this "identity crisis" is the development of specific goals. Such goals may include: knowing the dimensions of a self-concept (how we would like to be, how we perceive ourselves, how we think others perceive us, and how others do perceive us); understanding the role of interpersonal and intrapersonal communication in forming a self-concept; practicing empathic listening to help the speaker construct an accurate and satisfying self-image; revealing one's true self verbally and nonverbally, as opposed to putting forth false fronts; not hiding one's true self by engaging in neutral interpersonal behavior (noncommunication, monotone, etc.); achieving satisfaction with one's self-concept; gaining confidence in one's ability to communicate with others.

Adapted from Allan D. Frank, "A Communication Approach to High School Speech Curricula," The Bulletin of the National Association of Secondary School Principals, *1970, 54(350), 51–61.*

should participate in developing objectives for your course in interpersonal communication. In this chapter, then, you can find the background, the definitions, and the descriptions of interpersonal communication skills that will enable you to develop personal objectives for your course in interpersonal communication.

Summary

The development of public speaking techniques, and later of theories of speech communication, were derived from an initial concern with the methods of persuasion. Two main approaches to satisfying the need to achieve relevancy in communication courses are the communication theory approach and the small group communication approach. Whereas the goal of the former is to gain effectiveness in controlling one's environment, the goal of the latter approach is to achieve meaningful face-to-face encounters. There are two established methods for defining the purpose and function of interpersonal communication. The first method, an outgrowth of humanistic psychology, suggests that the contents for such a definition can be found in the therapeutic relationship such as exists between a therapist and a client. The second method purports that the function and purpose of interpersonal communication is to gain control over one's environment and thereby formulate a self-concept based on one's ability (or lack of ability) to gain such control. The approach to interpersonal communication taken by this text is based on the ability to determine how the process of communication shapes individual behavior. In order to communicate effectively, one must gain mastery over certain communicative skills. One successful method of achieving this goal is systematic desensitization, a technique developed by behavior therapists to help clients overcome their fear of anxiety-producing objects or events through a relaxation procedure. To achieve one's objectives in improving interpersonal communication, one must rely on giving and receiving feedback in an open and accepting setting.

Footnotes

[1] Gerald R. Miller and Mark Steinberg, *Between People: A New Analysis of Interpersonal Communication,* Chicago: Science Research Associates, Inc., 1975.

[2] Dean C. Barnlund, *Interpersonal Communication: Survey and Studies,* Boston: Houghton Mifflin Company, 1968, pp. 8–10.

[3] Bobby R. Patton and Kim Giffin, *Interpersonal Communication: Basic Text and Readings,* New York: Harper and Row, Publishers, 1974, p. 48.

[4] William D. Brooks, *Speech Communication.* Dubuque, Iowa: William C. Brown Publishers, 1971, p. 10.

[5] Gerald R. Miller, "Readings in Communication Theory: Suggestions and an Occasional Caveat," *Today's Speech,* 1971, 19(1), 8.

[6] Miller and Steinberg, p. 80.

[7] Donald P. Cushman and B. Thomas Florence, "The Development of Interpersonal Communication Theory," *Today's Speech,* 1974, 22(4), 12.

[8]Arthur P. Bochner and Clifford W. Kelly, "Interpersonal Competence: Rationale, Philosophy, and Implementation of a Conceptual Framework," *The Speech Teacher*, 1974, 23, 279–301.

[9]James C. McCroskey, David C. Ralph, and James E. Barrick, "The Effect of Systematic Desensitization on Speech Anxiety," *The Speech Teacher*, 1970, 19, 32–36; James C. McCroskey, "The Implementation of a Large-Scale Program of Systematic Desensitization for Communication Apprehension," *The Speech Teacher*, 1972, 21, 255–264; and

James E. Barrick, "A Cautionary Note on the Use of Systematic Desensitization," *The Speech Teacher*, 1971, 20, 280–281.

[10]Joseph Wolpe, *The Practice of Behavior Therapy*, New York: Pergamon Press, 1969.

[11]Gerald M. Phillips and Nancy J. Metzger, "The Reticent Speaker: Etiology and Treatment," *Journal of Communication Disorders*, 1973, 6, 11–28; and "The Reticent Syndrome: Some Theoretical Considerations about Etiology and Treatment," *Speech Monographs*, 1973, 40, 220–230.

Chapter

2

After reading chapter 2, you should be able to:
⸫ Describe how your reception of the external world is limited.
⸫ Describe the process of perceptual inference.
⸫ Identify and discuss two perceptual errors.
⸫ Describe the effects of altered states of consciousness on interpersonal communication.

PERCEPTION AND CONSCIOUSNESS

¶ As indicated in the preceding chapter, one of the most common approaches to understanding communication is to view it as a process of transmitting a message to a receiver in order to in some way change the receiver's beliefs, attitudes, or behaviors. For the purposes of this chapter on perception and consciousness, we are going to focus our attention on the receiver, who is capable of perceiving many possible communication messages from many possible communication sources.

In this context, Donald R. Gordon offers the following definition: "Communication is a *process* whereby the *sense and substance of a happening* (object, event, idea, motion) is *wholly or approximately perceived* (by the sensors of the happening itself or externally).[1] Gordon is referring to the communication that occurs within each individual, a process known as *intrapersonal* communication. Because communication originates internally, it is appropriate that we begin our exploration into interpersonal communication with a study of how we receive and react to external and internal *stimuli* (that is, those phenomena—that originate either from within or outside an organism—that are capable of evoking a response). This emphasis on ourselves as the active initiators and receivers of communication is the focus of the present chapter. We will examine how our senses of reception are limited, how we perceive others, and how our perceptual and communication skills are altered in nonordinary states of consciousness.

Our Senses of Reception and Perception

Throughout this chapter on perception and consciousness, it would be helpful to refer to the Barker and Wiseman model of intrapersonal communication reproduced as Figure 2.1. At any given moment, many external and internal stimuli are received by our body's sensory organs. The process of receiving stimuli through our senses is termed *reception* and is primarily a biological, or physiological, process. External receptors include the ears, nose, eyes, tongue, skin, and receptors beneath the skin that react to heat, pain, pressure, and so on. Internal receptors are the nerve endings that transfer messages about the stimuli to the brain; the messages then are translated into sensations, and are acted upon by the muscles and internal glands and organs.

Our ability to sense stimuli is impressive. For example, it has been estimated that we are physiologically capable of sensing 7,500,000 different, distinguishable colors.[2] We are capable of sensing 20 to 20,000 vibration cycles per second, in addition to partly

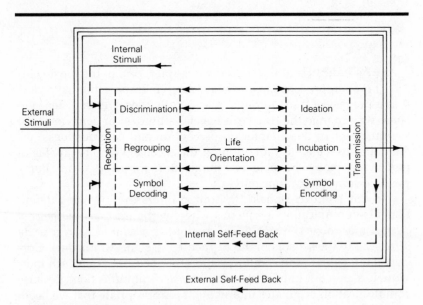

SOURCE: L. L. Barker and G. Wiseman, "A Model of Intrapersonal Communication," *Journal of Communication,* 1966, 16, 174.

FIGURE 2.1 The Barker and Wiseman model of intrapersonal communication distinguishes between reception and perception of stimuli. Two people, then, can perceive the same event differently.

conscious "sensing" of higher and lower frequencies that are often interpreted as the "presence" or "richness" of sound. We can differentiate among 5,000 different smells, down to as little as roughly 400 molecules of a given substance. The average non-smoker can differentiate about 10,000 taste sensations in combinations of the basic sensations of bitter, salty, sour, and sweet. Sensors in the tongue can sense objects as separate entities even when they are as little as 1.1 mm apart. Our fingers can distinguish objects with as little as 3 to 8 mm separation, and even parts of our back, our least sensitive area, can sense objects that are as little as 36 to 75 mm (roughly 1 1/2 to 3 inches) apart as separate entities.[3] In addition, it is possible to extend our biological senses by the use of mechanical or electronic aids. For instance, eyeglasses can extend or improve normal vision; telescopes enable us to view the macrocosm; microscopes allow us to view the microcosm; telephones, radios, and television put us instantly in touch with the rest of the world; and enormous radio transmitters and receivers may eventually put us in touch with distant parts of the universe.

But despite these impressive statistics, our ability to sense stimuli has limitations. The human organism is neither totally efficient nor sufficient to receive all possible stimuli. For example, we are rarely aware of automatic functions, such as our breathing and heart beat—unless we pay special attention to them, and we are never aware of the functioning of our glands and such internal organs as our liver and kidneys. We seldom notice such minor activities and habits as checking our watch, the steps involved in driving a car, or each movement of all the muscles involved in playing tennis or preparing a meal. Thus, we are constantly, actively involved in selecting, screening, and processing all the incoming stimuli. And there is good reason for our limited awareness. Imagine how inefficient we would be if we had to take in all possible inputs. We would be so consumed with trying to respond to the thousands of pieces of information, we would be unable to ever get anything done.

In order to "decide," then, what to react to and what to ignore, stimuli are screened for their relative strength and importance in a "discrimination" process that eliminates the weaker stimuli. This process, which narrows down the amount of input, is called *selective attention,* and it serves to give us a choice as to what we pay attention to. For example, imagine that you are in a busy airport waiting area. Your brain is automatically monitoring (but not necessarily responding to) many different sources of information: arriving and departing travelers, porters carrying luggage, activity at the ticket counter, the large clock (indicating how much time is left before the plane you are meeting arrives), and so on. Suddenly you hear your name announced over the loudspeaker. Immediately, your brain

We make assumptions about people based on all sorts of cues—such as those provided by the face. What could you assume about this person?

selects that sound as the most important stimulus and allows your attention to focus on it by eliminating the weaker, or less important, stimuli.

Another process of perception, one that determines how we interpret stimuli, is called *perceptual inference*. This 'means that we make assumptions about a given stimulus based on our past experiences. For example, when we pass a building, we do not have to walk around it to infer that it has four sides—we assume, from past experience, that it does—even though we can only see the front. However, the context, or environment, in which perception takes place is equally important. If we are on a movie studio lot, we may hesitate before assuming that a building has four sides, and want to walk around it before inferring that it does.

The Perception of Other People

We use perceptual inference to make assumptions about people, too. And we rely on all sorts of cues—dress, hairstyle, mannerisms, way of speaking, and so on—for making our assumptions. But the way in which we interpret these cues is affected by our experience, attitudes, and expectations. The way you perceive the ambiguous drawing in Figure 2.2A and Figure 2.2B will depend, in part, on what you expect to see.

Interpersonal perception, or the process of perceiving other people, also involves making inferences about the internal states of others—their attitudes, feelings, intentions, and so on. And the cues we select and the process by which we form our judgment involve an interplay of the characteristics or experiences of both the perceiver and the perceived. H. Cantril described this process as a

FIGURE 2.2(A) This illustration is like that used in research by Robert W. Leeper in the 1930s. What do you perceive the illustration to represent?

FIGURE 2.2(B) Leeper had the original drawing redrawn so that one version emphasized the young woman and the other the old hag as shown.

"transaction" between the perceiver and the perceived, a process of negotiation in which the perceptual end product is a result both of influences within the perceiver and of characteristics of the perceived.[4] For example, have you ever met someone you instantly liked or disliked because they physically resembled someone you know? In a very real sense, then, the judgments we make about other people reveal a good deal about ourselves.

Laing, Phillipson, and Lee describe interpersonal perception as a result of the experiences one brings to the encounter from one's culture and subculture. They give as an example a situation in which a husband begins to cry.

"The behavior is crying. This behavior must now be experienced by his wife. It cannot be experienced without being interpreted. The interpretation will vary greatly from person to person, from culture to culture. For Jill, a man crying is inevitably to be interpreted as a sign of weakness. For Jane, a man crying will be interpreted as a sign of sensitivity. Each will react to a greater or lesser extent according to a preconceived interpretive model which she may or may not be aware of . . . Jill may have been taught by her father that a man never cries, that only a sissy does. Jane may have been taught by her father that a man can show emotion and that he is a better man for having done so . . . Jill simply experiences her husband as weak; Jane simply experiences hers as sensitive. Neither is clear why."[5]

Two persons' interpersonal perceptions of a third person, then, may be diametrically opposed because each of the interpretations will be based on past learning, particularly from within the family but also from within the larger society.

What is the importance of stereotyping in how representatives of each group shown here perceive each other?

Perceptual Errors

Because people's judgments about others are often based on scanty information, their inferences are subject to error. Two common errors, which result from making generalizations, are *stereotyping* and the *halo effect*. The word "stereotyping" was first used by Walter Lippman in 1922 to describe judgments made about others on the basis of their ethnic group membership. Research conducted by Gordon Allport demonstrated that there need not be any truth even in a widely held stereotype. He showed, for exmple, that although the prevalent stereotype of Armenians labeled them as dishonest, a credit-reporting association gave them credit ratings as good as those given to others.[6] Stereotyping simplifies the task of making judgments about people, and therefore it is a commonly used device. Stereotyping is legitimate when forming first impressions; it becomes dangerous when the stereotypical image continues to operate beyond the initial contact. In Adapted Reading No. 2, a reporter writes about a sociologist's attempts to aid the defense in jury selection.

The desire to simplify the judgment process also results in the second type of perceptual error, the "halo effect." This term was first used in 1920 to describe the process in which a central trait or characteristic of a person (such as "kind" or "cold") greatly influences all other impressions of the person. In other words, once you decide that someone is "nice," you may find it difficult to see any negative qualities he might have. One study conducted in the U.S. Army showed that officers who were liked were judged to be more intelligent than officers who were disliked—even though they all made approximately the same score on intelligence tests.

★Probe Questions

Scientifically acquired knowledge of the biological and psychological sciences helps us to become more aware of the complexity and limitations of our receptive and perceptual capabilities. Such knowledge, however, merely makes interesting or uninteresting reading—and may seem to have little to do with "real life"—unless students can apply such knowledge to their everyday experiences. The following questions were designed to help make the preceding material more relevant to *you*. After thinking about the questions, you may want to discuss some of your thoughts about them with your classmates.

How much confidence do you customarily place in your ability to sense (receive and perceive) the way things really are or the way events really happen? Is such confidence justified or desirable?

Selecting a Favorable Jury

When a sociologist helps attorneys in jury selection, is the sociologist engaging in stereotyping? Does he have a basis for his judgments? Are the judgments any more accurate than those you and I would make of the same people?

Mr. Jay Schulman is a sociologist who's trying to even up the odds. And right now, he says, he faces the toughest set of odds he's seen. Dr. Schulman, 46, of New York has joined with the Attica Brothers Legal Defense to help the defense choose the right jurors in the prosecution of 61 former inmates of Attica prison charged with various crimes relating to the 1971 riot at Attica.

He has participated in a number of politically charged trials—charges from the occupation of Wounded Knee, S.D., the trials of Catholic anti-war activists in Harrisburg, Pa., and Camden, N.J., and Vietnam veterans in Gainesville, Fla.—but he said Attica will be the toughest.

"The issues here are deadly," he said in an interview outside the State Supreme Court in Buffalo, where his attempts to testify in a lawsuit challenging the makeup of the Erie County Jury. Pool had been limited by the judge.

"You have, first, riot; second, felons; third, murder; and fourth, blacks. This will be the toughest, there's no question. . . .

Schulman follows a lengthy four-part process: A community survey, close observation of in-court questioning of potential jurors, outside investigations of the individuals, and a consideration of the "group dynamics" of the final body of 12—how they will interact in deliberating.

As part of the challenge to the jury poll, a seven-month statistical study of the jury commissioner's records was made, showing women, the young, and the poor are under-represented. That finding was repeated in several months of actually observing

Adapted from Sheridan Lyons, "He's Trying to Even Odds," Rochester, New York Democrat and Chronicle, June 2, 1974, pp. 1B and 6B.

jurors in the court building, counting the numbers of women and blacks.

But Schulman also took a random telephone survey of 787 persons who served on juries in the first half of 1972. In addition to questions about age, income, and other data he asked about trust in the government, amnesty for conscientious objectors, and other questions designed to reveal a tendency not to question authority. . . .

He's worried about "the high percentage of Catholic ethnic groups in Buffalo—Slavs, Poles, Italians. . . ."

In the second phase, in court, he said, a bank of psychologists and "body language" experts will evaluate prospective jurors' faces and posture.

"The face, the eyes, blushing" are important, he said, but less so than posture and the way a person moves. . . .

Blacks particularly concern him, he said. Some are prone to acquit and others to convict other blacks.

"Every black who comes into this courtroom we have to know," Schulman said. "We can't make a mistake on a black."

Knowing these prospective jurors as individuals, rather than as generalizations of the telephone survey, will come from investigation outside, but not to the extent of jury tampering, he said.

"The other side is also doing as much as possible—running through the FBI computer and others . . . that we don't have access to."

The investigation will be used to exercise peremptory challenges of jurors (striking them without giving any reason) and in challenges for cause, in which the trial judge finds jurors ineligible for reasons, such as prejudice or a relationship to someone involved in the trial. . . .

The fourth phase, group dynamics, is a consideration from the beginning, he said. "No matter how bad or good they look, you have to think ahead to deliberations, what happens when the case is to the jury—a "theory of the jury." You have to get the right persons as strong leaders in the jury room. . . ."

Commenting on critics who charge he's taking the random element from the original concept of the jury, Schulman said, "I'll tell you this: if you were to bet on us, even with what I've told you, you'd be crazy. You have to bet on the government.

"We know that eight people of any 10 will favor the government. Now, with Watergate and Vietnam, that's dropped to four or five. But with Attica, it goes back to eight because of the load: riot; felons; murder; and blacks. . . .

If all of us are limited in our abilities to sense the world around us, what additional limitations are imposed by the conditions of blindness or deafness? Can you think of any advantages that these physical conditions may create? For instance, consider whether deaf and blind people are more or less likely than other individuals to commit the perceptual errors of stereotyping and the halo effect.

Do you often use stereotyping or the halo effect in your judgments of other people? How many instances can you think of in which errors were made as a result of employing these devices?

Are there significant people in your life (e.g., a parent, a sibling, or a friend) who seem to regard you so positively that you suspect the perceptual limitation of the halo effect? In what ways is such a perceptual bias an advantage for you? A disadvantage?

Can you think of specific ways in which your family, subculture, and culture have shaped your interpretations of certain behaviors?

In what circumstances, if any, do you, or does any other person, hold a moral obligation to correct the perceptual errors of others?

Altered States of Consciousness

You may wonder what a section on altered states of consciousness is doing in a book about interpersonal communication. What does dreaming, or getting high, or meditating, or being hypnotized have to do with how you relate to other people? Well, if you think about your own experiences for a moment you may be able to discover some connections.

In the first half of this chapter we discussed the relationship between physiological and interpersonal perception, and how our senses are responsible for bringing in information about the world. But thus far we have pretty much assumed that most people experience and interpret incoming stimuli in much the same ways. Your own experiences, however, undoubtedly tell you that such is not always the case. (How many times, for example, have you argued with someone over the merits of a particular flavor of ice cream, or disagreed about the color of a particular shade of blue-green?) Scientists of human behavior are interested in knowing how and why people can experience the same stimuli yet interpret or respond to them entirely differently.

In a previous section it was suggested that people make interpretations of other people's behavior according to the individual differences in their history and experience. Another factor that accounts for perceptual and interpretative differences is one's state of mind, or consciousness. For instance, we have all experienced how the world seems to change for the worse when we are having a "bad" day. We may think we look ugly, we seem to have less tolerance for other people, less interest in what's going on around us, and less inclination to be thoughtful or understanding. Thus, if our perception of the world, of ourselves, and of other people, is altered simply by being in a "bad mood," how much more is our perception altered when we are in truly unusual states of consciousness? One approach, then, to studying these alterations in perception is to study the states of consciousness that produce them.

Biological Rhythms

LeRoy Lane, in an article in a speech communication journal (see Figure 2.3) has argued that there are biological rhythms that influence communicative behavior. And these rhythms are revealed in variations in the individual's capacity to perceive, respond, and perform.[7] Humans do tend to observe a twenty-four-hour cycle of waking and sleeping, known as the *circadian rhythm*. Body temperature, brain activity, and muscular activity establish a rhythm which, when disturbed, can affect interpersonal behavior. For example, when a worker is switched from a day to a night shift, he is usually irritable for some days afterward because his bodily activity no longer corresponds to his established rhythmic cycle.

United Airlines, for example, keeps charts of the *biorhythms* (the individual biological rhythms) of its 18,000 employees in order to reduce air and ground accidents. At the National Airport in Washington, D.C., United has been keeping track of its employees' critical days since November, 1973. The airline reports that the number of accidents has been cut in half since the system began.

A Case for Altering Consciousness

What exactly is this phenomenon called consciousness? Philosophers, poets, and psychologists have been struggling with this question for hundreds of years. And although we still have no one definitive answer, most would agree that consciousness, at its least, is the ability of the mind to be aware of itself. We know, too, that consciousness exists in a variety of states: ordinary waking consciousness is but one of these varieties. Sleeping and dreaming is another commonly experienced, but nonordinary, state of consciousness. Other nonordinary states are those brought on by meditation, hypnosis, sensory deprivation (which results in hallucinations—such as "seeing" an oasis in a barren desert), and drugs.

In his landmark book *The Natural Mind*, Andrew T. Weil stated:

While I do not now have a special case to make for or against the use of drugs, I do have a case to make for something, i.e. that it is good to learn to spend time consciously in states of consciousness other than the ordinary waking hours.[8]

Weil argues that the human mind has an innate need, as basic as hunger and sex, to experience part of its time in dreams, fantasies,

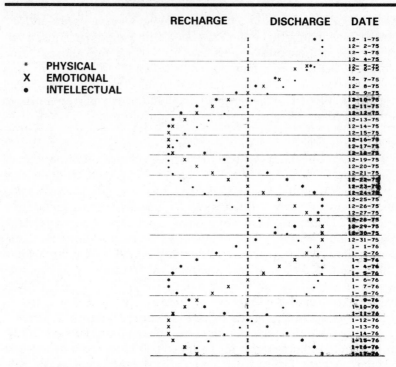

RECHARGE	DISCHARGE	DATE

* PHYSICAL
X EMOTIONAL
• INTELLECTUAL

FIGURE 2.3 Biorhythm cycles are divided into two periods. The discharge and the recharge periods. The discharge cycle indicates days when one feels more energetic, has more reserve power, and has greater endurance such that physical work seems easier. Selective surgery is most favorable during the middle days of this period. The second half of the physical cycle, the recharge period, indicates days when one feels less energetic, has less reserve power, and tires more easily. This period is most conducive to rest. Even though this period of the physical cycle shows less energy sources, one can train intellectually without overworking at this time and still be able to accomplish goals requiring physical work.

During the discharge period of the emotional cycle, one is more apt to be cheerful and have a positive outlook. One's creative activities are enhanced and one's ability to work and cooperate with others is more favorable during this period, also. The emotional recharge period shows tendencies to become irritable and negative. Special effort to coordinate and cooperate with others will be quite helpful.

The discharge period of the intellectual cycle indicates a time when one's memory is clearer and more spontaneous, as well as a time when one's ability to think is enhanced. This period is most advantageous for training intellectually for physical activity. The recharge period indicates a time when the ability to think is reduced and when it is best to review reading material and go over subjects which have already been studied.

So-called critical days in the cycles occur when the rhythms cross the median line between the discharge and recharge periods. One's reaction time is reduced on a critical day for that cycle, and therefore shows instability in one's biological system. These days are more accident prone, but this does not necessarily mean that they will always be bad days.

As the cycles vary from day to day, week to week, month to month, one notices a large number of possible cycle combinations. It is good to keep in mind that one's environment plays an important role. Make the most of both periods within the three cycles. You'll find that the recharge periods can be productive, as well as the discharge periods.

and other altered states of consciousness such as trance states, meditation, general anaesthesia, delirium, psychosis, mystic rapture, and varied chemical highs. Although drugs get one there quicker than perhaps any other approach, Weil believes that in the long run the use of drugs may lead the individual to assume that the only entry into altered consciousness is through drugs, not through the individual himself.

Perhaps the most well-known authority in the field of altered consciousness is Charles T. Tart. Tart believes that we create a consciousness that is adaptable to our environment. Thus, despite an almost universal assumption that all "normal" humans share similar world views, the fact is that since environments radically differ throughout the world, a multitude of different states of consciousness exist. Consider, for example, the different world views—and hence different states of consciousness—that exist between Peruvian Indians and residents of New York City. Consciousness, then, is a summation of our experiences with our environment. And if we fail to recognize the varying states of consciousness, we are denying a great deal of useful information about other people's cultures. One definition of consciousness, therefore, could be that it is the perception an individual has of his or her environment during waking hours that leads to the creation of and adherence to norms (socially acceptable standards of behavior) for that individual. [9]

Arnold Ludwig's definition of altered states of consciousness is more exact; that is, "any mental state induced by various physiological, psychological, or pharmacological maneuvers or agents, which can be recognized subjectively by the individual himself (or by an objective observer of the individual) as representing a sufficient deviation in subjective experience or psychological functioning from certain general norms for that individual during alert waking consciousness. This sufficient deviation may be represented by a greater preoccupation than usual with internal sensations or mental processes, changes in the format characteristics of thought, and impairment of reality testing to various degrees." [10]

What are these things, external to our bodies, that can affect our mental, emotional, and physiological states in such a way as to alter our consciousness so that there is an observable deviation from our everyday, waking experience and that also affect our interpersonal perceptual and communication skills? Certainly we are not aware of all the possibilities.

Some Effects of Drugs on Interpersonal Communication

Throughout history humans have taken chemical substances to change their perception and behavior. Although the use of many nonprescription chemicals to alter consciousness is illegal today in the United States, a survey by Response Analysis Corporation of Princeton, New Jersey, indicated that in 1972 at least 9.3 million

How have the alcohol-induced altered states of consciousness affected interpersonal communication at this office party?

Americans had tried hashish, 2.6 million had tried cocaine, 3.7 million had tried methamphetamines or "speed" for nonmedical purposes, and at least 24 million Americans had tried marijuana at least once and some 8.3 million continue to use it.[11] As Leo Hollister, a Stanford psychopharmacologist, remarked, "Obtaining drug-naive subjects these days is like recruiting virgins for a Black Mass."[12]

The author in no way means to advocate the use of drugs to alter consciousness; rather, it is felt that because drugs are an indisputable artifact of societies everywhere, it is to our advantage to learn as much about them as possible. At best we can infer that some apparent amplification, augmentation, and possible reorganization of sensory-cerebral activities take place when humans ingest chemical substances, including tranquilizers, barbiturates, opiates, cocaine, amphetamines, marijuana, psychedelics, amyl nitrite, glue, nicotine, caffeine, and alcohol.

Specifically, with respect to marijuana, the report to Congress, *Marihuana and Health*, from the Secretary of the United States Department of Health, Education and Welfare, dated March, 1971, lists some of the effects of marijuana use as: alteration of time and space perception, sense of euphoria, relaxation, well being and disinhibition, dulling of attention, fragmentation of thought, impaired immediate memory, an altered sense of identity, exaggerated laughter, increased suggestibility, and paranoid thinking.[13] In Adapted Reading No. 3, Andrew T. Weil and Norman E. Zinberg examine some of the effects of marijuana use on speech behavior.

Effects of Marihuana on Speech

*Our perception and interpersonal
communication behavior can be affected by
our state of consciousness. What
interpersonal communication difficulties
can occur when one in normal, waking
consciousness communicates with one
experiencing an altered state?*

I n a previous report of our . . . experiments with marihuana
in man[1], we noted that chronic users of the drug became high
in a neutral laboratory setting while marihuana-naive subjects
did not. We did not, however, attempt to define what being "high"
is.

The greatest puzzle about marihuana is the enormous
discrepancy between its subjective and its objective mental effects.
A person high on marihuana in a neutral setting may tell the
experimenter that he is "stoned" and is having a major
psychopharmacological experience, yet the experimenter is unable
to show objectively that the subject is different in any way from one
who is not high. In fact, all of the psychological testing done to date
on high subjects has picked up only the non-specific effects of any
intoxicant; it has not shown any specific or characteristic mental
change associated with being high.

The experience of previous researchers[2] has been that if tasks
are made complicated enough, subjects who are acutely intoxicated
on marihuana will show across-the-board decrements in
performance. Unusually high doses of marihuana given orally or of
potent synthetic derivatives cause similar non-specific performance
decrements, and the decrements are greatest in persons least
familiar with the effects of the drug. But experienced users seem to
be able to compensate for the acute effects of marihuana on ordinary
kinds of performance.

At the moment, the only way to know someone is high on

---

*Adapted from Andrew T. Weil and Norman E. Zinberg, "Acute Effects of
Marihuana on Speech," Nature, 1969, 222, 434–437. Some footnotes deleted.*

[1]Weil, A. T., Zinberg, N. E., and Nelsen, J. M., *Science*, 162, 1234 (1968).
[2]Mayor's Committee on Marihuana, *The Marihuana Problem in the City of New York*, 1944.

marihuana is for him to tell you so—hardly a satisfactory criterion for psychopharmacologists. It is therefore a matter of priority to find some specific, consistent change in mental function that can be taken as a reliable index of marihuana action.

On the basis of extensive interviews conducted with users of marihuana and of observations of volunteer subjects, we were led to look to speech as a possible territory in which to find such an indicative change.

Substantial indirect evidence makes this possibility likely. For example, even experienced marihuana users commonly report that they have difficulty talking to others when high. The essence of their difficulty is a fear of not making sense, of forgetting what one is saying and of saying "crazy things." Interestingly enough, very few non-users can actually detect any difficulty in a user's speech, but after listening to many high subjects we are convinced it is there. Consequently, we incorporated into our experiments the collection of a 5 minute verbal sample. . . .

Testing the Subjects

A full description of our experimental design has been reported previously.[1] Briefly, chronic user subjects were tested only once on high doses of marihuana (2.0 g of marihuana containing 0.9 per cent tetrahydrocannibinol). Naive subjects were tested three times on high dose, low dose (0.5 g) and placebo. . . . All drugs and placebos were administered as cigarettes to be smoked in a prescribed manner.

Immediately before smoking and at 50 minutes after completion of smoking, a verbal sample was collected from each subject. The subject was left alone in a room with a tape recorder and

Is communication improved or hindered by altering one's consciousness through drugs or alcohol?

instructions to describe "an interesting or dramatic experience" in his life until he was stopped. After exactly 5 minutes he was interrupted and asked how long he thought he had been in the recording room. . . .

Results of Tests

In view of the fact that the naive subjects had minimal subjective effects after smoking low or high doses of marihuana, it is not especially useful to look for changes in their verbal behavior. Even though changes did occur. . . , they cannot be taken as indices of being high simply because the subjects were not really high.

The chronic users, by contrast, all became quite high in their own judgment on the high dose of marihuana. In most instances their verbal samples changed grossly after smoking the drug; however, the changes were not consistent from subject to subject. . . .

Overall, the following patterns were noted: marihuana tended to cause grater and more vivid imagery, shift of time orientation from past or future to present, increased free associative quality and intimacy, and decreased awareness of a listener.

As an example of the kinds of changes seen, we reproduce here the full transcripts before and after a high dose of marihuana from one of our user subjects. . . .

(1) *Pre-drug* (dots indicate pauses): "Well, I guess the most interesting event recently that I can think of would have to do with turning my draft card in, which happened on January 29, 1968, and—uh—one of the most interesting things to me about handing in my draft card to the Resistance was that I hadn't planned to do so before I did it. In fact, the 29th was the day the—uh—Spock arraignment took place, and I had gone downtown to the Federal Building to the demonstration that was called for that event and—uh—went on to the Arlington Street Church without actually knowing that there was anything planned there. I just heard about it at the demonstration. And—uh—I had been anxious to turn my draft card in actually, just feeling that that was what I ought to be doing since October, but have been held back from it because I have this difficulty in my . . . my living situation where . . .where I'm raising my daughter myself. Uh—if I do happen to get arrested it could kind of mess up my life and hers a bit, and—uh—that had been holding me back up to that point, and I think that . . . I just began to feel more and more that . . . that . . . that that situation was really restricting my freedom to too great a degree and that I had to . . . I had to assert a freedom from their control over my life, and this really shifted my attitude after that . . . my attitude toward my situation and my existence was more one of that I had done something that I knew I should do and really the next move now is up to them. If they want to try to mess me up, then I'll have to deal with it when it comes. At least I've made a statement. It was Father Dan Berrigan . . . now let's see . . . Philip Berrigan . . . the Berrigan who's the priest from Baltimore who gave a talk that day. I think it's Philip Berrigan. He's the fellow who's been indicted for pouring blood on the draft board records in Baltimore, and it was really, I think, his talk at that service that . . . ! that kind

of convinced me because . . . well, his talk was different. It wasn't
a terribly emotional or passionate appeal, and it wasn't very . . . it
wasn't very sharply ideological. It was a kind of very matter-of-fact
tone. I was first of all impressed by the fact that Berrigan's
appearance would really put him far from me. He looks like a very
Irish sort of fellow, crew-cut—uh—and—uh—not at all the sort of
fellow that would be sympathetic to me if I'd seen him on the street.
But I was impressed with how matter-of-factly, how plainly he
stated the case. There really didn't seem to be more than one thing
to do. Uh . . . he talked about being jailed in Baltimore for his little
draft board episode and about how the Irish cops—Catholic
cops—were rather appalled to find a priest in jail for this kind of
thing and how it was his realization that they should have been
appalled several years ago, that he wasn't there several years ago
rather than that he was there now. And—uh—by the time his talk
was over, I began to feel simply that he was kind of saying to me
personally something like—uh—in a very low-keyed manner,
something like, 'Well, you up there, what are you doing with your
draft card in your pocket?' or 'Have you still got your draft card in
your pocket? Why?' Something on that score."

(2) *Post-drug:* "Uh . . . yes . . . well, the present is a kind of
interesting event in my life with A.——(an experimenter) going out
the open door. He's now closing it behind him with a kind
of . . . how shall I say? . . . an endearing little smile, full of care,
full of the doctor's care for his patient (laughs) . . . . I guess . . . I
guess that's about all the interest I can drum up for that little
moment. What is h₂ going to do now with the door closing? . . .
Yes, well, an interesting or dramatic event . . . Hell, you know,
they're all alike (chuckles) . . . . Um . . . okay . . . beginning
of event . . . quote . . . (apparently, subject goes to washbasin
and runs water at this point) . . . You think that's something, wait
till you hear the cold (runs water again) . . . . Yes, well—uh—I'd
better fill some of this up, I guess, because you're probably getting
very bored listening to it. Oh—(clears throat)—you know, the
tro- . . . the trouble is that—uh—the present is more interesting
now than events in the past. I mean the idea of sitting here and
talking about something that's already happened instead
of—uh—you know—instead of happening now—instead of just
being now—the present—is kind of ridiculous. It doesn't really
make sense to do that, so I guess I'll—uh—just sort of being
now—things that are going through my mind—uh—(clears
throat) . . . okay . . . a lot of Yeats . . . a lot of . . . Yeats
going through my mind, which is funny because I don't usually
think about that. Recently, . . . it's just been a couple of years that
I think about that kind of thing much . . . . 'A shudder in the loins
engenders there/The broken wall, the burning roof and tower/And
Agamemnon dead.' Like that . . . (long pause) . . . It's
interesting to wonder what you could tell from the room . . . . The
tape recorder has been going rather steadily. The room . . . the
room is just so goddam confused and noisy—noisy in a visual
sense. This whole thing—it's hard to get any sense of it at all. It's
just kind of like an absolutely random collection of things. It's hard
to get a sense of people living in here. This is obviously a laboratory,

where . . . where nobody permanently has their office, it would seem. It doesn't look like any person really lives in here all day. It looks just like a general kind of a room that a lot of people use. . . . I think they're coming after me. Yes, they're coming after me. They're here. He's return—— . . . ."

Speech Difficulty

The [study] described here show something of the nature of the differences in speech samples before and after intoxication, but these differences would not account for the difficulty marihuana users report they feel in talking when they are high. The difficulty was detected by the judges on all samples and can be noticed in the example given here. If the existence of this subtle speech retardation is demonstrable, what, then, is the source of it?

On the basis of careful listening to users high on the drug, we think the problem is this: a high individual appears to have to expend more effort than when not intoxicated to remember from moment to moment the logical thread of what he is saying. Our subjects reported this need for increased effort whatever highly variable mood change occurred, which leads us to suspect an actual change in brain function rather than a change resulting from a difference in motivation because of an affectful response to drug intake. This speech difficulty has two principal manifestations: simple forgetting of what one is going to say next and a strong tendency to go off on irrelevant tangents because the line of thought is lost. As a result, in the post-drug speech sample given here, the subject typically sticks to the concrete present by commenting on the room. These comments have a greater free associative quality than in the pre-drug narrative about his draft card and, when the post-drug present oriented pattern falters, the flight is to a highly evocative poetic image which contrasts with his pre-drug concern with the priest's matter-of-fact tone. This post-drug sample maintains an awareness of the listener, which many do not, although the concern with the listener has a curious concrete quality. This sample does not have the quality of personal intimacy which many other samples showed. It must be emphasized, however, that these manifestations are fine and not readily apparent except to persons who listen very carefully for them.

Here are descriptions of the phenomenon by two heavy users of marihuana. (1) (24-year-old male medical student): "I've learned to do a lot of things when I'm stoned and seem to be able to function quite well in all spheres of activity. I can also 'turn off' a high when that seems necessary. The one problem I have, however, is talking to straight people when I don't want them to know I'm stoned. It's really scary, because you constantly imagine you're talking nonsense and that the other person is going to realize you're high. That's never happened, though, so I conclude that I don't sound as crazy to others as I do to myself. It's worst on the telephone. Someone will call up and be talking to me, and when he stops I'll have no idea what he just said. Then I don't know what I'm supposed to answer, and I have to stall until I get a clue as to what's expected of me. Again, even though this is very disconcerting, the other party never seems to notice that anything's wrong, unless he's a heavy grass smoker, too, and then it doesn't matter." (2) (25-year-old male lawyer): "I very much agree with the idea that marihuana does something to memory when you're trying to talk normally. For one thing, I've noticed that conversations in groups where everyone has been smoking marihuana are peculiar in a specific way that supports this hypothesis. Very often, the last statement made by a member of the group is totally ignored, as if everyone had just forgotten it, and the next remark refers to something said a minute or so earlier. But, eventually, conversation returns to the forgotten statement. Also, I've found myself that if I'm distracted or interrupted in any way while talking when I'm high, I forget what I was saying and have to wait a minute or so to get it back. Most people I know have had the same experience."

The next step is to document these effects in the laboratory in appropriately controlled conditions. One of us is about to start another series of . . . human experiments in San Francisco, a principal goal of which will be to show that persons high on marihuana have this kind of difficulty speaking. A simple test is suggested in the second description given: interrupting a subject during a narrative and then asking him what he was about to say.

If this effect can be demonstrated, it is likely that it is, itself, a manifestation of a more general acute effect of marihuana on a specific mental function: namely, an interference with ultra-short-term (or immediate) memory. By immediate memory we mean memory over the past few seconds. To be more precise, the interference seems to be with retrieval of information while it is in an immediate memory storage; once it passes into the next (recent-memory) storage, it again seems to be easily accessible to consciousness. Indirect evidence for this kind of interference is abundant. (1) (28-year-old male physician): "I often drive my automobile when I'm high on marihuana and have never had any actual problems doing so. But I do have some purely subjective difficulty, which perhaps you'll understand. My reflexes and perception seem to be O.K., but I have problems like this: I'll come to a stop light and have a moment of panic because I can't remember whether or not I've just put my foot on the brake. Of course, when I look down, it's there, but in the second or two afterwards I can't remember having done it. In a similar way, I can't recall whether I've passed a turn I want to take or even whether I've made the turn. So all of this difficulty must have something to do with some aspect of memory." (2) (26-year-old male graduate student—a naive subject in the previous experiments describing his reaction to the high doses): "Time seemed very drawn out. I would keep forgetting what I was doing, especially on the continuous performance test, but somehow every time an 'X' (the critical letter) came up, I found myself pushing the button. . . ."

Generalizations can be misleading; however, some generalizations—based on the readings in Tart's *Altered States of Consciousness*—may be made and applied to interpersonal communication. For instance, because certain chemical substances—particularly marijuana—are typically used in social settings, it may be inferred that these drugs facilitate interpersonal relationships. It may *not* be assumed, however, that enhanced communication is a feature of these relationships. The major factors that determine whether communication will be affected seem to be the environment in which the drug is used and the particular effect the drug has on the individual user.

It may be said that awareness is heightened. A person may become more aware of automatic and other nonconscious events and actions, and he may sense more detail to the movements of self and others. In this regard, a greater awareness of verbal and nonverbal feedback, feelings, and emotions may be available to the user. This awareness could be thought to help communication since feedback control can be achieved and an empathy between the communicators can be established more readily. However, this increased awareness could serve to hinder communication. Recall the distinction made earlier in this chapter between reception and perception. In other words, to say someone is more aware of nonverbal and verbal behavior does not imply one is able to *interpret* such behavior more accurately. If the user allows his mind to be distracted, let's say by one facial expression of which he suddenly becomes aware, his mind will wander away from the communication and focus exclusively on, perhaps, the movement of the speaker's eyebrows. Thus, the communication may be useless.

Another effect of "social" drugs may be a loss of inhibitions. With this loss, communication may become more open. That is, participants may express their true opinions more readily because they have lost their fear of offending others. Stronger emotional responses ay be made, and even nonverbal actions may become more uninhibited. However, if other participants in the communication are offended by such openness, then communication will undoubtedly be hindered. Further, with this loss of inhibitions, a person may not feel the customary social pressure to communicate; thus, he may only participate if and when he wants to participate, which may in turn lead to more meaningful and relaxed communication.

Time distortions can also affect communication. Since time may seem to pass very slowly for someone under the influence of a drug, a few minutes of boring conversation may seem like hours to him. Often this may cause the person to become distracted and to ignore the conversation. If, however, he uses his lack of inhibitions to end the boring and meaningless conversation, the communication may be enhanced.

Thus, it may be said again that the effects of these "social" drugs can either enhance or inhibit communication depending on the environment and the way in which they affect the user.

There are three drug effects, mentioned in most studies, that seem to have adverse effects on communication. These are fragmentary thoughts, loss of short-term memory, and paranoid thinking. Fragmentary thoughts distract the speaker's or listener's mind and cause him to pause frequently while communicating in order to refocus his attention on the subject at hand. A short-term memory loss may cause a person to forget what he or she was talking about and, again, serve to disrupt the flow of communication. Often a person with a short-term memory loss may be unable to answer a direct question simply because he or she is unable to remember the question. Paranoid thinking—specifically a fear of discovery—may frequently cause a drug user to avoid communication with others. The person may fear that he will not make sense, that he will be disfluent, or that he will forget questions asked of him.

Meditation

Another way of altering consciousness is through meditation. Meditation is and must be a private experience. The individual in a meditative state must shut out all other people from his thoughts. In this state, then, the individual may be said to be communicating *intra*personally. Meditation is seen as a way of eliminating the need for an individual to see himself only through the eyes of other people. The effects of meditation on communication may be related to the self-discovery possible during the experience. Once returning to normal consciousness, increased awareness may allow for closer and more meaningful relationships with others.[14]

The benefits of meditation have been well-publicized by the followers of Maharishi Mahesh Yogi, who view their technique—transcendental meditation—as the answer to a great many ills afflicting society today. Though presented as benefits produced solely by their technique, the following list of advantages may be derived from any number of techniques or practices. The Maharishi is quoted as saying: "Meditating thirty to forty minutes a day would reduce anxieties, tensions, depression, irritability, inhibitions, and psychosomatic diseases, at the same time increasing self-assuredness, good humor, creativity, spontaneity and expressiveness."[15] The ability to communicate more effectively might easily be added to the list provided by the Maharishi. Meditation may facilitate more effective communication as a result of an increased awareness—associated with many altered states of consciousness—or simply because it provides an opportunity for rest and recuperation. After all, interpersonal communication demands energy expenditure, and self-reflection may allow the body to recharge.

★Probe Questions

In this section your attention has been directed to several factors or events, such as drugs and meditation, which have been topics of interest in our culture during the last few years. However, there are many other ways in which consciousness can be altered—for example, high body fever, brain concussions, severe dieting, and extended solitary confinement. Try to identify and define as many of your own non-drug-induced states of altered consciousness as you can remember. It might be interesting to compare your experiences with those of some of your classmates.

In what ways have you benefited from experiencing an altered state of consciousness?

Which of the following do you consider to be the more important problem an individual faces: consciously developing one's perceptual skills, or finding safe and satisfying ways of escaping from the biological factors that limit one's ability to perceive and know? What are some of the ways of resolving each of these problems?

How often is the desire to gain insight and knowledge the motivating factor for seeking an altered state of consciousness? What are other reasons for altering consciousness?

Summary

Reception is the process of receiving stimuli through our senses. Although our senses are capable of detecting enormous amounts of stimuli, they are not totally efficient—there is much of which we are unaware. *Selective attention* makes it possible to pick and choose among the vast amounts of incoming stimuli, and *perceptual inference* allows us to interpret the stimuli based on our past experiences. Errors in perception occur as a result of making generalizations. Two common errors are *stereotyping* and the *halo effect*. Altered states of consciousness also affect our perceptions. *Biorhythms* is one way to keep track of our changing internal states. States of consciousness are adapted according to the needs of one's particular culture. Consciousness is said to be altered when an individual's mental state represents a significant deviation from his normal waking state. Aside from sleeping and dreaming, the most common ways to alter consciousness are through the ingestion of drugs and by meditating.

Footnotes

[1]Donald R. Gordon, *The New Literacy*, Toronto: University of Toronto Press, 1971, p. 17.

[2]Frank A. Geldard, *The Human Senses*, New York: John Wiley & Sons, Inc., 1953, p. 53.

[3]Gordon, pp. 25–47.

[4]H. Cantril, "Perception and Interpersonal Relations," *American Journal of Psychiatry*, 1957, 114, 119–126.

[5]R. D. Laing, H. Phillipson, and A. R. Lee, *Interpersonal Perception: A Theory and a Method of Research*, New York: Harper & Row, 1966.

[6]G. Allport, *Nature of Prejudice,* Reading, Mass: Addison-Wesley, 1954.

[7]LeRoy L. Lane, "Communicative Behavior and Biological Rhythms," *The Speech Teacher,* 1971, 20, 16–20.

[8]Andrew T. Weil, *The Natural Mind,* Boston: Houghton Mifflin, 1972.

[9]Charles T. Tart, ed., *Altered States of Consciousness: A Book of Readings,* New York: John Wiley & Sons, Inc. 1969.

[10]Arnold M. Ludwig, "Altered States of Consciousness," *Archives of General Psychiatry,* 1966, 15, 225–234, and reprinted in Tart, pp. 9–22.

[11]"1.5 Million Youths 'Have Tried Heroin'" (AP article), Cleveland, Ohio: *The Plain Dealer,* May 10, 1972.

[12]Leo Hollister quoted in Solomon H. Snyder, "Work With Marijuana: I. Effects," *Psychology Today,* May, 1971, 4(12), 37.

[13]Report to Congress from The Secretary of the Department of Health, Education, and Welfare, March 1971.

[14]Edward W. Maupin, "On Meditation," in Tart, pp. 177–186.

[15]William Cromie, "Meditation, Can It Help You?" *Let's Live,* December 1972, 40(12), 65–69.

Chapter

After reading this chapter, you should be able to:

¶ Discuss language development in humans and cite research conducted with chimpanzees.

¶ Analyze the significance of "filler" words and profanity for interpersonal communication.

¶ Illustrate the differences between verbal and nonverbal communication.

¶ Give examples of and define the various forms of nonverbal communication.

¶ Discuss the significance of nonverbal communication for interpersonal relationships.

VERBAL AND NONVERBAL COMMUNICATION

¶ Interpersonal communication may be divided into two major categories: verbal and nonverbal. Verbal communication refers to words, and is dependent on symbolic content for meaning. Thus, verbal communication is not only the words we speak, but is also printed material and sign language (in which the signs represent words). Nonverbal communication refers to non-word vocalizations (such as laughter, the use of "ers" and "ahs," voice inflections, tone, and pitch), proxemics (the amount of physical distance one maintains while communicating), facial expressions, and other forms of body language, such as posture and gestures. Nonverbal communication is at least equally as important as verbal communication, and often it is more important. How many times, for instance, have you heard someone say "It doesn't matter," but have known from their tone of voice or downcast eyes that what the person really means is "It matters very much"? The subject of this chapter, then, is the many (often contradictory, and often unconscious) ways in which we communicate.

The Use of Words in Conversation

During an average day on a college campus, you might hear as many as 100,000 words. Not all of these words are different, however. We repeat many words, rearranging them in almost infinite combinations to express a countless number of ideas. In a frequency count of conversational English of university students (see Figure 3.1), Kenneth Berger reported that the words "I" and "you" accounted for 7.2 percent of all words counted, that a mere twelve words accounted for 25 percent, and that fifty words accounted for 46.5 percent of all the words counted.[1] Obviously, we *know* a great many more words than we tend to *use* in our everyday conversations.

You and the Chimps

Because speech implies thought, and because it is assumed that animals do not think, humans tended to disregard the idea that animals can speak. But perhaps we have been wrong.

In 1944, Leslie White wrote that the real difference between human and animal communication is that humans alone can use *symbols* (abstract units of thought used to represent a thing or a quality) whereas animals are limited to *signs,* that is, signals made in response to a specific situation.[2] Animal communication, according to White, is a sterile and closed system in that each species inherits a limited number of signals—distinct to the species and produced under highly stereotypic conditions—conveying unambiguous and highly limited information.

But recently it has been demonstrated that White's definition is insufficient. Since 1968, David Premack, of the University of California at Santa Barbara, has been teaching a chimpanzee named Sarah to read and write by using plastic symbols of various shapes and colors to represent words. Sarah has learned about 130 symbols.[3] At the Yerkes Primate Research Center in Atlanta, Georgia, the chimpanzee Lana has learned to use symbol-coded buttons on a computer console to compose sentences. Lana uses about eight word-symbols and is able to invent new words by combining previously unrelated words. For instance, upon seeing a swan for the first time, Lana punched out "water bird" on the computer, thus joining two words she had known independently. Lana's reactions have gradually come to resemble those of a small child who constantly asks, "What's this?"[4] Another chimpanzee who has learned to "talk" is Washoe, whose life with Beatrice and Allen Gardner was documented in "The First Signs of Washoe" by WGBH-TV in the Public Broadcasting System's series *Nova.* Washoe has learned over 160 words in American Sign Language. She is able to combine two words to create a third, new one, for example, sweet and water were combined to indicate soda pop, and she has invented an entirely new word for "bib."[5]

Do these studies mean that chimps can learn language? The answer to that question is unclear. Although Washoe has demonstrated an ability to communicate about objects that are not present or events that are not happening ("You me go there in"),

Word Frequency of University Students' Conversations, Telephone Conversations, and Printed English

Present Study		Printed		Telephone
Order	% of Total	Order	% of Total	Order
I	3.68	the	7.31	I
you	3.53	of	3.99	you
the	3.33	and	3.28	the
it	2.48	to	2.92	a
a	2.48	a	2.12	on
to	2.28	in	2.11	to
and	1.48	that	1.34	that
in	1.23	it	1.22	it
of	1.23	is	1.21	is
is	1.11	I	1.16	and
that	1.08	for	1.04	get
have	1.00	be	.85	will
this	.97	was	.84	of
get	.91	as	.78	in
was	.83	you	.78	he
going	.77	with	.73	we
we	.77	he	.68	they
do	.69	on	.64	see
for	.69	have	.62	have
he	.69	by	.60	for
on	.69	not	.59	know
did	.66	at	.59	don't
like	.66	this	.57	do
they	.66	are	.54	are
what	.66	we	.53	want
it's	.60	his	.52	go
if	.57	but	.50	tell
she	.57	they	.48	with
be	.54	all	.47	me
but	.54	or	.46	him
up	.54	which	.45	about
here	.51	will	.45	at
how	.51	from	.43	think
your	.51	had	.41	this
I'm	.49	has	.39	day
not	.49	one	.37	thing
see	.49	our	.33	say
at	.46	an	.33	can
just	.46	been	.33	call
than	.46	no	.32	would
all	.43	their	.32	them
are	.43	there	.31	was
go	.43	were	.31	now
know	.43	so	.30	from
out	.43	my	.30	what
there	.43	if	.26	morning
about	.40	me	.26	an
can	.40	what	.25	just
good	.40	would	.25	over
had	.40	who	.25	be

SOURCE: Kenneth Berger, "Conversational English of University Students," *Speech Monographs*, 1967, 34, 70.

FIGURE 3.1 A comparison of three different frequency counts shows that we use certain words much more than others.

Two important studies have demonstrated that chimps can learn to use symbols—a behavior long thought to be exclusively human.

her ability to use symbols is very limited compared to that of a normal human child.

How Humans Acquire Language

Human speech is made possible by the coordinated use of our diaphragm, lungs, chest muscles, vocal cords, mouth, lips, and tongue. Most children begin to babble at about six months (Figure 3.2); by about one year of age, children have managed their first word, and by eighteen to twenty-four months they begin to combine words. Between the age of four to five years, the child is using the basic grammar characteristic of adult speech. With speech, the child is able to interact with adults and other children as one important means of developing a self-concept. And through speech the child is *socialized,* that is, taught the rules of behavior of the culture, by his or her parents.[6]

Eric H. Lenneberg has suggested that speech can be attributed more to our genetic make-up than to environmental training. Lenneberg has attempted to distinguish between the innate, biological factors and the cultural, social-training factors that together may account for the origin of speech and language.[7] If Lenneberg is correct, his theory could account for the folk stories of abandoned "wolf" children who seemed to possess some communication skills. Lenneberg does concede, however, that normal adult speech and language are dependent upon a continuous interaction between our inherited physiological mechanisms and the stimulating effects of the environment during childhood. That is, during maturation, the speech and language environment surrounding the child automatically interacts with certain of the child's innate traits to produce

Age	Form of Vocalization
One–two weeks	Irregular, intense, frequent (including during sleep), largely monotonic, frequently "no apparent reasons."
Mostly crying	*Mostly "frontal vowels" a-e-i.*
Two–four weeks	Begins to taper off; waking at night less frequent; different "cries" begin to be distinguishable.
Two–three months	"Instrumental crying" (begins and ends more predictably with a need and its satisfaction, respectively).
Three months	Babbling begins (simple vowel-consonant combinations, later become repetitive).
Four months	Shouts (as distinct from crying).
Six months	Most vowels, about half of the consonants produced ("back" consonants before "frontal" consonants, which require teeth and tongue control); simple sounds imitated orally but no ability to imitate words.
Eight months	"Babbling" at its peak.
Nine–twelve months	"Imitation readiness," successful attempts to imitate simple words, understands gestures.
Twelve months	Concrete meanings learned through association; responds to simple commands accompanied gestures.
Twelve–fourteen months	The first five or six words mostly nouns—objects in environment—the "single word sentence."
Eighteen months	Verbs, adjectives and adverbs applied to familiar objects—"good," "hot," "give ball"; formation of simple phrases.
Twenty-four months	Simple sentences including pronouns, articles, conjunctions and prepositions.
Two–three years	Rapid increase in vocabulary, use of many descriptive adjectives, acquisition of fundamental grammar.
Four–five years	Complete sentences, all parts of speech.

SOURCE: Bernard Berelson and Gary A. Steiner, *Human Behavior: An Inventory of Scientific Findings,* New York: Harcourt, Brace & World, Inc., 1964, p. 59.

FIGURE 3.2 Various aspects of children's speech typically appear at a certain time.

normal adult speech and language. Notice that Lenneberg argues that this process is more or less automatic; that normal speech and language are not the product of any "planned" behavior of the parents, but that parents (or other caretakers) necessarily provide, or control, much of the child's speech and language environment. Thus, an adult's speech will undoubtedly reveal much of his past speech environment.

Lenneberg's theory is borne out in a now famous study conducted by the British sociologist Basil Bernstein. Bernstein described two language codes—the *restricted* and the *elaborated*—which he observed when comparing the speech of British lower- or working-class people and British middle-class people.[8] The restricted code, according to Bernstein, is that form of speech used in situations in which both the source and receiver of the communication have such a high degree of shared experiences that speech is abbreviated. It is likely that all of us can think of instances in which we have had such a close relationship with a friend or co-worker that communication often took the form of a kind of shorthand. Thus, in situations of social linkage, such as among close friends or such as are defined formally by prescribed roles, a restricted code is characteristic of communication. There are implications here for interpersonal communication. For instance, consider the possible relationship between the importance or intimacy of a friendship and the use of the restricted code.

The elaborated code, on the other hand, does not require a high degree of shared experiences between the speaker and the listener because the meaning is made quite explicit through the use of detailed language. Examples of the use of the elaborated code are formal argument, university lectures, and even the language used in this textbook.

Given this distinction, Bernstein goes on to equate the restricted code with closed social roles, or roles that are characterized by strict and formal patterns of conduct. And he equates the elaborated code with open social roles, or those that allow for an attitude of "Let's discuss it." Bernstein's major thesis is that the learning of restricted, elaborated, or a combination of both codes is the major way by which social structures are perpetuated. Such learning originates within the family structure, and the roles and codes one learns there are in turn transmitted to the next generation. Bernstein observed that the British working class tend to use the restricted code whereas the middle class tend to use a combination of both. According to Bernstein, the British working-class family is typically characterized by closed social roles, or an authoritarian family structure—that is, by family communication that is mainly direction-giving and does not require or encourage verbal elaboration. Thus, it employs the restricted code. British working-class children are therefore socialized into the use of a restricted code in their pre-school years and the elaborate code requirements of school may seem irrelevant or become frustrating to them. Hence, there is an almost built-in predetermination to not succeed academically.

Thus, while it may not be entirely accurate to say that our speech directly reveals who we are, it may be accurate to say that our speech can reveal much of what our past environment has been.

The Meaning of What We Say

As we have already implied, there is more to interpersonal communication than just the content of the message. And even describing an encounter between only two persons can be an extremely complicated task. An incredible amount of data can be generated during only a few moments of interaction. For example, Pittenger, Hockett, and Danehy have devoted an entire book to an analysis of only the opening moments of a conversation between a therapist and a patient. Figure 3.3 offers an analysis of one statement spoken by a patient to a therapist.

Filler Words and Forms of Address

I once asked the departmental secretary to transcribe a tape recording of a lecture I had given to a class of dormitory resident advisers. Several hours later, she presented me with the transcription of the tape along with a criticism of my presentation. It seems that, at least in that lecture, I punctuated every statement with "okay." She said my excessive use of that word reminded her of lecturers who used one word or phrase so repetitively that students would keep tallies. Not to be taken aback, I explained that what I was really trying to do was to encourage feedback from the class on what I was saying. Okay?

Patient: I don't feel like talking, (pause) right now.

ANALYSIS

Therapist: This is a momentary withdrawal of (the patient) from the situation into embarrassment with overtones of childishness. Everything about the delivery of the sentence is congruent with the words: the slight oversoft, the breathiness, the sloppiness of articulation, and the incipient embarrassed giggle on the first syllable of *talking.* The timing of this last phenomenon may not be independently significant; it may fall on *talk* simply because that is the syllable that bears the primary stress. However, it is also possible that the timing somehow underscores *talking,* as symbolic for any variety of exportation from the body.

The intonation at the end of *talking* is indeterminate, suggesting that only as she says the words does she decide to tack on the qualifying phrase *right now.* If that phrase were part of the sentence as "planned" from the outset, the intonation at the end of *talking* would be unambiguous. Whenever (I) find evidence suggesting that the wording towards the end of an utterance is not what the speaker had "planned" it to be at the outset of the utterance, (I) shall speak of FRACTURE. In this instance, the fracture is entirely appropriate to the momentary childish embarrassment.

The withdrawal may stem simply from the general situation in which (the patient) finds herself—entering into an intimate interview, about troublesome matters, with a man she scarcely knows. But the nature of (what I said to her earlier) cannot be ignored: However conducive to this sort of reaction the general setting may be, (what I said) probably helps to trigger her into it. Another contributing factor may be her own perception, via feedback of (her earlier statement): In part she may be saying, "I haven't said much yet, really; that is because I am not in the mood to say much, since I don't know you nor how you will respond."

(The patient's statement) gives (me) two alternative openings. (I) can respond to the avowed disinclination to talk, or to the *right now.*

SOURCE: Robert E. Pittenger, Charles F. Hockett, and John J. Danehy, *The First Five Minutes: A Sample of Microscopic Interview Analysis,* Ithaca, New York: Paul Martineau, Publisher, 1960, pp. 23a, 25a, 30, 31b, and 32.

FIGURE 3.3 A therapist may learn much about a patient from what the patient says.

According to the linguist Mario Pei, the "okay" is an *intercalation*—something thrown in for good measure when you really don't need it. In an article in the *Los Angeles Times*, in 1972, Pei called attention to our use of "you know." Admitting that the recent overuse and constant repetition of "you know" may be partly due to imitation and force of habit, Pei also suggested that "you know" (with its equivalents in several foreign languages) is really an appeal for support whereby the speaker is trying to enlist the hearer's sympathy for his or her point of view by implying that the hearer already knows what is being told him and is already in agreement.

Carrying this one step further, the psychiatrist Brendan Maher suggests that compulsive "you-knowers" could be latent schizophrenics. Schizophrenic speech is often characterized by a repetition of words, phrases, or other verbal units recurring at shorter intervals than in the talk of normal individuals. According to Maher, such repetitions may be evidence of excessive rigidity, a need for security, and an anxiety-reducing symptom.[9] Maher's thesis is somewhat related to George Mahl's earlier study in which it was found that persons in anxious or conflictful states have significantly more silent periods and significantly greater percentage of speech disturbances, such as "ah," repetitions, and the like, than do persons in a relaxed state.[10]

Even such seemingly straightforward communication as forms of address can be meaningfully analyzed. A study by Roger Brown and Marguerite Ford, for example, showed that mutual or one-sided use of titles, last names, or nicknames are reliable indicators of interpersonal distance.[11] The forms of address used by students and instructors can be a meaningful indicator of interpersonal distance inside and outside the classroom. For example, as a beginning college instructor, I remember suggesting that students address me as "Fred." My reasoning was that I was not *that* much older than my students and I did not want to erect the meaningless barrier of title in our relationships. In retrospect, I didn't realize that I was attempting to force a close relationship that had the effect of making some students uncomfortable. Now when introducing myself I suggest that students address me as they feel comfortable. And I am aware of a more natural progression from "Dr. Jandt," to no direct address, such as references only to "you," and then to "Fred."

Profanity: or, "What the Hell's Going on?"

It is a fact that people use profanity as part of their verbal communication. And as such, it is useful to study this phenomenon in order to further define the dynamics of interpersonal relationships.

In a two-year field study, Paul Cameron determined that the occurrence of profanity or swearing in interpersonal communication may, in specific instances, approach the frequency of one swear

Graffiti may be as old as the cave dwellers. What function does the anonymous swearing in graffiti serve for the communicator?

word out of every five words spoken. *Time* magazine quoted Cameron as estimating that among construction workers, swearing accounts for 24 percent of their conversation, and that among white-collar professionals, swearing accounts for 1 percent of their conversation in the office and 3 to 4 percent of their conversation at parties.[12]

Part of Cameron's study, reprinted as Adapted Reading No. 4, was a frequency count to determine the one hundred most frequently used words by college students at a small midwestern college in the late 1960s. Swear words accounted for approximately 8 percent or one out of every fourteen words spoken. In the early 1970s, Nicholas Hipskind and Patrick Nerbonne of the Department of Speech at the University of Massachusetts used tape recorders and microphones hidden in camera cases and coatsleeves to listen in on students in the student union and in the lobby at concerts at the University of Massachusetts.[13] They collected some 5,000 words and determined 7.44 percent of them to be profane—a figure almost identical to Cameron's. However, Hipskind and Nerbonne maintain that the vocabulary used by college students in unguarded conversations is *not* representative of typical informal American speech.

It seems surprising that so few communication scholars have attempted to deal with such a widespread phenomenon as swearing or profanity. In Summer 1974, many Americans seemed shocked and puzzled by the number of times the phrase "expletive deleted" appeared in former President Nixon's transcripts.

On the Use of Profanity

In this chapter, the uses of profanity in interpersonal communication have been discussed. Compare the list of most frequently used words in this reading to that shown in this chapter by Berger. How does the author of this reading argue that Berger's count is incorrect? Is his argument legitimate in terms of what you know about interpersonal communication?

One does not need a high degree of sensitivity to notice that profanity is not necessarily the "mark of the uneducated" or even that it is not necessarily socially taboo. In our society "profane" or "taboo" words fulfill many functions—if you don't know someone or only know him to a modest degree, calling him an "old bastard" is apt to elicit a sore nose; on the other hand, the same phrase may constitute endearment to a friend. Situationally we well know that taboo words *are* taboo on the airways, in formal or quasi-formal gatherings (such as professional or religious assemblies), or in most written communication. At the same time taboo words are often *demanded* if one is to be "one of the boys" at a party, or on an assembly line, or a comedian at night clubs. Then, too, if special force or emphasis is to be given to an utterance in a formal gathering, nothing will do quite as well as a profanity. On the assembly line floor a similar contrast is often effected by a "straight" statement.

Examples as the above illustrate the importance of verbal behavior, including profanity, in social research. In fact, verbal behavior is probably the most frequent kind of behavior, and profanity a commonplace in many situations. Yet, for three decades psychologists, sociologists, teachers, and philologists have been using the Thorndike-Lorge (1944) word frequency count—even though it includes almost no profanity and is based entirely on written English—as "gospel." Although it is obviously a serious

Adapted from Paul Cameron, "Frequency and Kinds of Words in Various Social Settings, or What the Hell's Going On?" Pacific Sociological Review, *1969, 12(2) 101–104. Used by permission of the publisher Sage Publications, Inc. Footnotes deleted and renumbered. Table showing frequency count of profanity deleted.*

methodological error to assume the equivalence of written and spoken English, even the more recent efforts to sample spoken English have betrayed such a bias.

In the most ambitious undertaking to date, French, Carter, and Koenig (1930) sampled 80,000 words used over the phone in New York business conversations in the year 1929. Though the expenditure of time and energy had to be considerable to produce such an array of data, the investigators *deliberately excluded 25 per cent* of the words heard from their sample and yet had the temerity to claim that their sample was ". . . a good representation of the main body of telephone conversation (p. 292)." More recently, an English professor (Berger, 1968) collected a sample of words spoken by college students in predominantly mixed groups in his or a female associate's presence and, having found his sample in major agreement with the Dewey (1923) and French *et al* (1930) studies, concluded that . . . "printed and oral English are generally alike in word frequency . . . (p. 71)." It seems highly probable that these and other (Fairbanks, 1944; Haggerty, 1930; Uhrbrock, 1935) word-samples were gathered in such pristine situations and/or in such a biased manner that they couldn't possibly represent typical U.S. speech patterns; hence this study.

Method

Sample 1: College Student Usage

If you want a *representative* sample of college students' word-usage, you must sample their speech proportionate to the amount of time they spend in each segment of their life space. It is highly improbable that a professor or a female associate can gather a representative sample by wandering about the campus "listening-in" on what students say. The very presence of either would change the range of vocabulary. Further, unlike the Berger (1968) study you cannot allow the sampling to depend on your judgment of what you will record (i.e., at what moment you will start and stop recording), because you will not be sure whether the data was "out there" or a function of your selective process. To solve the first sampling problem, we utilized 47 Stout State student "overhearers" (25 were female, a third upperclassmen) who were instructed to carry out their normal activities over a week's time while surreptitiously recording the speech they overheard. Great emphasis was put upon remaining undetected and keeping the sampling proportionate to actual behavior. By having a relatively large number of overhearers we assured ourselves that any one person's life-space pattern would not unduly influence our results. We largely eliminated the measurement of personal selective process by having the overhearers record the first three words they heard during the conversation at 15-second intervals as determined by the sweep-second hand on their watches. In the choosing of conversations to record from, it was further stipulated that overhearers were to sample speech: (a) in as many locations as possible, (b) to spend no more than 10 minutes sampling from the same conversation, (c) to attempt to listen in on conversations between members of the same sex about two-thirds of the time (which a pre-sample had suggested would approximate normal speech patterns), (d) to spend about half their time listening to members of the opposite sex, and (e) to choose the moment of first sampling *before* entering into the vicinity where recording would take place.

Sample II: Adults at Work

As we wanted a sample of non-college-student words-at-work we had 22 Wayne State University students (2/3 male, all upperclassmen) sample speech on their part-time jobs. Only employee-employee conversation out of ear-shot of customers was sampled. All of the previous strictures were applied where possible, although the student was allowed to adjust the interval between time samples to his particular job with consideration to retaining it and remaining an unknown recorder. Part-time jobs being what they are, we oversampled white collar situations. (Samples were from two factories, three eating establishments, seven retail stores and a clinic.)

Sample III: Adults at Leisure

The adult leisure sample was drawn in Detroit by seven Wayne students from shoppers, telephone conversations of their parents, a party, and a pool hall. . . .

Results

We got a sample of 48,912 words of college student-usage; 16,323 adult on-the-job-between-employees usage, and a 1,532 word sample of adults-at-leisure. The number of different words from each sample was 1668, 668, and 404, respectively. Table 1 lists the 30 most frequent words for each of the three samples. Comparing our top 30 with any of the previous investigator's top 30 levels leaves little doubt that there are significant discrepancies. The most obvious is the almost complete lack of profanity-taboo words, or whatever you choose to call them, in all the other published lists. Taking Berger's (1968) recent list, for instance, we find no such words in his top 50, yet our college sample had the following profanities in their top 50: damn, hell, Jesus, fuck, shit, bastard, and God. Profanity accounted for 8.1 per cent of the college, 12.7 per cent of the adult leisure, and 3.5 per cent of the on-the-job samples. . . .

The obvious decrement of profanity on-the-job is highlighted by the interviewer's . . . . sample of the same medical professionals working and at a party. The incidence of profanity was 1.1 per cent at the clinic; 3.3 per cent at the party. Although our sample is as yet too small for the parameters to have normative weight, overhearers estimated the profanity rate on-the-job at about 1 per cent for white-collar proletarians; about 5 per cent for common service occupations; and around 10 per cent for blue-collar workers.

"Damn" is apparently the most popular profanity, possibly among the 15 most frequent words in spoken English. . . .

In the college sample a subsample of about 5,000 words was drawn exclusively from female-female conversation with the finding that the words they used did not seem to differ appreciably from a like subsample of male-male interaction. . . .[1]

[1]Which seems in harmony with Stoke and West's (1931) finding that Ohio University female students told about the same proportion of "shady" stories in bull sessions as male students.

TABLE 1. 30 MOST FREQUENTLY USED WORDS

College Students at Leisure		Adults at Work		Adults at Leisure	
word	times used	word	times used	word	times used
a	1341*	the	1154**	I	77**
you're	1226	school	801	you	43**
you	1212**	please	781	she	33**
I	896**	book	799	it	31**
the	866**	tomorrow	673	damn	31**
is	633**	and	648**	your	30*
what	517**	you	570**	shit	26
that's	509*	a	505**	mother-	
it	500*	was	452*	fucker	26
I'll	481**	people	452	Christ	25
to	434**	to	398**	to	25**
damn	404**	really	327*	of	25**
he	397**	these	290	and	25**
I'm	395	he	271**	that	24**
and	391**	that	245**	the	21**
don't	380*	she	215**	a	21**
hell	378*	damn	212**	bitch	20
do	369**	your	208*	know	19
in	358*	I	204**	fuck	18**
beer	347	stamp	199	Jesus	17*
no	340**	broad	175	so	15
of	339**	what	172**	God	15*
did	328*	oh	158*	he	14**
Jesus	321*	me	139*	son	14*
fuck	311**	there	128	for	13
have	306	of	128**	no	13*
was	305	fuck	127**	get	12*
we	305	think	125	have	12**
not	304	shit	120**	is	12**
they	302	kids	119	do	12**

** in most frequent 50 of both other lists
 * in most frequent 50 of one other list

Discussion

The explanation for the difference between our and the other published spoken-English word lists is not hard to find. The studies of Haggerty (1930) and Uhrbrock (1935) were performed upon the speech of children under the age of six—we really wouldn't expect children to use the same vocabulary as adults. The French *et al.* (1930) study suffers from a representative standpoint in (a) sampling business conversation 89 per cent of the time, (b) choosing a phone sample in 1929 when a majority of the population didn't have a phone, (c) the deliberate exclusion of 25 per cent of the words overheard, and (d) a strange method of gathering words to be counted (all the nouns one time, all the verbs the next). There is every reason to believe that the kind of vocabulary one would record under such a regimen would approximate written English. Again we would expect a close match between the kind of vocabulary employed and written English for the Fairbanks (1944) sample of words used by university freshmen in an extemporaneous speech situation. Such a situation could hardly be

54

called "informal." The recent Berger (1968) study which purports to sample the "conversational English of university students (p. 65)," suffers representatively in: (a) the deliberate exclusion of "many" samples because they were not complete sentences (an admittedly common occurrence), (b) the choice of a professor and female graduate student as samplers, (c) the very long recording time necessary most of the time (he reports that the average sentence was 7.8 words, a difficult recording task compared to our 3-word samples), and (d) the lack of a control against selection-bias.

Explanations for discrepancies aside, what the hell's been going on in the study of real people's speech? Something is decidedly off-kilter among sociolinguistic scientists when they allow the peculiar conventions of a society to blind them to an actual situation. And we are not talking here about some mystical, ethereal, subliminal, subconscious event, but honest-to-goodness objective, countable, observable human behavior. . . .

References

Berger, K. "Conversational English of University Students." *Speech Monographs* 34 (July): 65–73, 1968.

Dewey, G. *Relative Frequency of English Speech Sound*. Cambridge: Cambridge University Press, 1923.

Fairbanks, H. "The Quantitative Differentiation of Samples of Spoken Language." *Psychological Monographs* 56: 19–38, 1944.

French, N. R. and C. W. Carter, Jr. "The Words and Sounds of Telephone Conversations." *Bell System Technical Journal* 9 (April): 290–324, 1930.

Haggerty, L. C. "What a Two-and-one-half-year-old Child Said in One Day." *Journal of Genetic Psychology* 37 (January): 75–101, 1930.

Stoke, S. M. and E. D. West. "Sex Differences in Conversational Interests." *Journal of Social Psychology* 2 (February): 120–126, 1931.

Thorndike, E. L. and I. Lorge. *The Teacher's Word Book of 30,000 Words*. New York: Columbia Teachers College Press, 1944.

Uhrbrock, R. S. "The Vocabulary of a Five-year-old." *Educational Research Bulletin* 14 (January): 85–92, 1935.

In a recent study conducted among college students, two University of Wyoming researchers asked some students to write down obscene words and other students to tape record them.[14] The results indicated that gender significantly affected the quantity of obscene words—males admitted to knowing approximately 50 percent more obscene words than did females. Additionally, those females who were asked to *write* obscene words admitted to knowing more of them than did the female students who were asked to *speak* them. A second part of the investigation was to have the students fill out a questionnaire. The majority of the students involved in this study recalled being verbally or physically punished by their parents for using obscenity as children, and many reported that they now rarely or never swear in front of their parents. Although all but one of the students reported to swearing at least occasionally, over half the students would not swear in the presence of children. Over 75 percent reported they rarely or never resented obscenity used by a friend and overwhelmingly indicated that they themselves used obscenity for emotional release rather than to convey literal meaning. Interestingly, it has been suggested that as women become more emancipated they tend to use more obscene language.

As part of our culturally learned language code, swearing has meaning both for the communication source and for the communication receiver. The receiver of the communication responds physiologically to hearing swear words, just as one responds physiologically to *any* communication message. The galvanometer and lie detector (or polygraph) are used to record our physiological responses to communication messages. A simple galvanometer, borrowed from an audiological laboratory, can be used in the classroom to demonstrate the class members' physiological reactions to swearing.

But it is not enough just to show that a response occurs, it is also necessary to determine *what is being communicated* by the source. In one study of swearing under conditions of stress, Helen Ross kept records of the number of swear words used by a group of five men and three women between the ages of nineteen and twenty-four who were undertaking an Arctic Norway expedition.[15] The total amount of swearing varied as shown in Figure 3.4. Under conditions of very low stress, swearing was almost entirely social. But with increasing stress, social swearing diminished and annoyance swearing increased. The drop-off of the former was more rapid than the rise of the latter, resulting in an overall decrease of swearing under conditions of medium stress. Under higher stress, social swearing almost entirely disappeared and annoyance swearing increased until it, too, reached a peak and began to drop. Under conditions of serious stress, however, there was silence. Ross concluded that silence during serious stress suggests that swearing is a

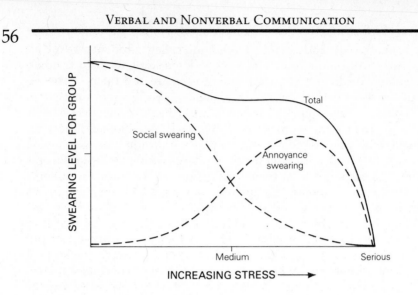

SWEARING LEVEL FOR GROUP

Total

Social swearing

Annoyance swearing

Medium

Serious

INCREASING STRESS

SOURCE: *Atlas,* 1961, I, 78.

FIGURE 3.4 On an expedition, a researcher charted how the amount of two different kinds of swearing varied according to the amount of stress people were experiencing.

sign that a disagreeable situation is bearable; in fact, that swearing may even help to reduce stress.

Years earlier, Delbert Miller and William Form suggested that swearing by factory workers and soldiers may serve as a means of expressing hostility.[16] Additionally, the clinical psychologist Marvin J. Feldman points out that obscene words carry emotional weight when they are used in particular interpersonal relations between children and parents.[17] For example, obscene words spoken by a child typically result in direct verbal or physical punishment or other indications of prohibition. Thus, through the disapproval of certain words by *significant others*, these words acquire emotional tones of shame and embarrassment.

Swearing among peers may be a way of communicating to certain people that one would like to be friends with them. In other words, if one of the norms of a group to which you would like to belong is swearing, then by exhibiting swearing behavior, you are showing group members that you are like them and would like to affiliate with them. If you are already a member of a group that has a norm of swearing, then peer-group pressure to conform to that norm will be high and you may use profanity as a way to maintain your status within the group. The behavior we exhibit among our peers, however, is often different from our behavior elsewhere. For instance, chances are you use different language in the presence of your family or in the classroom than you do on the football field or at a party.

★Probe Questions

Why were Americans so distressed upon discovering that a President of the United States uses swear words? How did the *context* within which they were discovered add to the climate of shock? How does the indication of swearing on Nixon's tapes relate to our earlier discussion of the "halo effect"?

The data on swearing imply that "everybody (at least enough important everybodies) does it" and the interpretations of the functions of swearing include some rather worthy purposes. The message seems clear: *Conform* to the social consensus of your peer group by swearing and you'll gain social approval for adhering to group norms and thus helping to maintain the group.

Another message is also clear. Swearing serves to distinguish you as a certain type of person: Either you swear or you don't swear. That is, you may swear to gain admission into one group at the expense of denying yourself admission into another group. Many people resolve the problem by swearing in the presence of some people and not swearing in the presence of others. In each case, conformity seems to be the dominant criterion.

The question, then, is who is to determine the individual's language behavior? Do you conform to the subtle, but persistent demands of others, or do you establish convictions regarding personal demands on yourself? In other words, what are you trying to prove by either swearing or not swearing? To help you determine the answers to these questions, it might be informative to keep track (perhaps in the form of a daily log) of when you swear. What situations (people?) provoke swearing behavior, which preclude it?

Quantity of Verbal Output

You have undoubtedly observed (and perhaps have been concerned about) differences among your peers, classmates, and others in the amount or frequency of communicative behavior; that is, some people seem always to be talking while others rarely participate. Aside from differences in quantity (who speaks how much), you may also be aware of the direction (who speaks to whom) of communication. We know that one's relative quantity of interaction is to some extent determined by one's early learning experiences within the home and by early peer-group socialization. But we also know that the quantity of a person's verbal communicative behavior is related to power—talking takes up time; talking also takes time and attention away from other people, some of whom may want to speak themselves. Talking, then, can be an exercise of power over others, regardless of the content of the communication. For example, from a study of married couples in three cultures, Fred Strodtbeck found that the spouse who talked most also carried the greater weight in making decisions for the couple.[18]

It might be interesting to analyze the verbal communicative behavior of your class. You can plot the amount of time each person talks on a graph to determine how styles of interaction affect other people. From this information you can determine what behaviors (in yourself and in your classmates) may be changed, and you may also become aware of certain keys to the use of power: Do people use power constructively or destructively? Is the amount of verbal communicative behavior a sign of complementarity or symmetry in interpersonal relationships? In other words, are quiet people attracted to other quiet people? Talkative people to other talkative people?

Leave-Taking

One recent study by speech communication researchers has demonstrated the importance of leave-taking as a form of communication behavior. How we take leave of one another is one of those little noticed but highly important interpersonal maneuvers by which we structure and maintain our social contacts. Mark Knapp has defined leave-taking as that unit of interaction best suited for expressing our pleasure (or displeasure) for having been in contact and for indicating our desire (or lack of desire) for renewed contact in the future. Knapp and his associates thereby identified three uses for leave-taking: to warn of future inaccessibility; to reinforce relationships and to support future encounters; or to summarize the substantive portions of the interaction.

We all seem to be able to "know" when an interaction is ending, but can you identify the behaviors that provide us with the cues? From their study, Knapp and his associates determined that leave-taking seems to consist primarily of a combination of *reinforcement* (short words or phrases that serve to give outright or tacit agreement to remarks previously made by another, such as "yeah," "right," and "uh-huh"), *professional inquiry* (a statement seeking a response about one's professional role), *buffing* (short words or phrases that serve to "bridge" thoughts or change the topic under discussion, such as "uh," "er," and "well"), and *appreciation* (statements serving to express satisfaction or enjoyment at having participated in the interaction). Leave-taking consists of those behaviors that occur during the time that a person is "tending toward" the direction of his or her proposed exit. These behaviors include breaking eye contact, left positioning (that is, feet positioned toward the door and away from the other person), leaning forward, and head nodding.[19]

To summarize, the discussion of leave-taking shows us at least two things: (1) that there are many verbal and nonverbal communication symbols whose meanings we have learned and that we respond to but which we are only "unconsciously" aware of as symbols that regulate our interpersonal communication behavior; and (2) that to study verbal and nonverbal communication separately is an artificial division—verbal and nonverbal communication occur simultaneously and interrelate with each other.

Forms of Nonverbal Communication

Probably no area of communication has received more popular interest in recent years than the area of nonverbal communication. Nontechnical books on the subject, such as Julius Fast's *Body Language*, have even become best sellers. Perhaps one of the reasons for this surge of attention can be attributed to the popularity of encounter and sensitivity-training groups that have emerged throughout the country since the 1960s. (These groups will be discussed later in Chapter 5.)

Nonverbal communication may be defined in different ways. But the broadest definition is that nonverbal communication involves all forms of communication other than the spoken or written word. And as suggested at the beginning of this chapter, nonverbal communication includes such behaviors as voice tones, facial expressions, gestures, and body posture. In his list of eighteen dimensions of nonverbal communication, G. Borden includes, among others, grooming and apparel, environmental surroundings, space, and time.[20] There has been a tendency to use the term *nonverbal communication* synonymously with the term *nonverbal behavior*. But, actually, nonverbal communication, as can be seen from the above description, is the broader term and includes many things that are not strictly behaviors.

What are some functions of nonverbal communication? Randall Harrison describes its function as defining and regulating the communication system as well as communicating specific content.[21] Knapp wrote that nonverbal communication can repeat, contradict, substitute, complement, accent, and regulate verbal signals.[22] Knapp is referring here to *metacommunication*, or communication about communication, or to cues as to how the message is to be taken. Most such cues are nonverbal.

What happens though when the verbal message is contradicted by the nonverbal message? Well, think about what happened, in terms of the expression "credibility gap," to American politics as a result of Eisenhower and his U-2 plane, Kennedy and his Bay of Pigs invasion, Johnson and his Tonkin Gulf incident, and Nixon and his Watergate. Did Americans perceive a contradicting nonverbal message? Albert Mehrabian states that when any nonverbal communication contradicts verbal communication, the nonverbal message may determine the total impact of the message.[23] In other words, chances are that nonverbal communication is more revealing than verbal communication.

Nonverbal communication may be, in fact, the primary mode we have for communicating feelings and attitudes. Examine the English language for words communicating affective states. It is relatively sparse; we have, for example, only about four or five words describing different feelings of love. Perhaps, then, we may very well depend on nonverbal means to define our interpersonal relationships.

The published literature on nonverbal communication is extensive and much of it is especially relevant to interpersonal communication. In Adapted Reading No. 5, the Iranian-born Albert Mehrabian summarizes some of the well-known literature in this area. There are additional topics, however, that we will examine here in more detail from the perspective of interpersonal communication.

Laughter

Laughter is a form of nonverbal communication and is predominantly a human behavior. Before the human infant can speak, it can communicate and be communicated to through laughter. With growth and social development, laughter becomes more of a social response, yet some of the characteristics of an involuntary convulsive reaction remain. In a review of laughter in young children, psychologist Mary K. Rothbart found that babies generally smile as early as five to nine weeks and actually laugh about a month later.[24] Generally, children laugh when they experience sudden, intense, or incongruent stimuli but only after they are sure the situation is safe or inconsequential. Rothbart thus concluded that children laugh as a release from tension.

What nonverbal message is being communicated through these people's laughter?

Communication Without Words

An expert in nonverbal communication, Professor Mehrabian believes that we use it for certain kinds of messages. What are these and what examples and evidence does he present? What effect does socioeconomic background have on the use of nonverbal communication?

Suppose you are sitting in my office listening to me describe some research I have done on communication. I tell you that feelings are communicated less by the words a person uses than by certain nonverbal means—that, for example, the verbal part of a spoken message has considerably less effect on whether a listener feels liked or disliked than a speaker's facial expression or tone of voice.

So far so good. But suppose I add, "In fact, we've worked out a formula that shows exactly how much each of these components contributes to the effect of the message as a whole. It goes like this: Total Impact = .07 verbal + .38 vocal + .55 facial."

What would you say to *that*? Perhaps you would smile good-naturedly and say, with some feeling, "Baloney!" Or perhaps you would frown and remark acidly, "Isn't science grand." My own response to the first answer would probably be to smile back: the facial part of your message, at least, was positive (55 per cent of the total). The second answer might make me uncomfortable: only the verbal part was positive (seven per cent).

The point here is not only that my reactions would lend credence to the formula but that most listeners would have mixed feelings about my statement. People like to see science march on, but they tend to resent its intrusion into an "art" like the communication of feelings, just as they find analytical and quantitative approaches to the study of personality cold, mechanistic, and unacceptable.

The psychologist himself is sometimes plagued by the feeling that he is trying to put a rainbow into a bottle. Fascinated by a complicated and emotionally rich human situation, he begins to study it, only to find in the course of his research that he has destroyed part of the mystique that originally intrigued and involved him. But despite a certain nostalgia for earlier, more intuitive approaches, one must acknowledge that concrete experimental data have added a great deal to our understanding of how feelings are communicated. In fact, as I hope to show, analytical and intuitive findings do not so much conflict as complement each other.

It is indeed difficult to know what another person really feels. He says one thing and does another; he seems to mean something but we have an uneasy feeling it isn't true. The early psychoanalysts, facing this problem of inconsistencies and ambiguities in a person's communications, attempted to resolve it through the concepts of the conscious and the unconscious. They assumed that contradictory messages meant a conflict between superficial, deceitful, or erroneous feelings on the one hand and true attitudes and feelings on the other. Their role, then, was to help the client separate the wheat from the chaff.

The question was, how could this be done? Some analysts insisted that inferring the client's unconscious wishes was a completely intuitive process. Others thought that some nonverbal behavior, such as posture, position and movement, could be used in a more objective way to discover the client's feelings. A favorite technique of Frieda Fromm-Reichmann, for example, was to imitate a client's posture herself in order to obtain some feeling for what he was experiencing.

Thus began the gradual shift away from the idea that communication is primarily verbal, and that the verbal message includes distortions or ambiguities due to unobservable motives that only experts can discover.

Language, though, can be used to communicate almost anything. By comparison, nonverbal behavior is very limited in range. Usually, it is used to communicate feelings, likings and preferences, and it customarily reinforces or contradicts the feelings that are communicated verbally. Less often, it adds a new dimension of sorts to a verbal message, as when a salesman describes his product to a client and simultaneously conveys, nonverbally, the impression that he likes the client.

· A great many forms of nonverbal behavior can communicate feelings: touching, facial expression, tone of voice, spatial distance from the addressee, relaxation of posture, rate of speech, number of errors in speech. Some of these are generally recognized as informative. Untrained adults and children easily infer that they are liked or disliked from certain facial expressions, from whether (and how) someone touches them, and from a speaker's tone of voice. Other behavior, such as posture, has a more subtle effect. A listener may sense how someone feels about him from the way the person sits while talking to him, but he may have trouble identifying precisely what his impression comes from.

Correct intuitive judgments of the feelings or attitudes of others are especially difficult when different degrees of feeling, or contradictory kinds of feeling, are expressed simultaneously through different forms of behavior. As I have pointed out, there is a distinction between verbal and vocal information (vocal information being what is lost when speech is written down—intonation, tone, stress, length and frequency of pauses, and so on), and the two kinds of information do not always communicate the same feeling. This distinction, which has been recognized for some time, has shed new light on certain types of communication. Sarcasm, for example, can be defined as a message in which the information transmitted vocally contradicts the information transmitted verbally. Usually the verbal information is positive and the vocal is negative, as in "Isn't science grand."

Through the use of an electronic filter, it is possible to measure the degree of liking communicated vocally. What the filter does is eliminate the higher frequencies of recorded speech, so that words are unintelligible but most vocal qualities remain. (For women's speech, we eliminate frequencies higher than about 200 cycles per second; for men, frequencies over about 100 cycles per second.) When people are asked to judge the degree of liking conveyed by the filtered speech, they perform the task rather easily and with a significant amount of agreement.

This method allows us to find out, in a given message, just how inconsistent the information communicated in words and the information communicated vocally really are. We ask one group to judge the amount of liking conveyed by a transcription of what was said, the verbal part of the message. A second group judges the vocal component, and a third group judges the impact of the complete recorded message. In one study of this sort we found that, when the verbal and vocal components of a message agree (both positive or both negative), the message as a whole is judged a little more positive or a little more negative than either component by itself. But when vocal information contradicts verbal, vocal wins out. If someone calls you "honey" in a nasty tone of voice, you are likely to feel disliked; it is also possible to say "I hate you" in a way that conveys exactly the opposite feeling.

Besides the verbal and vocal characteristics of speech, there are other, more subtle, signals of meaning in a spoken message. For example, everyone makes mistakes when he talks—unnecessary repetitions, stutterings, the omission of parts of words, incomplete sentences, "ums" and "ahs." In a number of studies of speech errors, George Mahl of Yale University has found that errors become more frequent as the speaker's discomfort or anxiety increases. It might be interesting to apply this index in an attempt to detect deceit (though on some occasions it might be risky: confidence men are notoriously smooth talkers).

Timing is also highly informative. How long does a speaker allow silent periods to last, and how long does he wait before he answers his partner? How long do his utterances tend to be? How often does he interrupt his partner, or wait an inappropriately long time before speaking? Joseph Matarazzo and his colleagues at the

University of Oregon have found that each of these speech habits is stable from person to person, and each tells something about the speaker's personality and about his feelings toward and status in relation to his partner.

Utterance duration, for example, is a very stable quality in a person's speech; about 30 seconds long on the average. But when someone talks to a partner whose status is higher than his own, the more the high-status person nods his head the longer the speaker's utterances become. If the high-status person changes his own customary speech pattern toward longer or shorter utterances, the lower-status person will change his own speech in the same direction. If the high-status person often interrupts the speaker, or creates long silences, the speaker is likely to become quite uncomfortable. These are things that can be observed outside the laboratory as well as under experimental conditions. If you have an employee who makes you uneasy and seems not to respect you, watch him the next time you talk to him—perhaps he is failing to follow the customary low-status pattern.

Immediacy or directness is another good source of information about feelings. We use more distant forms of communication when the act of communicating is undesirable or uncomfortable. For example, some people would rather transmit discontent with an employee's work through a third party than do it themselves, and some find it easier to communicate negative feelings in writing than by telephone or face to face.

Distance can show a negative attitude toward the message itself, as well as toward the act of delivering it. Certain forms of speech are more distant than others, and they show fewer positive feelings for the subject referred to. A speaker might say "Those people need help," which is more distant than "These people need help," which is in turn even more distant than "These people need our help." Or he might say "Sam and I have been having dinner," which has less immediacy than "Sam and I are having dinner."

Facial expression, touching, gestures, self-manipulation (such as scratching), changes in body position, and head movement—all these express a person's positive and negative attitudes, both at the moment and in general, and many reflect status relationships as well. Movements of the limbs and head, for example, not only indicate one's attitude toward a specific set of circumstances but relate to how dominant, and how anxious, one generally tends to be in social situations. Gross changes in body position, such as shifting in the chair, may show negative feelings toward the person one is talking to. They may also be cues: "It's your turn to talk," or "I'm about to get out of here, so finish what you're saying."

Posture is used to indicate both liking and status. The more a person leans toward his addressee, the more positively he feels about him. Relaxation of posture is a good indicator of both attitude and status, and one that we have been able to measure quite precisely. Three categories have been established for relaxation in a seated position: least relaxation is indicated by muscular tension in the hands and rigidity of posture; moderate relaxation is indicated by a forward lean of about 20 degrees and a sideways lean of less than 10 degrees, a curved back, and, for women, an open arm position; and extreme relaxation is indicated by a reclining angle greater than 20 degrees and a sideways lean greater than 10 degrees.

Our findings suggest that a speaker relaxes either very little or a great deal when he dislikes the person he is talking to, and to a moderate degree when he likes his companion. It seems that extreme tension occurs with threatening addressees, and extreme relaxation with nonthreatening, disliked addressees. In particular, men tend to become tense when talking to other men whom they dislike; on the other hand, women talking to men *or* women and men talking to women show dislike through extreme relaxation. As for status, people relax most with a low-status addressee, second-most with a peer, and least with someone of higher status than their own. Body orientation also shows status: in both sexes, it is least direct toward women with low status and most direct toward disliked men of high status. In part, body orientation seems to be determined by whether one regards one's partner as threatening.

The more you like a person, the more time you are likely to spend looking into his eyes as you talk to him. Standing close to your partner and facing him directly (which makes eye contact easier) also indicate positive feelings. And you are likely to stand or sit closer to your peers than you do to addressees whose status is either lower or higher than yours.

What I have said so far has been based on research studies performed, for the most part, with college students from the middle and upper-middle classes. One interesting question about communication, however, concerns young children from lower socioeconomic levels. Are these children, as some have suggested, more responsive to implicit channels of communication than middle- and upper-class children are?

Morton Wiener and his colleagues at Clark University had a group of middle- and lower-class children play learning games in which the reward for learning was praise. The child's responsiveness to the verbal and vocal parts of the praise-reward was measured by how much he learned. Praise came in two forms: the objective words "right" and "correct," and the more affective or evaluative words, "good" and "fine." All four words were spoken sometimes in a positive tone of voice and sometimes neutrally.

Positive intonation proved to have a dramatic effect on the learning rate of the lower-class group. They learned much faster when the vocal part of the message was positive than when it was neutral. Positive intonation affected the middle-class group as well, but not nearly as much.

If children of lower socioeconomic groups are more responsive to facial expression, posture and touch as well as to vocal communication, that fact could have interesting applications to elementary education. For example, teachers could be explicitly trained to be aware of, and to use, the forms of praise (nonverbal or verbal) that would be likely to have the greatest effect on their particular students.

Another application of experimental data on communication is to the interpretation and treatment of schizophrenia. The literature on schizophrenia has for some time emphasized that parents of schizophrenic children give off contradictory signals simultaneously. Perhaps the parent tells the child in words that he loves him, but his posture conveys a negative attitude. According to the "double-bind" theory of schizophrenia, the child who perceives simultaneous contradictory feelings in his parent does not know how to react: should he respond to the positive part of the message, or to the negative? If he is frequently placed in this paralyzing situation, he may learn to respond with contradictory communications of his own. The boy who sends a birthday card to his mother and signs it "Napoleon" says that he likes his mother and yet denies that he is the one who likes her.

In an attempt to determine whether parents of disturbed children really do emit more inconsistent messages about their feelings than other parents do, my colleagues and I have compared what these parents communicate verbally and vocally with what they show through posture. We interviewed parents of moderately and quite severely disturbed children, in the presence of the child, about the child's problem. The interview was video-recorded without the parents' knowledge, so that we could analyze their behavior later on. Our measurements supplied both the amount of inconsistency between the parents' verbal-vocal and postural communications, and the total amount of liking that the parents communicated.

According to the double-bind theory, the parents of the more disturbed children should have behaved more inconsistently than the parents of the less disturbed children. This was not confirmed: there was no significant difference between the two groups. However, the *total amount* of positive feeling communicated by parents of the more disturbed children was less than that communicated by the other group.

This suggests that (1) negative communications toward disturbed children occur because the child is a problem and therefore elicits them, or (2) the negative attitude precedes the child's disturbance. It may also be that both factors operate together, in a vicious circle.

If so, one way to break the cycle is for the therapist to create situations in which the parent can have better feelings toward the child. A more positive attitude from the parent may make the child more responsive to his directives, and the spiral may begin to move up instead of down. In our own work with disturbed children, this kind of procedure has been used to good effect.

If one puts one's mind to it, one can think of a great many other applications for the findings I have described, though not all of them concern serious problems. Politicians, for example, are careful to maintain eye contact with the television camera when they speak, but they are not always careful about how they sit when they debate another candidate of, presumably, equal status.

Public relations men might find a use for some of the subtler signals of feeling. So might Don Juans. And so might ordinary people, who could try watching other people's signals and changing their own, for fun at a party or in a spirit of experimentation at home. I trust that does not strike you as a cold, manipulative suggestion, indicating dislike for the human race. I assure you that, if you had more than a transcription of words to judge from (seven per cent of total message), it would not.

The psychologist Anthony J. Chapman has concluded that laughter is not simply a natural result of a humorous situation, but that it has a lot to do with the social context. As proof he offers the results of one study in which he had seventy boys and seventy girls, ages seven and eight years old, listen to "funny" audio tapes through headphones. In some instances the children listened alone; in others, the children sat next to another child who observed but who could not hear the humor; and in a third condition, a companion listened with the child on a second pair of headphones. Chapman found that the children laughed more when there was a nonlistening companion in the same room than when they were alone. But they laughed the most when a companion was also listening and laughing along.[25]

It seems, then, as nonverbal communication, laughter is social: people that laugh together may be communicating the affective message, "I enjoy sharing this experience with you."

Adult human laughter is always a potential form or manner of communication. Yet, it is not always clear just what is being communicated. Theorists of small-group communication have attempted to categorize the intent or purpose of laughter. For example, Robert F. Bales describes laughter as a sudden escape into a motor discharge of conflicted emotional states that can no longer be contained. Laughter, according to Bales, is a momentary breaking of states of tension or a discharge of such emotions as anxiety, aggression, affection, and so on.

Edgar F. Borgatta describes laughter that goes back and forth between individual members of a group as assertive, supportive communications. In this sense, says Borgatta, laughter goes beyond mere responsiveness in that initiative is taken by one individual in support of another individual. Thus, laughter has the effect of communicating unity and solidarity.

An example of an attempt to gain solidarity through the use of laughter in an interpersonal setting is given by Franklin Roosevelt in Adapted Reading No. 6.

As an illustration of Bales' analysis of laughter as a momentary breaking of states of tension or a discharge of emotions, the anthropologist Margaret Mead provides us with an example from Balinese society. In Bali, the social structure is highly stratified and rigid, but in their theater there is allowed parodies of rank. The parodies may take the form of dances in which people stand on their heads, use their feet as hands, and place masks on their pubes. Mead suggests that the theatrical caricatures, which provoke much laughter, provide a release for the latent hostilities generated by the rigid stratified society.[26]

Because laughter is a definite form of communication, it has been the subject of several behavioral studies. Rose Coser, for example, studied laughter that occurred in hospital staff meetings.

In the tradition of Freud's analysis of wit as aggression and as a release of hostility, Coser observed humor and laughter at twenty scheduled staff meetings in a mental hospital. The hospital organization included a hierarchy of different status positions, and Coser concluded that laughter served to reduce the social distance between persons occupying different positions in the social structure. Laughter served the useful function of relaxing the rigidity of the social structure without upsetting it. Interestingly, it was found that the target of a witticism, if present, was never in a higher position of authority than the initiator of the witticism. Coser saw humor used as an invitation to those who are present to join in laughter, and that it highlighted or created group consensus while permitting all group members to withdraw together from the seriousness of the concerns of the group.[27]

Environment

Architecture and the objects within an environment affect interpersonal communication. Aware of this relationship, the architect Oscar Newman, in conjunction with New York University's Institute of Planning and Housing, studied the crime rate in public housing developments. Newman concluded that design of the space in which people live is a critical factor in determining the amount of crime that is generated. High-rise projects, such as the Rosen houses in Philadelphia and the Van Dyke in New York, had higher crime rates than those adjacent projects with similar population densities and socioeconomic-class residents but that were built lower and broken up into smaller units. Newman felt that as high-rise projects got bigger and higher, with angled corridors and blind public areas, they also became more and more anonymous, had no defensible space, and, hence, promoted a higher crime rate.[28] An extreme in architectural design is described in Adapted Reading No. 7.

Making Stalin Laugh

*Laughter can be spontaneous, but it can
also be the result of an intentional
interpersonal strategy. In the Teheran
conference, President Franklin D.
Roosevelt was meeting with Churchill and
Stalin. Roosevelt tells how he made Stalin
laugh. Why do you think he did this? How
do you think this incident affected their
later deliberations?*

You know, the Russians are interesting people. For the first three days I made absolutely no progress. I couldn't get any personal connection with Stalin, although I had done everything he asked me to do. I had stayed at his Embassy, gone to his dinners, been introduced to his ministers and generals. He was correct, stiff, solemn, not smiling, nothing human to get hold of. I felt pretty discouraged. If it was all going to be official paper work, there was no sense in my having made this long journey which the Russians had wanted. They couldn't come to America or any place in Europe for it. I had come there to accommodate Stalin. I felt pretty discouraged because I thought I was making no personal headway. What we were doing could have been done by the foreign ministers.

I thought it over all night and made up my mind I had to do something desperate. I couldn't stay in Teheran forever. I had to cut through this icy surface so that later I could talk by telephone or letter in a personal way. I had scarcely seen Churchill alone during the conference. I had a feeling that the Russians did not feel right about seeing us conferring together in a language which we understood and they didn't.

On my way to the conference room that morning we caught up with Winston and I had just a moment to say to him, "Winston, I hope you won't be sore at me for what I am going to do."

Winston just shifted his cigar and grunted. I must say he behaved very decently afterward.

Adapted from Frances Perkins, The Roosevelt I Knew, *New York: The Viking Press, 1946, pp. 83–85. Copyright 1946 by Frances Perkins, Copyright © renewed 1974 by Susanna W. Coggeshall. Reprinted by permission of The Viking Press, Inc.*

I began almost as soon as we got into the conference room. I talked privately with Stalin. I didn't say anything that I hadn't said before, but it appeared quite chummy and confidential, enough so that the other Russians joined us to listen. Still no smile.

Then I said, lifting my hand up to cover a whisper (which of course had to be interpreted) "Winston is cranky this morning, he got up on the wrong side of the bed."

A vague smile passed over Stalin's eyes, and I decided I was on the right track. As soon as I sat down at the conference table, I began to tease Churchill about his Britishness, about John Bull, about his cigars, about his habits. It began to register with Stalin. Winston got red and scowled, and the more he did so, the more Stalin smiled. Finally Stalin broke out into a deep, hearty guffaw, and for the first time in three days I saw light. I kept it up until Stalin was laughing with me, and it was then that I called him "Uncle Joe." He would have thought me fresh the day before, but that day he laughed and came over and shook my hand.

From that time on our relations were personal, and Stalin himself indulged in an occasional witticism. The ice was broken and we talked like men and brothers.

Although few of us can afford to design our own world, most of us can shape what we have in order to accommodate our needs and desires in a way that conforms to our personalities.

How does the environment affect interpersonal communication? Look around your classroom. How are the seats arranged? In traditional rows? In a circular fashion? R. Sommer studied the interaction that occurred in six different types of classrooms, ranging from seminar rooms with moveable chairs to laboratories equipped with straight-row seating. Sommer was interested in studying the amount and type of student participation in the different classroom environments. He found that in the seminar environment fewer students actively participated and those who did participate were most often those who were seated across from the instructor. In the seminar environment, students tended to avoid the seating space on either side of the instructor and those who eventually were to occupy those spaces were more often silent. In the rooms containing straight rows of seats, Sommer found that most participation came from those students seated within a distance that allowed for eye contact with the instructor. Students seated in the center position of the rows participated most often, and participation decreased from the front to the back of the room as the distance between the student and instructor increased.[29]

Where do you choose to sit when you walk into a classroom? What factors determine your decision? Do you notice a correlation between where people sit and the amount of talking they do? All of these behaviors have a learned symbolic meaning in our culture. We are aware of them and we respond to them although perhaps we do not always do so "consciously."

One study by Maslow and Mintz illustrates how the environment can affect interpersonal communication. It was designed to discover the effect that "beautiful" and "ugly" rooms would have on human interaction. In each of these environments subjects were asked to rate photographs of various male and female faces in terms of "energy" and "well-being." Maslow and Mintz found that the subjects in the "beautiful" room rated the photographs higher than did those in the "ugly" room. Additionally, "ugly"-room subjects reported feelings of monotony, fatigue, headache, discontent, hostility, sleepiness, and irritability, whereas "beautiful"-room subjects reported feelings of pleasure, comfort, enjoyment, and an apparent desire to continue with the task.[30] How do these findings relate to your own experience? Are there places that you know that seem to evoke warm, friendly feelings? Places that are sterile or dingy that make you feel uncomfortable? Where do you go when you want to have an intimate conversation? Think about its architecture and decor. Why does it make you feel safe?

Perhaps the most well-known study dealing with the effect of architecture on interpersonal communication was conducted by Festinger, Schachter, and Back. These researchers questioned married students residing in a housing project about the people they saw socially most often and about how they chose their friends. They found that friendships occurred most often between people who were physically close to one another and that friendships rarely occurred between people who were separated by four or five apartments. The researchers used the term "functional distance" to determine the number of contacts that were encouraged between people as a result of their positions in the overall design of the housing structures. Functional distance, which greatly influenced the process of making friends, was particularly influenced by such variables as the direction in which apartments faced, the location of exits and entranceways, stairways, and mailboxes.[31] In other words, it was found that the more contacts between people (such as coming in or out of adjacent doorways, meeting on the stairs or at the mailbox, etc.), the greater the likelihood of striking up a friendship. Think about the implications of this study in terms of your own choice of friends. To what extent has environment played a role in initiating friendships? Probably it has been a key factor.

Proximity

The last study demonstrated the importance of environmental proximity to interpersonal relationships, but proximity also plays a role in interpersonal communication on another level.

Whatever the environment, we move within it and we position our bodies in relation to others. Where a person sits in a room, how close he stands when talking with others, and how he defends or yields "personal space" are all forms of *proxemic communication* (that is, how we communicate through the use of space). Edward T. Hall has described various distance relationships and what they mean. In our North American culture, for instance, intimate distance is considered to be from between full contact to a distance of eighteen inches apart; casual-personal distance is between eighteen and forty-eight inches; and social-consultative distance is between four and twelve feet. Public distance extends from twelve feet to the maximum carrying distance of the voice.[32] In other cultures, the distance relationships will vary. For Germans, the space between people will be greater; for Arabs, it will be smaller. Hall maintains that each of us carries around a "bubble of privacy" that we increase or decrease depending on various factors, such as the perception we have of a particular relationship, our personality, and so on. Hall also has a concept of territoriality that has to do with the belief that each of us tends to identify with certain spatial areas to the extent of actually claiming ownership of them and demonstrating a willingness to defend that territory against invasion by others. For exam-

Design Your Own Private World

*If architectural design can affect
interpersonal communication, what would
be your designs for environments for
facilitating different types of interaction?*

Privacy, that most elusive and sought after quality, can now be bought. It can be shaped to suit you—but it doesn't come cheap.

Starting at $80,000, an Atlanta company will design your own private world, the complete retreat, where nobody can get to you and you may have utter silence. Or only the sounds and scenery you desire.

It comes in an oval- or egg-shaped, self-contained, life-supporting capsule. In it you can lie on a couch and plan, work, meditate, dream, invent. Or luxuriate in utter darkness and privacy. Your own personal space.

"People are looking for a place to go, to retreat, to relax," said William Pulgram, president of Associated Space Design Inc., which specializes in interior architecture.

"We're living right now in 'future shock'—it's not in the future," said Pulgram. "We're already suffering from urbanization and from all the masses."

Private World can be designed to fit in a business firm or in a home, or even perch on a cliff. It's a room usually about 12 by 5 feet, insulated, inpenetrable, cut off from the hurly-burly of life.

What goes on inside is strictly what turns the owner on.

You have your choice of linear designs for the couch—a recliner, upright, water bed, cushions or, like an astronaut's, shaped to you.

You can lean back, push a button and a sliding panel reveals the sky. Or push another and have a seascape flash on, if that's what is soothing to you.

Adapted from "Your Own World for $80,000," Rochester Democrat and Chronicle, *March 24, 1974, p. 7C. Reprinted by permission of The Associated Press.*

Given the resources, how would you design your own private, ideal world? How would it affect intra- and interpersonal communication?

"We build an environment to serve the person who wants it," said Pulgram.

"For example, a stamp collector can project stamps on the sloping wall, so blown up he can see watermarks.

"A producer can push a button and turn on projector equipment and hold his own private screenings. A drinking man can have a bar."

Other gadgets can turn out your favorite scent—violets, lemon, orange blossoms, whatever.

In order to design the capsule to control your environment, the company will hold a number of interviews to find out what technically best suits you. And even consult psychologists to talk with you to determine what that is.

"It's a brain and senses we're playing with, also comfort," said Pulgram. "It's not an executive sandbox, a toy or a gimmick."

ple, how many times have you "marked off" a territory—for instance at a study table in a library—by erecting boundaries with your personal belongings, or felt intruded upon when the stranger next to you in a movie theater attempted to use "your" armrest?

J. Williams conducted an experiment to test the relationship between proximity and personality type. After classifying his subjects as introverts or extroverts, he placed each subject in an experimental room and then walked toward the person telling him to speak out as soon as he came too close. Williams then reversed the experiment by moving away until the subject reported that he was too far away for comfortable conversation. As might be expected, Williams' results showed that introverts keep people at a greater conversational distance than do extroverts.[33]

Although it is true that intimates sit closer together, sitting closer to someone won't make you intimate. For example, clinical psychologist Carol Lassen has shown that in psychiatric interviews conducted at three, six, and nine feet apart, the farther the client sat from the interviewer the greater was his anxiety. Perhaps the anxiety was a result of the long-range clients being in full view and thus more aware of being observed. But Lassen also found that clients at the shortest distance were the most reluctant to reveal personal matters. She explained this finding in terms of three feet being a culturally unacceptable distance for a psychiatric setting and, hence, one that generated the least intimacy.[34]

Clothing

Stop for a moment now to think about your clothing. What criteria do you use when choosing what you put on in the morning? Personally, I admit to thinking about what I'm going to be teaching in a class before I select my clothes for the day. Clothing may serve as decoration, physical and psychological protection, a display of status, or as a means to attract sexual attention. A study conducted by Lefkowitz, Blake, and Mouton demonstrated that the extent of one's influence in getting others to cross a street against the signal depended on how the person was dressed. People were more prone to violate the signal light if someone else went before them—particularly if this someone else was dressed in the manner of a high-status person.[35]

In response to a dress-code requirement for instructors imposed by his college administration, Wayne Bartz decided to test how students in two of his classes reacted to him as a teacher in two different styles of dress—"semi-casually" and "very casually." As you may have guessed, Bartz found that the more casually he dressed the more effective he was in communicating with students and in achieving his teaching and educational goals.[36] On this basis, I could argue that I am an extremely effective instructor. (But remember there are other factors involved.)

Eye Contact

Do you ever feel uncomfortable talking to someone who is wearing dark sunglasses? If you do, you are not alone. Eye contact is one of the most significant aspects of interpersonal communication, and people depend on it for a great many cues. According to M. Argyle and J. Dean, more eye contact is engaged in by the listener than by the speaker; people tend to look up at the conclusion of phrases and speeches and look away at the beginning of long utterances; more eye contact occurs during a discussion of an impersonal subject than during a personal discussion; women have been observed to make more eye contact than men; and eye contact occurs more often between individuals experiencing a positive relationship than between individuals in conflict. And, according to these researchers, the main function of eye contact is that it serves as a feedback mechanism that enables a speaker to determine how his message is being received. Eye contact is an indication of whether the communication channel is open or closed; it is evidence to those who want to be seen that the other is attending to them; and it allows interacting individuals to establish the terms of their relationship, be it sexual attraction, friendship, hate, dominance, or submission.[37]

Psychologist Zick Rubin, in a study designed to differentiate feelings of "liking" and "loving," found that couples who made

Why is it said that politicians are careful to maintain eye contact?

high scores on his "love scale" spent more time gazing into each other's eyes than did couples who made lower scores.[38] On the opposite end of the spectrum, it has been noted that strangers on elevators, buses, and so on go to great lengths to avoid eye contact.

But what happens when we defy the taboo of making eye contact with a stranger? Three Stanford University researchers stationed themselves at a busy street corner in a small Northern California city. When a driver stopped for the light at the intersection, one of the researchers, either on foot or on a motor scooter, fastened his eyes on him and stared long and hard. The researchers observed that the stared-at drivers fumbled with their car radios, raced their engines, struck up a conversation with imaginary passengers, sneaked glances back to see if the researcher was still staring, and finally sped away significantly faster than did drivers who were not stared at.[39]

Touch

Perhaps, though, the most intimate nonverbal form of communication is touch. Touching as a form of interpersonal communication is dealt with at great length by Ashley Montague. He remarks that touch is experienced not simply as a sensation but also as an emotion. Tactile communication is viewed by Montague as being essentially an interactional process (that is, a means of communication—as between a parent and a child). The process begins when the infant first comes in contact with the hands of the delivering person at birth and extends to contact made with the mother's body. Montague contends that if infants fail to receive these early contacts then the possibility arises that later in life he or she may have difficulty with interactional relationships. To stress this point, Montague refers to Alexander Lowen's comments in *The Betrayal of the Body* regarding confused, schizophrenic experiences. Lowen contends that one's sense of identity is directly related to the kinds and amounts of body contact he or she has experienced. A person's feeling state, then, is dependent on whether and how he or she has been touched. And in order to know who one is, one must be aware of what one feels. Lowen maintains that the schizophrenic, although not knowing self, is aware of a body that is oriented in time and space. But because the ego is not identified with the body, the schizophrenic does not feel a relationship with the world and with the people in it. Put succinctly, once touch with the body is lost, touch with reality will follow.[40]

An interesting characteristic pattern of sense development in humans is pointed out by Montague. During infancy senses develop in the order of tactile, then auditory, and then visual. However, by adolescence this order is reversed in terms of predominance, and visual sense comes first, then auditory, and then tactile. Thus, the sense of communication that is so vital during the early years of life (touch) is given less emphasis later, and, at least in our culture, tactile communication is discouraged and highly regulated by societal norms.

Kenneth J. Gergen and his associates found a correlation between the amount of touching between people and the absence of light. They asked four male and four female students individually to slip off their shoes, empty their pockets, and leave whatever they might have been carrying behind. They then took them individually to an absolutely dark, padded chamber ten feet wide and twelve feet long. The researchers were interested in studying what effects anonymity, produced by the totally dark environment, would have on interpersonal behavior. Comparing tape recordings of these groups with other groups in lighted rooms, Gergen and his associates found that conversation in the lighted room was continuous, but in the darkened room conversation slacked off dramatically after the first thirty minutes. Comparing infrared photographs and post experience essays written by the students, Gergen and his associates were able to show that the darkened environment had indeed affected interpersonal behaviors, as shown in Figure 3.5.

Almost 90 percent of the dark-room participants touched one another on purpose, whereas almost none of the light-room subjects touched one another. Almost 50 percent of the dark-room participants reported hugging another person, and almost 80 percent of the dark-room participants reported feeling sexually excited. Thus, with the simple subtraction of light from the environment, these groups of strangers within an hour moved to relationships characterized by a high degree of intimacy.[41]

★Probe Questions

As mentioned in Adapted Reading No. 5, it has been suggested that one of the conditions that may produce mental disorders is overexposure to conflicts in communication. A *double-bind situation* is typical of such a conflict. In a double-bind situation, an individual receives a command he can neither obey nor disobey and from which he cannot escape. Typically, such situations involve a verbal message and a contradictory nonverbal message. For example, a mother may resent her daughter and feel threatened by her yet also feel true maternal love for her. Thus, she may say, "Come here and give me a kiss" but stiffen her body and withdraw when the daughter approaches her. If similar situations repeat themselves throughout childhood, the individual may come to see the world as a confusing and disconnected place and she may believe that her actions and those of others have little significance or meaning. Thus she may develop what Maher calls the language of schizophrenia as a result of social and emotional disorder.

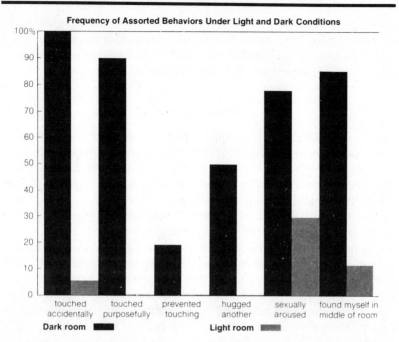

Frequency of Assorted Behaviors Under Light and Dark Conditions

Dark room ■   Light room ▨

SOURCE: *Psychology Today*, 1973, 7(5), 130.

FIGURE 3.5 In one experiment comparing students observed in a lighted room and in an absolutely dark room, students in the dark room felt more free to touch each other.

But on lesser levels, we all have faced double-bind situations at various times in our lives. How many examples from your own experience can you think of that illustrate some form of the double-bind situation? How did you resolve the conflicts? Can you see patterns of responses developing?

Knowledge of the components and uses of nonverbal communication helps us to understand the diversity of means that are available to us for communicating and for being communicated to. In order to put to use what you have learned here, spend some time observing your family, friends, and classmates in an attempt to gain a more thorough understanding of your interpersonal relationships. Try to ignore verbal communication and concentrate instead on nonverbal cues, such as voice inflection, eye contact, proximity, posture, facial expression, and so on. How well are you able to interpret body language? Do you notice contradictory verbal and nonverbal messages? (Remember that it is possible to lie nonverbally as well as verbally.)

Remembering the research studies cited in this chapter, mentally design an ideal environment for optimum interpersonal contact. How does your ideal compare and contrast to the ideals of your classmates? What reasons can you give for the differences?

Summary

Verbal communication is unique to humans, but chimpanzees have been taught to communicate through the use of symbols. Although it is not clear whether their "language" is meaningful, chimps are able to combine already known words to form new words, and they are able to communicate about objects that are not present and events that are not happening. Humans acquire language through a combination of maturation and learning. One's early speech environment is crucial to his or her use of language, and an adult's speech can reveal much of what his past environment has been. Intercalculations, such as "okay," may be a means of reducing anxiety, and they may be used as a way to obtain reassurance; they may also reflect the speaker's need for security. Profanity plays a large role in interpersonal communication. It is part of a culturally learned language code and may develop as a result of peer-group pressure to conform. Quantity of verbal output may be related to an exercise of power. That is, the more one talks, the more power he has over those who talk less. Leave-taking involves both verbal and nonverbal communication and is used to signify a variety of feelings about the preceding interaction. Laughter is a form of nonverbal communication and serves many different purposes. It is, primarily, a release from tension, but it also serves as a means for achieving solidarity. Other important forms of nonverbal communication include environment, proximity, clothing, eye contact, and touch. Of these, the two most important are eye contact and touch. The former is a good indicator of the degree of intimacy between two people, and the latter is instrumental in the formation of a self-concept.

Footnotes

[1]Kenneth Berger, "Conversational English of University Students," *Speech Monographs*, 1967, 34, 65–73.

[2]Leslie A. White, "The Symbol: The Origin and Bases of Human Behavior," *Rev. Genl. Sem.*, 1944, 1, 229–237.

[3]D. Premack, "A Functional Analysis of Language," *Journal of Experimental Animal Behavior*, 1970, 14, 107–125, and A. J. and D. Premack, "Teaching Language to an Ape," *Scientific American*, October 1972, 227(4), 92–99.

[4]"A Chimp Has a Lot on His Mind," *The New York Times*, June 2, 1974, and "A Chimp Reveling in the Abstract," *The New York Times*, December 8, 1974.

[5]R. A. and B. T. Gardner, "Teaching Sign Language to a Chimpanzee," *Science*, 165, 664–672.

[6]A. Luria, *The Role of Speech in the Regulation of Normal and Abnormal Behavior*, New York: Liveright, 1961.

[7]Eric H. Lenneberg, "Language, Evolution, and Purposive Behavior," in

Culture in History: Essays in Honor of Paul Radin, S. Diamond, ed., New York: Columbia University Press, 1960, and "On Explaining Language," *Science,* 1969, 164, 635–643.

[8]Basil Bernstein, "A Sociolinguistic Approach to Socialization: With Some Reference to Educabillty," in *Language and Poverty: Perspectives on a Theme,* F. Williams, ed., Chicago: Markham, 1970.

[9]Brendan Maher, "The Language of Schizophrenia: A Review and Interpretation," *British Journal of Psychiatry,* 1972, 120, 13–17.

[10]George F. Mahl, "Disturbances and Silences in the Patient's Speech in Psychotherapy," *Journal of Abnormal and Social Psychology,* 1956, 53, 1–15.

[11]R. Brown and M. Ford, "Address in American English," *Journal of Abnormal and Social Psychology,* 1961, 62, 375–385.

[12]"X-Rated Expletives," *Time,* May 20, 1974, 103(20), 72–73.

[13]G. Patrick Nerbonne and Nicholas M. Hipskind, "The Use of Profanity in Conversational Speech," *Journal of Communication Disorders,* 1972, 5, 47–50.

[14]Russell Foote and Jack Woodward, "A Preliminary Investigation of Obscene Language," *Journal of Psychology,* 1973, 83 (second half), 263–275.

[15]Helen E. Ross, "Patterns of Swearing," *Discovery* (London), 1961, 1, 40, and *Atlas,* 1961, 1, 77–78.

[16]Delbert Miller and William H. Form, *Industrial Sociology,* New York: Harper Bros., 1951, pp. 291–292. The same observation was made by Hans Gerth and C. W. Mills, *Character and Social Structure,* New York: Harcourt Brace Jovanovich, 1953, p. 285.

[17]Marvin J. Feldman, "The Use of Obscene Words in the Therapeutic Relationship," *American Journal of Psychoanalysis,* 1955, 15, 45–58.

[18]Fred L. Strodtbeck, "Husband-Wife Interaction over Revealed Differences," *American Sociological Review,* 1951, 16, 468–473.

[19]Mark L. Knapp, Roderick P. Hart, Gustav W. Friedrich, and Gary M. Shulman, "The Rhetoric of Goodbye: Verbal and Nonverbal Correlates of Human Leave-Taking," *Speech Monographs,* 1973, 40, 182–198.

[20]G. Borden, "Current Developments in Communication Research," *Journal of Communication,* 1965, 15, 110–117.

[21]Randall Harrison, "Nonverbal Behavior: An Approach to Human Communication," in *Approaches to Human Communication,* R. Budd and B. Ruben, eds., New York: Spartan Books, 1972, pp. 253–268.

[22]Mark Knapp, *Nonverbal Communication in Human Interaction,* New York: Holt, Rinehart and Winston, 1972.

[23]Albert Mehrabian, *Silent Messages,* Belmont, California: Wadsworth, 1971.

[24]Mary K. Rothbart, "Laughter in Young Children," *Psychological Bulletin,* 1973, 80, 247–255.

[25]Anthony J. Chapman, "Social Facilitation of Laughter in Children," *Journal of Experimental and Social Psychology,* 1973, 9, 528–541.

[26]Margaret Mead and Gregory Bateson, *Balinese Character.* Special Publication of the New York Academy of Science, Vol. II, 1942.

[27]Rose Laub Coser, "Laughter Among Colleagues: A Study of the Social Functions of Humor Among the Staff of a Mental Hospital," *Psychiatry,* 1960, 23, 81–95.

[28]Oscar Newman, *Defensible Space: Crime Prevention Through Urban Design,* New York: Macmillan, 1972.

[29]R. Sommer, *Personal Space,* Englewood Cliffs, New Jersey: Prentice-Hall, 1969, pp. 110–119.

[30]A. Maslow and N. Mintz, "Effects of Esthetic Surroundings," *Journal of Psychology,* 1956, 41, 247–254.

[31]L. Festinger, S. Schachter, and K. Back, *Social Pressures in Informal Groups,* New York: Harper & Row, 1950.

[32]E. T. Hall, "Silent Assumption in Social Communication," in *The Human Dialogue,* F. W. Matson and A. Montague, eds., New York: Free Press, 1967.

[33]J. Williams, "Personal Space and Its Relation to Extroversion-Introversion," in M. L. Patterson, "Spatial Factors in Social Interaction," *Human Relations,* 1968, 21, 350–361.

[34]Carol L. Lassen, "Effect of Proximity on Anxiety and Communication in the Initial Psychiatric Interview," *Journal of Abnormal Psychology,* 1973, 81, 220–232.

[35]M. Lefkowitz, R. Blake, and J. Mouton, "Status Factors in Pedestrian Violation of Traffic Signals," *Journal of Abnormal and Social Psychology,* 1955, 51, 704–706.

[36]Wayne R. Bartz, "Impressions of a College Instructor as a Function of Attire," *College Student Journal,* 1971, 5(3), 31–32.

[37]M. Argyle and J. Dean, "Eye-

Contact, Distance, and Affiliation," *Sociometry*, 1965, 28, 289–304.

38Zick Rubin, "Measurement of Romantic Love," *Journal of Personality and Social Psychology*, 1970, 16, 265–273.

39Phoebe C. Ellsworth, J. Merrill Carlsmith, and Alexander Henson, "The Stare as a Stimulus to Flight in Human Subjects," *Journal of Personality and Social Psychology*, 1972, 21, 302–311.

40Ashley Montague, *Touching: The Human Significance of the Skin*, New York: Columbia University Press, 1971.

41Kenneth J. Gergen, Mary M. Gergen, and William H. Barton, "Deviance in the Dark," *Psychology Today*, 1973, 7(5), 129–130.

Chapter

After reading this chapter, you should be able to:

¶ Identify the principal socializing agents in your life and discuss how interactions with them have helped shape your place in society.

¶ Describe how your self-concept is affected through interaction with others.

¶ Identify the factors that have contributed to your choice of friends and lovers.

SOCIALIZATION, SELF-CONCEPT, AND INTERPERSONAL ATTRACTION

¶ Chapter 1 pointed out that this volume is organized around a central perspective on interpersonal communication; that is, that every individual develops uniquely as a result of interpersonal contacts. In this chapter we will further develop this perspective in terms of the process of socialization through communication, the resulting formation of self-concept, and, in turn, an examination of the factors that determine our choice of friends and lovers. Because these three major areas of study are closely interrelated, I have presented them together in one chapter. As a result, however, there is a great deal of material to absorb. For better comprehension, then, you might want to read this chapter in two or three separate study sessions.

Socialization Through Communication

Socialization is a continuing process that begins at birth and does not stop until we die. It is the process through which we learn our culture and the social rules of our society and come to behave in a manner appropriate to that society's values and roles. Somewhere toward the beginning of this learning process an idea of "self" emerges. But how, and why, does it emerge? Paul Pfuetze has said that "speech communication is the chief mechanism constitutive of self-hood, language is the mark of man, . . . man is literally talked into self-hood."[1] Additionally, Frank Dance and Carl Larson, of the University of Denver, maintain that a primary function of interpersonal communication is to link the human with his total environment.[2] In other words, once the human infant is born, he is required a priori to form relationships with other humans. And once these relationships are formed, a self-concept emerges in direct relation to the communication he receives about himself from other people.

Because most of our behaviors seem to happen spontaneously, it is easy to make the mistake of assuming that they are innate, or inherent in the human species. But, in fact, nearly all behavior is learned. This does not mean that a formal training process is necessary in order to learn every behavior, but it does mean that through human contact—watching and absorbing what others do—we come to imitate and be like the others of our species. In other words, we learn by example. And it has been shown that "normal" adult behavior develops only through the process of communicative contact. Although no one would deprive a child of human contact in order to test this theory, we can find evidence to support it in the reports of the retarded development of children who have been separated from human contact and have survived in the wilderness. When discovered, these so-called "feral children" showed few if any human capabilities or responses. For example, in 1921 in India, Amala and Kamala were found living among wolves. The medical missionaries who found the two girls recorded the circumstances of their discovery and provided documents of the girls' medical histories. Amala died soon after being found. And although Kamala lived a number of years afterward, she was never able to learn a language or develop anything approximating a normal relationship with her surroundings.[3] A more recent report of a discovery of a "feral" child appeared in *Medical World News* and is reproduced as Adapted Reading No. 8.

The History of a Wolf Boy

From this fairly complete history of a wolf boy, determine what effects the absence of human interaction had had? Could the boy be considered "human?"

From the day in 1954 that the strange child was brought in, it was difficult for the staff at Balrampur hospital to keep from staring at him. Though severely crippled he had somehow dragged himself to a third class waiting room in a nearby Lucknow station and passed out. When found, the boy was naked and starving.

Starvation is hardly unique in India, but even the most experienced physicians on the staff flocked to the boy's bedside.

Underlying their eagerness were rumors that, like Rudyard Kipling's fictional Mowgli, the boy had been raised by wolves. But unlike Mowgli, the Lucknow boy never returned to the jungle.

During the years that he remained at the hospital, the belief that he was a feral child was never dispelled. The hospital staff and the many other Indian physicians who examined him were convinced that he was indeed *ghadya ka bacha*—the wolf boy.

"It was difficult to believe otherwise," recalls Dr. D. N. Sharma, the boy's first physician. The child had scars on his neck, suggesting that he may have been dragged in an animal's jaws over a long distance. And he had incisors that protruded animal-like from his mouth.

Couldn't Sit Up

One time the boy sank those teeth deep into the arm of a nurse who tried to feed him. From then on, the nurses would do no more than place food beside him. Like an animal, the boy would rip his portion of meat apart and lap his beverages from a bowl.

"False ankylosis prevented him from ever straightening his limbs," says Sharma, "even though we put him through countless hours of physiotherapy."

Adapted from "Death Ends India Wolf Boy Mystery Case," Medical World News, *Copyright © 1968, McGraw-Hill, Inc.*

He could not even sit in a wheel chair without support, and he spent most of his days curled up in bed, playing with a stuffed animal or an empty container. One physician speculated that "this could have been the way he spent part of his day in the wolf lair."

But the child was not always so passive. He once leaped out of his wheel chair to attack a dog. And when taken to see the wolves in a zoo, he became unusually excited.

"The boy had an extraordinary sense of smell," says Sharma. "Whenever raw meat was being cut in the hospital kitchen, he would howl hungrily, even though the kitchen was more than 100 yards from his room."

Skeptics Unconvinced

Though there were always skeptics who suggested that he was a deformed child kept in hiding and later abandoned by sick and unhappy parents, most of the doctors who examined him concluded that he had grown up in an animal environment.

Thick calluses on his elbows and knees suggested that he had long used both to move about. X-rays of his bones indicated that he was about 11 years old when found.

The Lucknow physicians guessed that he must have been dragged off by some animal when about 1 year old.

The wolf child of Lucknow was clearly retarded and aphasic. He could howl and grunt, but he never learned to communicate in a human way, not even with gestures. But his hearing and sight were not impaired. And although he had epilepsy, neurological studies never turned up any evidence of a brain lesion.

Among the many specialists called in to examine the boy were Dr. B. B. Bhatia, one of India's leading physicians, and Sir Philip Manson-Bahr, director of the tropical medicine clinic at the London School of Hygiene and Tropical Medicine.

Both men concluded that he was a child of the jungle rather than a neurological or psychological cripple.

No Claimant Found

No one ever came to claim the boy, and the staff at the hospital grew fond and protective toward him. Out of affection they named him Ramu, after Rama, one of the incarnations of the Hindu god Vishnu.

But Ramu never returned any affection for the doctors or nurses who cared for him. In fact, he never showed any sign of human emotion. He never laughed and tears never welled in his eyes.

Ramu was plagued by bouts of fever, constipation, epileptic seizures, and a chronic respiratory infection. . . . after years of struggling against his ailments and a seemingly hostile environment, he died.

Altogether, he had lived at the hospital for 14 years, approximately the length of time that a wolf survives in captivity.

A similar example is the case of Anna. Although not a "feral" child, in that she did not survive in the wilderness, Anna was an illegitimate child who was hidden away in her mother's house. Left completely alone except for feedings and enough minimal care to keep her alive, she apparently had some small amount of friendly contact. She was nearly six years old at the time she was discovered, and she could not talk or walk, and she showed no overt signs of intelligence. She was emaciated and undernourished, appeared to be deaf and blind, and was unable to do anything for herself. When she died four and a half years later, she had progressed to the level of a normal two- or three-year-old.[4]

Much of what we know about the more normal human socialization process comes from theories of *symbolic interactionism,* a distinct perspective in social psychology that can be found in the works of John Dewey, Charles Horton Cooley, and most notably, George Herbert Mead. Mead lectured at the University of Chicago between 1893 and 1931. Books based upon lecture notes taken by his students were published after his death. Mead contended that our mind and our self are socially developed through interaction with others.

Through watching and absorbing what others do, we come to imitate and be like those others.

It is important for you to develop an understanding of Mead. Therefore, please give particular attention to Adapted Reading No. 9, which is a summary and interpretation of Mead's *Mind, Self, and Society*.

We interact with others in our families, in groups of our peers, and in institutional or organizational settings throughout our lifetime. This continuous flow of contacts permits learning, modeling, and modification of our behaviors to enable us to "fit" into the predominant societal context. Socialization is a circular process: by "fitting" people into the society it insures that the values and roles of the society are perpetuated. Thus, there is a continuation and strengthening of the framework upon which the society is built.

Socialization does not happen at random. Rather it is carefully built into the structure of the society in the form of nuclear families, schools, advertising, and so on. These institutions are all, in one way or another, agents of socialization. A primary intent of this chapter is to assist you in identifying your principal socializing agents.

Socialization by Parents

Not surprisingly, the primary socializing agent is the immediate family, or the interactions between parent(s) and child. When the child is born, he or she begins to perceive and respond to stimuli. This is the beginning of the process of socialization; a cycle of stimulus-response relationships between the child and others. The primary contact (or stimulus) is usually the mother. This early interaction, of course, is primarily a servicing of the child's physiological and comfort needs.

Eventually this physical dependence leads to emotional involvement as the parents become the source of both frustration and satisfaction. As this new relationship develops, the child begins to learn through interaction with others that he or she may be denied love, affection, and physical needs based on role-appropriate behavior. If the child's behavior becomes excessive or deviant he or she is told by parents to be a "good little boy" or a "nice little girl." Even if at the time the child is not really sure how a "good little boy" or a "nice little girl" should behave, the child is relatively certain about how *not* to behave. Thus, through parental intervention the child gradually begins to realize the parameters of acceptable "boy" and "girl" behaviors. These sex-role parameters may vary depending on age, ethnic background, birth order, socioeconomic status, geographic region, and so on. But, generally, they are well-defined and distinct from each other.

The Theories of George Herbert Mead

George Herbert Mead never presented his ideas in book form, and the four volumes published under his name are for the most part stenographic reports of lectures. *Mind, Self and Society* represents notes taken during 1927 and 1930 in Mead's social psychology lectures, a course he had given since 1900.

Both as philosopher and social psychologist, Mead was concerned with socialization. As a philosopher he was interested in the question: Which came first, the individual or society? Many philosophers, in trying to account for the existence of society, assumed that individuals endowed with mind and self-consciousness could exist prior to or outside society. According to Thomas Hobbes's version of the contract theory of society, man first lived in a state of nature in which each individual pursued his desires as best he could. This wholly individual pursuit of satisfaction resulted, however, in "the war of all against all." Therefore, in the interests of self-preservation and to render their satisfactions more secure, men "contracted" with each other to accept authority and live according to rules—they agreed to create society.

Sophisticated contract theorists probably did not believe that a pure state of nature ever actually existed, and in any case they were more concerned to *justify* social norms than to trace their historical origins. Nevertheless, their argument assumes a "natural man," who had mind and selfhood prior to and outside society.

92

Mead considered the human individual endowed with mind and self as the *product,* not the creator, of society. "The self . . . is essentially a social structure, and it arises in social experience. After a self has arisen, it in a certain sense provides for itself its social experiences, and so we can conceive of an absolutely solitary self. But it is impossible to conceive of a self arising outside of social experience" (1934:140).

Mead thought the distinctive task of social psychology is to explain how society "gets into" the individual, determines his behavior, and thus becomes part of his psychology, or of his "selfhood." He also advanced specific hypotheses concerning stages in the development of the self from the narrow capacity to take on the attitudes of other individuals to the more generalized capacity to relate to the community.

The essentials of Mead's point of view may be stated in a few key propositions. These are briefly presented and explained in the following discussion.

Preverbal Interaction

Social interaction precedes language, mind, and self-consciousness. Among many animal species sexual union and care of the young make necessary at least some continuing interaction with another individual; thus, rudimentary family life exists among species lower than man. In most cases common cooperation is made necessary by biological differences in capacity or function, of which sexual differentiation is the most striking example.

Among ants and bees, some individuals are biologically specialized to perform a single function, such as reproduction or food-getting. The survival of both individual and species depends upon the interaction of highly specific biological roles in a complex pattern of co-operative acts. In this way ant and bee "societies" arise. But their organization is, strictly speaking, a biological one, and interaction is based on physical and chemical cues.

Nonverbal communication must precede language. Interaction, even on the biological level, is a kind of communication; otherwise, common acts could not occur. A dancing male bird does not deliberately intend to communicate a readiness to mate; yet communication occurs because it is more or less guaranteed by the nervous system of the species. As a rule, the dance does arouse an appropriate response in a female, much as if she "understood" the meaning of the male's behavior.

The dance communicates because it stands for something else. It is not an isolated, meaningless bit of behavior. It is a *natural sign,* a product and manifestation of a state of organic tension, of a physiological readiness to mate. The tensions behind the mating dance require for their relief appropriate behavior on the part of another. Thus, because the dance is a natural sign directed toward another, it can be viewed as a *gesture,* that is, as nonverbal communicative behavior.

If man could not first participate in a nonverbal "conversation" of gestures, he could never communicate by means of language. Before language can convey meaning *to* the child, the behavior of his mother must have meaning *for* him. He could never understand the meaning of *"angry"* or *"hungry"* unless he first understood an angry or a nurturing gesture. Nor would his mother's gesture have meaning for the child unless both were participants in a joint activity. The emergence of language depends upon the existence of already established, albeit primitive, social interaction.

The Importance of Language

Language creates minds and selves. Despite interaction and communication, neither mind nor self-consciousness need be present in these primitive social acts; indeed without language they cannot be. Language alone makes possible ideas and communication by ideas.

The male bird's mating dance has meaning for the female when it prompts an answering response from her, but it cannot be said to have meaning for the dancing male. He is simply behaving. *He* is not telling the other he is ready to mate; if anything "tells" the other, it is the dance and not the dancing bird. The bird's behavior communicates, but not the bird.

Language makes it possible to replace behavior with ideas. Though the mother can teach her child the meaning of "I am angry" only by behaving in appropriate ways, once the child learns the words, the mother need not behave in an angry fashion in order to communicate displeasure. Having learned what the words mean, the child now has the *idea* of anger. Because mother and child now share an idea, the child can respond to what the mother says as well as to what she does. It is the mother (not merely her behavior) that now communicates.

Furthermore, having the idea of anger, the child can *think* about his mother's anger; it can have meaning for him even when she is absent or not angry. Thus as the child acquires language he acquires mind. He also becomes self-conscious as he reflects not only about his mother's anger but about himself and his own behavior. Thus he acquires a self. The attitudes of others, such as his mother's anger, lead him to modify his inner self as well as his external actions. As he matures, the child no longer adjusts merely to the immediate expression of approval and disapproval; he changes himself and his ways in order to achieve a stable adjustment to other people and his environment. He *takes the attitudes of others* into himself as enduring guides and standards, as part of his own personality.

The Social Self

Mind and self are social. Much of language is factual, simply identifying objects about which people communicate. Though factual, these meanings are nevertheless social; they are shared and common meanings. In time "dog" and "cat" and "cow" come to have the same factual meaning for the child that they do for others.

Through language the child also learns the attitudes and emotions with which objects are viewed by his parents and others. The factual and emotive meanings of words are separable in analysis, but in practice they are learned together, and language transmits not only names of objects but appropriate or prescribed

Do you see in this photograph an example of socialization by a parent as well as an attention-getting interpersonal communication strategy?

attitudes toward the objects named. Some of these are designed to enable the child better to deal with his physical environment; for example, attitudes of wariness and caution may go along with "dog" and "fire". Others are more distinctively social. Factually "cow" means the same to a Hindu as to an American, but to the Hindu child the meaning of "cow" also includes attitudes of religious reverence and respect. Thus as he learns language the child is initiated into a world of social meanings; he shares the meanings that objects have for his social group.

Just as the child learns to take the same attitudes toward objects in his environment that others take toward them, so he learns to take the same attitudes toward himself that others take toward him. When the mother tells the child that he has done something good or bad, right or wrong, she is trying to teach him merely what the words mean. She treats the child as an object toward which she takes a certain attitude, and tries to induce the child to do the same. He is encouraged *to take himself as an object*. He evaluates and controls himself in the same way that he evaluates and controls other objects, and he does so from the standpoint of someone else. He is taught, in short, to make appropriate or prescribed responses to his own behavior just as he has been taught to make appropriate or prescribed responses to other objects in his environment.

Because this control occurs through taking the attitudes of others toward oneself, because it is control from the standpoint of someone else, it is distinctively social in nature. This is how society "gets into" the individual. Of all the animals, man alone is able to exercise self-criticism; but all self-criticism is social criticism insofar as the principles that guide it are the result of internalizing the attitudes of others toward oneself.

Prior to using the attitudes of others to think about himself, the young child is not *self*-conscious. As an animal, the human child is conscious. He has sensations, feelings, and perceptions of which he is aware. It is by thinking about himself in the light of the attitudes of others toward him that the individual becomes self-conscious and begins to acquire a social self.

Maturation and Response to the Other

As the individual matures he develops the capacity to respond to significant others and to *a generalized other*. All higher forms of communication depend upon the capacity of each to put himself in the place of the other, that is, to control his own responses in terms of an understanding of what the other's responses are likely to be. As he learns to control his behavior in the light of another individual's attitudes either toward that behavior or toward the environment, the individual can be said to be learning to take the role of the other. He responds to himself and to the world as he anticipates the other would respond. The capacity to put oneself in the place of the other emerges only with maturity and in the process of social interaction and communication.

The child first internalizes the attitudes of particular individuals, primarily his parents, toward himself. At this stage he does not have the capacity to participate in organized group life or to engage in complex, co-operative games governed by impersonal rules. Social interaction is limited to interaction with specific individuals, and behavior is largely determined by the child's experience with those who are not merely others but *significant* others for him. At this stage of development, his play consists largely of simple role-taking. He plays at being a mother, father, doctor, or postman. He re-enacts the behavior and attitudes of others as individuals.

The child gradually learns, however, a less personalized, more complex form of role-taking as expressed in his developing ability to participate in organized games. In baseball, for example, the acting out of a highly specific individual role is not required. The player adjusts his behavior from moment to moment, and does so in the light of what a number of others are doing and of the rules and purposes of the game. In performing his role, he responds to a *generalized other*.

Mead used this term to designate "The organized community or social group which gives to the individual his unity of self . . ." (1934:154). One who takes the standpoint of the generalized other knows what is required to keep the group to its distinctive aims and rules. He sees not only his own role, not only the roles of particular others, but the ways roles are related in determining the outcome of group acticity. Gradually the individual becomes capable of taking on the point of view of the community as a whole.

The 'I' and the 'Me'

The social self has a creative, spontaneous aspect. To stress the essentially social nature of the self may seem to imply that the self is completely determined by the internalized attitudes of others. This is not so. To be sure, the internalized attitudes of others represent what the individual takes into account when he acts; they are the demands that group life actually or supposedly makes upon him. Nevertheless, his behavior has a large element of freedom and spontaneity. The demands of the social situation pose a problem to the acting individual, but there is considerable leeway in how he meets the problem. Furthermore, the individual can never predict precisely what his response in a given situation will be. The baseball player wants to play good ball; in this sense his behavior is determined by accepting the demands and standards of the group. But whether he will make a brilliant play or an error neither he nor anyone else knows beforehand.

Mead called the acting self the 'I.' The 'me,' on the other hand, is that part of the self that is an organization of the internalized attitudes of others. The 'I' represents the self insofar as it is free, has initiative, novelty, and uniqueness. The 'me' represents the conventional part of the self. The 'I' responds to the 'me' and takes it into account, but it is not identical with it.

There may be varying amounts of 'I' and 'me' in behavior. In impulsive behavior, the 'me' is absent; in Freudian language, the 'I' is not being censored by the 'me.' Social control is present to the extent that the 'I' is controlled by the 'me'. The oversocialized individual is overdetermined by his 'me'. In more normal circumstances, the individual responds to a situation in its social aspects but does so with some regard for his own unique capacities and needs. The most gratifying experiences are those in which the demands of the 'me'—or of the social situation—permit the expression and realize the potentialities of the 'I.'

In primitive society the individual self is more completely determined than in civilized societies by the 'me,' that is, by the particular social group to which the individual belongs. Primitive society offers much less scope for the 'I.' Indeed, the development of civilization is largely dependent upon the progressive social liberation of the individual self. The 'I' is the innovator, the source of new ideas and energy to initiate social change.

The enlargement of the self is dependent upon and in turn supports the breadth of community values. What the self is and how it develops depends upon the nature of the community whose attitudes the individual has internalized. Membership in a community is more than physical presence in it; the small boy belongs to his gang, not to the city in which he lives: " . . . until one can respond to himself as a community responds to him, he does not genuinely belong to the community" (1934:265).

The self will be isolated and alienated from other selves if it is a member of a socially isolated group or one with narrow or provincial values. The self becomes enlarged to the extent that it belongs to a group engaged in activities that bring it into contact with other groups. The rise of national states, which seems to be and often is a constraining and limiting influence, nevertheless encourages the development of internationalism and the extension of man's effective community. It does so because it fosters communication among nations rather than limiting it to communication among intra-national groups. Similarly the self becomes enlarged to the extent that it belongs to a community that subscribes to universal values, such as the objective standards of science or a religious belief in human brotherhood.

Summary

1. Language is a biologically given potentiality of man. But man could not develop this potentiality without first being able to interact socially and communicate with others in a nonverbal, gestural way within shared, ongoing activities. Without social interaction, language would not be possible. Out of social interaction, accompanied by language, human reason and self-consciousness emerge.

2. Social interaction, when accompanied and facilitated by language, leads "naturally" to social control and the development of human society.

3. Through language the individual takes on or internalizes the attitudes of others toward both the environment and himself. In this way, the human being acquires a social self. The young child internalizes the attitudes of those who are significant others to him. With maturity the individual learns to relate to a generalized other, that is, to organized group activity and the community as a whole.

4. The individual need not and indeed cannot be totally controlled by the internalized attitudes of others, that is, by the 'me' part of the self. The individual is also an 'I,' that is, someone who takes account of the 'me' but is not necessarily dominated by it. The 'I' may act upon, influence, and modify the social process.

In language development, the learning process enables the human infant to progress from early babbling noises to symbolic communication (as defined in Chapter 3), which extends the scope of the child's reality far beyond his immediate experience. That is, the child learns such abstract concepts as justice and truth, and also learns to think and talk about the past and the future, thus he eventually develops a concept of history. Figure 4.1 traces the development of human infant communication from birth to age two and one half. But how do we actually learn this wonderful thing called language? In fact, the learning process is enormously complex and there are many theories that attempt to describe it—each one of which would constitute a volume in itself. What follows are very brief summaries of five of the major theories, adapted from the work of Robert Hopper and Rita Naremore.

The behaviorists B. F. Skinner and his followers argue that learning occurs as a result of *operant conditioning,* which is a form of training that rewards or punishes certain of the child's spontaneous behaviors, resulting in corresponding increases or decreases of those behaviors. For example, if a child is thirsty and says "wa-wa" and is rewarded, or reinforced, by receiving a glass of water, it is likely that the next time he is thirsty he will say "wa-wa" again.

Social-learning theorists also believe that children learn by receiving rewards for the "right" behaviors. But they contend that much of what children do or say is in *imitation* of what they observe in adults. For instance, how did the child in the above example come to say "wa-wa" in the first place if not by imitating the adult word "water"?

Courtney Cazden has tried to teach language to children by using a technique she calls *modeling.* Modeling teachers never repeat or expand upon a child's utterances, rather they comment on what the child said by answering his questions, offering contributions on related topics, and so forth.

Another way that children learn to acquire language is by the simple act of repeating, over and over again, what they have heard. This repetition seems to be intrinsically rewarding to the child and hence the term *self-motivated practice.* Children seem to enjoy playing with words, and if you have ever been around a small child you have probably observed him endlessly repeating or creating variations on one or two words or phrases he has picked up from adult speech.

Finally, Roger Brown and Ursula Bellugi wrote about *rule-induction.* This term refers to the theory that children acquire grammatical rules about their language by making generalizations about what they hear. For instance, children soon learn that past tense is formed by adding *ed* to the end of words. As a result, they

Age in Months

Behavior	0	6	12	18	24	30
First noted vocalizations	xxxxxxxxxx					
First responds to human voice	xxxxxx					
First cooing	xxxxx					
Vocalizes pleasure	xxxxxxxx					
Vocal play	xxxx					
Vocalizes eagerness and displeasure		xxx				
Imitates sounds		xxxxxxxxx				
Vocalizes recognition		xx				
Listens to familiar words		xxxx				
First word		xxxxxxxxxx				
Expressive sounds and conversational jargon			xxxxxxxxxxxxxxxxxxxx			
Follows simple commands			xxxxxxx			
Imitates syllables and words			xxxxxxxx			
Second word			xxxxx			
Responds to "no" and "don't"			xxxxxxxxxxxxxx			
First says more than 2 words				xxxxx		
Names object or picture				xxxxxxxxxxxx		
Comprehends simple questions				xx		
Combines words in speech					xxxxxxxxxx	
First uses pronouns					xxxxxx	
First phrases and sentences					xxxx	
Understands prepositions					xxx	

SOURCE: "Composite Table Showing Age in Months at which Selected Items are Reported in Eight Major Studies of Infant Development," George A. Miller, *Language and Communication*, New York: McGraw-Hill Book Company, Inc., 1951, p. 142.

FIGURE 4.1

will add *ed* to everything when they want to talk about the past. For example, "We goed to the park yesterday," or "Daddy buyed me a cookie." These errors eventually disappear when the child is corrected enough times, but the general rule has been incorporated into his vocabulary.[5]

Which of these theories are valid and which are not is still an open question. Likely, we learn as a result of a combination of all of them. In any case, the influence of the parents or caretakers is great. With increasing age, the child learns to communicate symbolically. Figure 4.2, as a follow-up to Figure 4.1, further traces the communication strategies of children.

Communication Strategies

Group	Eating	
	Task	*Strategy*
I	Get attention	Throws spoon
	Get food	Asks for it by name
		Pulls M* into kitchen
		Cries
		Has temper tantrum
II	Get food	Cries and screams
		Says it's for someone else
		Says he is *sick* and food
		will make him feel better
	Avoid food	Says, "It tastes horrible!"
III	Get food	Looks expectant
	Avoid food	Gags
IV	Get food	Asks repetitively

Group	Sleeping	
	Task	*Strategy*
I	Prolong the	Plays independently
	bedtime hour	Asks for toys
		Goes to F*
		Asks for hugs
	Get M into	Throws things on floor
	bedroom	Asks for water
		Screams

SOURCE: From Royce Rodnick and Barbara Wood, "The Communication Strategies of Children," *The Speech Teacher*, 1973, 22, 120.

FIGURE 4.2 Group I describes the strategies of children one to two years old. Group II describes communication strategies of children three to four years of age. Group III describes strategies for five to six year olds. And Group IV describes strategies for seven to eleven year olds.

Socialization by Peers

Between the ages of five and sixteen the social institution of the school, which provides opportunities for peer-group relationships and the formation of a youth subculture, competes with the family as a socializing agent. In fact, the school may become the predominant influence.

By late adolescence there is generally even less contact with the parents than in early adolescence, and the youth's self-concept is characterized by ambivalence between wanting to be an independent adult and needing the security and support of his family.

Group	Sleeping	
	Task	*Strategy*
II	Prolong the bedtime hour	Asks for hugs
		Asks to watch TV
		Throws things
		Tells F she's afraid of M
	Get someone into bedroom	Says there are monsters
		Asks for water
		Yells, "Bad Mommy!"
III	Prolong the bedtime hour	Tells M that he loves it when she reads
IV	Prolong the bedtime hour	Yells at brother in next room until F comes in
		Says she wants to wait up until F gets home

Group	Playing	
	Task	*Strategy*
I	Get M to play	Pulls on M
		Talks loudly
		Climbs and pulls
		Bangs toys
	Get something forbidden	Nags
		Asks M to leave room
II	Get M to play	Becomes affectionate
		Says he is lonely
		Pulls at clothes
		Bangs toys
		Asks questions repeatedly
	Get attention	Climbs on lap
III	Get M to play	Says he is lonely
IV	None mentioned	None mentioned

*M = mother; F = father.

FIGURE 4.2 (cont'd)

Adolescence is a time of conflict and contradictions, and the young person's internal struggle is often mirrored in his unpredictable behavior, which is sometimes categorized as "adolescent rebellion."

The pressure of the peer group is strong in any historical period, but perhaps coming of age in the 1960s was particularly rough. Joyce Maynard humorously describes the 1960s as a period in which everyone knew each other's faces and bodies and wardrobes so well that any change was noticed at once. She recalls that in the lunchroom, the girls with too-long dresses and hair "that curled in the bent, squared-off way that came from using bobby pins" sat at tables separate from the girls with matching mohair skirts and sweaters and shoulder bags bursting with notes and cosmetics. And when a special event took away some of the lunchroom tables, the whole ecology collapsed. Each September in locker rooms girls pulled off shirts and revealed what had happened over the summer to determine who could join that particular club started by some girls who, as early as the third grade, hunched over from the weight and shame of early bras. But, it happened too often to be a coincidence that the same people who were cool, cute, bright, and popular were always the ones who got picked first or who were captains of teams.[6]

It is clear that no other time of life is quite as emotionally painful as adolescence can be. The signs of seeking an identity are clearly evident during late adolescence. The young person typically is concerned with cultural values and with the choices that his society's institutions make available to him. If he is committed to certain ideals he may find it easier to make the transition to an increasing independence from his parents. It is also important that there are other people with whom he can discuss his beliefs and concerns—a group he belongs to not so much for social purposes but because the members share mutual ideals.[7]

With increasing independence from the family, the adolescent becomes more and more involved with society at large. And as his world expands and he encounters a wide variety of people, subcultures, and institutions, the young person modifies and redefines his attitudes and beliefs to accommodate this new input. In early adolescence, one is still accorded some of the privileges of childhood. But as one approaches twenty-one, he is expected to adopt mature attitudes and "put away childish things." Inherent in this expectation is that the youth will choose a future occupation. Such a choice is, of course, a major life decision, and it will, in part, be determined by all of the relevant influences that have preceded it—parental values, sex-role identification, peer-group attitudes, and so on. Once a choice is made, the youth's self-concept will be substantially revised to include a definition of himself in terms of the work he has chosen.

Socialization now continues within the context of the work environment. In other words, the individual is socialized into the rules and values of his work group. Again, through interactions with others—the foreman, the plant supervisor, the office manager, or the union shop steward—the individual learns what is considered appropriate. Often, for example, new employees are taught not to work too hard, not too many hours overtime, lest management begin to expect it of everyone. Similarly, junior executives learn that one does not improve upon suggestions made by vice-presidents of the company. In moving from one occupation to another, new behaviors and attitudes must be learned. A college professor learns new behaviors when he becomes a faculty dean, a Vietnam veteran learned to leave the norms of warfare behind in order to resume life as a civilian, and a woman who has spent many years as a housewife adopts new rules and values when she enters the work force. This process of resocialization may be rather difficult since it requires the stripping away of previous behaviors which are inappropriate. It is not uncommon for a freshman college student, on his first visit home, to remark upon the immature, "high-school" behaviors of individuals who just a few months ago were his classmates and friends. The fact that the student's own behaviors no longer mirror those of his younger friends is not evidence of any maturational benefits of a few months on a college campus. Rather, it displays quite clearly the manner in which behaviors may be modified when an individual finds himself interacting with a new group of peers in a new situation or environment.

★Probe Questions

American society places much emphasis on the individual. The predominance of the pronouns *I* and *you* in college student's language usage (as noted in Chapter 3) is one indication of that emphasis. Thus, rewards are typically recognized as such only when meted out on an individual basis. For example, if all members of a work group receive the same amount of salary increase, the pay raise is not usually considered a reward for the group. And although there is a "public domain" and there are recognitions of communal property, possessions are primarily personal. One says "my group" rather than the "group's me."

A Congressional Medal of Honor is bestowed on an individual soldier, not on the group of officers and other soldiers who trained him. Capital punishment is an individual fate, not the destiny of parents, teachers, siblings, and associates who interacted with him. Mothers, fathers, or, at the most, both parents receive credit for rearing "good" children and receive blame for rearing obnoxious delinquents.

Against this climate of individuality, then, consider the following questions:

When a member of a bowling team ends the season with a higher average than any of his teammates, should he treat his teammates to a beer or should his teammates treat him?

When a son or daughter behaves in a manner that is consistent with the behavior of his or her peers but that is different from the behavior approved by the parents' peers, who faces a problem of identity?

Society seems to place heavy emphasis on a theory of individual responsibility. Some social scientists are emphasizing a theory of socialization. Which of these two opposing theories is a cop-out, an excuse or rationalization for problems that so far have defied solution?

The Socialization of Sex Roles

During the first student rebellion at Columbia University in the Spring of 1968, after the administration buildings had been taken, the male militants blandly turned to their sisters-in-arms and assigned them the task of preparing the food while they planned further strategy. "And Stokely Carmichael observed, taking the logical point of view, before marrying a woman older, richer, and more famous than himself, that women indeed had a place in the Movement—on their backs."[8] Males have learned their male roles well, and human liberation has to contend with the consequences of the socialization process.

Probably one of the most stable aspects of socialization is the learning of sex-role-appropriate behavior. It is hard to imagine any other social role that has a greater impact on an individual's behavior, emotional reactions, cognitive organization, and general psychological and social development.[9] A person's gender may become a factor in determining occupational choice, personal life style, relations with others, membership and status in various organizations, automobile insurance premiums, ability to own credit cards, and on and on. The socialization of sex roles, like most other aspects of socialization, begins almost from the time of birth. Baby girls are dressed in pink and treated more delicately than blue-garbed baby boys. Soon, little girls are put in dresses and given dolls to play with while little boys wear pants and play with balls and trucks. Parents further differentiate sex-role-appropriate behavior by establishing a system of rewards and punishments that serve to reinforce the sex role. Thus, little boys learn to be aggressive, independent, and gregarious, while little girls learn to be passive, dependent, and demure. Figure 4.3 delineates some of the early sex differences that result from socialization.

Boys	Girls
Testosterone	
More physical activity	Less physical activity
Greater aggressiveness	Less aggressiveness
Less pain sensitivity	More pain sensitivity
More insistent sexual impulses	Lower sexual impulses
More masturbation	Less masturbation
Figure Ground*	
More inclined to focus on figure as distinct from ground	More influenced by entire context
More likely to ignore what is irrelevant to problem being solved or to goal	More attention to complexity, to visual, aural, social stimuli
Personality	
More intent on own purposes, more likely to be unaware of or resistant to parental demands	More aware of social demands, better able to assess parental wishes and anticipate them
Receives more parental pressure to inhibit or channel aggressiveness; more likely to be rewarded for achievement, to have to struggle for sense of autonomy against parental pressure	More likely to conform, to be rewarded for goodness, to remain dependent on others for self-esteem
Higher self-esteem based on achievement	Higher self-esteem based on being loved
Independence, achievement, objectivity	Interdependence, conformity, subjectivity

*AUTHOR'S NOTE: In the term "Figure Ground," Figure refers to the foreground of a perceptual field and Ground refers to the background of the same perceptual field.

SOURCE: "Socialization of Early Sex Differences," in Judith M. Bardwick, *Psychology of Women: A Study of Bio-Cultural Conflicts*, New York: Harper & Row, Publishers, 1971, p. 94.

FIGURE 4.3 Bardwick identified these differences between boys and girls.

Social-Learning Theory

Social-learning theorists believe that children acquire appropriate sex-role behaviors through the active teaching by parents, peers, and teachers and through imitating the behaviors of these influential persons. The teaching aspect of this socialization process may be subtle or overt, but in either case it involves the administration of rewards (for appropriate behaviors) and punishments (for inappropriate behaviors). Through imitation, children pattern their behaviors after those they observe in adults. A little girl will model, or imitate, her mother or female teacher, and a little boy will do the same with his father or male teacher. And as long as the child's imitations of and interactions with the model continue to be pleasant (rewarding), he or she will continue to emulate the model's behaviors and mannerisms. In this way, the act of imitating itself becomes a rewarding experience. [10]

Cognitive-Development Theory

The psychologist Lawrence Kohlberg offers another theoretical explanation of sex-role acquisition in terms of *cognitive development;* that is, the process by which a person acquires knowledge or becomes aware. Kohlberg believes that sex-role development begins when children first understand the meaning of the labels "boy" and "girl," which apparently happens by the age of two or three. They then use these labels to define themselves and others. By the fifth or sixth year the labels are a significant part of their self-concept, and they are then motivated to adopt the attitudes, values, and behaviors that the society associates with being "male" or "female."[11]

Consequences of Sex-Role Training

In studies that examined the behavioral differences between pre-school boys and girls, researchers have observed that boys are more aggressive (especially to other boys) and more interested in physical activities than are girls. Girls were found to be more complacent and more likely to be cooperative than boys.[12] Similar studies with nursery-school children have shown that children learn quite early to choose sex-appropriate toys as their playthings. In one study, young boys experienced considerable anxiety and even discredited their favorite teacher (an accomplice in the experiment) when she picked out a girl's toy for them to keep.[13] In another study children were observed playing in a room with a mixture of "masculine" and "feminine" toys. After being allowed to play alone for awhile, the parents of the children were instructed to enter and act as if they were at home. In many instances upon the entrance of the parents, the young boys would drop the sex-inappropriate toy with which they had been playing and begin to play with a truck or space rocket.[14]

The process continues in the schools. A first-grade teacher, for example, may ask for "two strong boys to carry some boxes" as though it were not noticed that most of the six-year-old girls seated in the same classroom are larger and stronger than the boys. And the socialization of sex roles continues, as do other forms of socialization, throughout life.

How Sex Roles Are Perpetuated Through Language

In the emerging climate of increasing human awareness, it is becoming ever more apparent how even language itself fosters and maintains the process of socialization. For instance, how great is the effect on women of the use of the word *"man*kind," as opposed to the seldom-used word *"human*kind"? And to what extent is a woman's individuality neglected by labeling her Miss or Mrs. (that is, without a man or with a man) instead of, simply, Ms.? Men, on the other hand, are labeled Mr., whether they are married or not. What is the underlying significance of a woman adopting the name of the man she marries? Does it mean he owns her?

Job titles, too (until the recent movement for the Equal Rights Amendment), have perpetuated the notion that women should not aspire to certain positions of authority. For example, if a woman desires to be the chair*man* of the board of a company or corporation, does it mean she is somehow not a woman? Why are the labels "teacher" and "secretary" almost always followed by the pronoun "she," and the labels "professor" and "boss" almost always followed by "he"?

Consider, too, the words that men use to refer to women: "chick," "fox," "pig," "pussy," "dog," "bird," and so on. It seems no coincidence that women are equated with animals (or somehow as less than human) whereas men are often referred to as "dude" (cowboy) or "stud" (breeder).

As a result of the growing awareness of the consequences of language as a reflection of cultural attitudes—largely as one outcome of the Women's Liberation Movement—our language is gradually beginning to reflect a more equalitarian and accepting attitude toward women. Job titles have been changed to words ending in "—person," many women refer to themselves as Ms., and more and more women are keeping their maiden names when they marry. For to the extent that cultural attitudes are reflected in the language, so too can cultural attitudes be shaped by the language.

Judith M. Bardwick of the University of Michigan has made a thorough study of sexism, and her book *The Psychology of Women*, published in 1971, is a careful and well-known review of psychological literature up to that date. Although much has changed since then, Adapted Reading No. 10, in which Ms. Bardwick discusses the socialization of women, is a useful compendium on the subject.

The Socialization of Women

In this adapted reading first published in the early 1970s, the socialization of women in our society is discussed. According to this reading, how does the socialization process affect the self–concept and interpersonal communication behavior of women in our society? Do you feel that there have been changes in the last few years?

What are big boys made of? What are big boys made of? Independence, aggression, competitiveness, leadership, task orientation, outward orientation, assertiveness, innovation, self-discipline, stoicism, activity, objectivity, analytic-mindedness, courage, unsentimentality, rationality, confidence, and emotional control.

"What are big girls made of? What are big girls made of?" Dependence, passivity, fragility, low pain tolerance, nonaggression, noncompetitiveness, inner orientation, interpersonal orientation, empathy, sensitivity, nurturance, subjectivity, intuitiveness, yieldingness, receptivity, inability to risk, emotional liability, supportiveness.[1]

These adjectives describe the idealized, simplified stereotypes of normal masculinity and feminity. They also describe real characteristics of boys and girls, men and women. While individual men and women may more resemble the stereotype of the opposite sex, group differences between the sexes bear out these stereotypic portraits. How does American society socialize its members so that most men and women come close to the society's ideal norms?

From infancy children have behavioral tendencies that evoke particular types of responses from parents, older siblings, and anyone else who interacts with the child. Such responses are a function of both individual values—whether the particular person values outgoing extroverted behavior, for example—and widespread social values of acceptable child behavior. Socialization

---

Adapted from Judith M. Bardwick and Elizabeth Douvan, "Ambivalence: the Socialization of Women," Chapter 9 of Woman in Sexist Society, *pp. 147–159, edited by Vivian Gornick and Barbara K. Moran, New York: Basic Books, Inc., 1971. Footnotes deleted and renumbered.*

refers to the pressures—rewarding, punishing, ignoring, and anticipating—that push the child toward evoking acceptable responses. . . .

When people find their ways of coping comfortable and gratifying, they are not motivated to develop new techniques which in the long run might be far more productive. All very young children are dependent on adults for their physical well-being and for the knowledge that they exist and have value. Girls' self-esteem remains dependent upon other people's acceptance and love; they continue to use the skills of others instead of evolving their own. The boy's impulsivity and sexuality are sources of enormous pleasure independent of anyone else's response; these pleasures are central to the early core-self. Negative sanctions from powerful adults against masturbation, exploration, and physical aggression threaten not only the obvious pleasures, but, at heart, self-integrity. Thus, boys are pressured by their own impulses and by society's demands to give up depending predominantly on the response of others for feelings of self-esteem. Adult responses are unpredictable and frequently threatening. Forced to affirm himself because of the loss of older, more stable sources of esteem, the boy begins, before the age of five, to develop a sense of self and criteria of worth which are relatively independent of others' responses. He turns to achievements in the outer and real world and begins to value himself for real achievements in terms of objective criteria.

On the other hand, neither the girl's characteristic responses nor widespread cultural values force her to give up older, more successful modes of relating and coping. Her sexuality is neither so genital nor so imperative,[2] but, rather, an overall body sensuality, gratified by affection and cuddling. Since girls are less likely to masturbate, run away from home, or bite and draw blood, their lives are relatively free of crisis until puberty. Before that girls do not have to conform to threatening new criteria of acceptability to anywhere near the extent that boys do. When boys are pressured to give up their childish ways it is because those behaviors are perceived as feminine by parents. Boys have to earn their masculinity early. Until puberty, feminity is a verbal label, a given attribute—something that does not have to be earned. This results in a significant delay in the girl's search for identity, development of autonomy, and development of internal criteria for self-esteem. Because they continue to depend on others for self-definition and affirmation and are adept at anticipating other people's demands, girls are conformist. Girls are rewarded by good grades in school, parental love, teacher acceptance, and peer belonging. As a result, girls remain compliant and particularly amenable to molding by the culture. . . .[3]

Schools are generally feminine places,[4] institutions where conformity is valued, taught largely by conformist women. The course content, the methods of assessing progress, and the personal conduct required create difficulties for boys who must inhibit impulsivity, curb aggression, and restrain deviance. The reward structure of the school system perpetuates the pattern set by relationships with the parents—boys are further pressured to turn to their peers for acceptance and to develop internal criteria and objective achievements; girls are further urged to continue the non-deviant, noninnovative, conformist style of life.

Girls are rewarded with high grades in school, especially in the early years of grammar school. What do girls do especially well in? What are they being asked to master? Grammar, spelling, reading, arithmetic—tasks that depend a great deal upon memorization and demand little independence, assertiveness, analysis, innovativeness, creativity.[5] The dependent, passive girl, cued into the affirming responses of teachers, succeeds and is significantly rewarded in school for her "good" behavior and her competent memorizing skills.

It appears that until puberty academically successful girls evolve a "bisexual" or dual self-concept. Both sexes are rewarded for achievement, especially academic achievement. Girls, as well as boys, are permitted to compete in school or athletics without significant negative repercussions. The girl who is rewarded for these successes evolves a self-concept associated with being able to successfully cope and compete. While there are no negative repercussions and there is a high probability of rewards from parents and teachers as long as her friends are similarly achieving, this girl will also feel normally feminine (although questions of feminity are probably not critically important in self-evaluation of prepubertal girls unless they are markedly deviant). With the onset of the physical changes of puberty, definitions of normalcy and feminity change and come precipitately closer to the stereotype. Now behaviors and qualities that were rewarded, especially successful competing, may be perceived negatively.[6] Femininity also becomes an attribute that has to be earned—this task is made crucially difficult because of the girl's ambivalent feelings toward her body.[7]

The maturation of the girl's reproductive system brings joy and relief, feelings of normalcy, and the awareness of sexuality. Simultaneously, in normal girls the physical changes are accompanied by blood and pain, the expectation of body distortion in pregnancy, the threat of the trauma of birth, and the beginning of sexual desirability. In addition, the physical changes of menstruation are accompanied by significant and predictable emotional cycles sufficiently severe to alter the perception of her body as secure or stable.[8] Simultaneously joyful and fearful, the young adolescent girl must begin to evolve a feminine self-concept that accepts the functions and future responsibilities of her mature body; at the same time these physical changes are cues for alterations in the demands made upon her by the culture.[9] From the very beginning of adolescence girls, as potential heterosexual partners, begin to be punished for conspicuous competing achievement and to be rewarded for heterosexual success. Socialization in adolescence emphasizes the use of the cosmetic exterior of the self to lure men, to secure affection, to succeed in the competition of dating. At the same time the girl is warned not to succeed too much: conspicuous success in competitive dating threatens her friendship with girls. She learns in puberty that she is likely to be punished for significant competition in either of her important spheres.

Thus, for a long time, even the girls who are competitive, verbally aggressive, and independent can feel normal, but with the onset of puberty girls are faced with their first major crises: they must come to terms with and find pleasure in their physical femininity and develop the proper psychological "femininity." Since they are still primarily cued to others for feelings of esteem, and largely defined by interpersonal relations, under the stress of their evolving, incomplete feminine identity, most girls conform to the new socialization criteria. While girls characteristically achieved in grade school because of rewards for this "good" behavior from others (rather than for achievement's own sake), in adolescence the establishment of successful interpersonal relationships becomes the self-defining, most rewarding, achievement task.[10] When that change in priorities occurs—and it tends to be greatest in the later years of high school, and again in the later years of college—personal qualities, such as independence, aggression, and competitive achievement, that might threaten success in heterosexual relationships, are largely given up.

While boys are often afraid of failing, girls are additionally afraid of succeeding.[11] The adolescent girl, her parents, her girl friends, and her boy friends perceive success, as measured by objective, visible achievement as antithetical to feminity. Some girls defer consciously, with tongue in cheek, but the majority, who were never significantly aggressive, active, or independent, internalize the norms and come to value themselves as they are desired by others. The only change from childhood is that the most important source of esteem is no longer the parents but the heterosexual partner.

The overwhelming majority of adolescent girls remain dependent upon others for feelings of affirmation. Unless in early life the girl exhibited the activity, aggression, or sexuality usually displayed by boys, and thereby experienced significant parental prohibitions, there is little likelihood that she will develop independent sources of esteem that refer back to herself. Instead, the loss of love remains for her the gravest source of injury to the self and, predictably, she will not gamble with that critical source of esteem.[12]

In the absence of independent and objective achievements, girls and women know their worth only from others' responses, know their identities only from their relationships as daughters, girl friends, wives, or mothers and, in a literal sense, personalize the world. When we ask female college students what would make them happy or unhappy, when would they consider themselves successful, both undergraduate and graduate students reply: "When I love and am loved; when I contribute to the welfare of others; when I have established a good family life and have happy, normal children; when I know I have created a good, rewarding stable relationship."[13] During adolescence as in childhood, females continue to esteem themselves insofar as they are esteemed by those with whom they have emotional relationships. For many women this never changes during their entire lifetime.

Girls are socialized to use more oblique forms of aggression than boys, such as the deft use of verbal injury or interpersonal rejection. Their aggression is largely directed toward people whose return anger will not be catastrophic to self-esteem—that is, other females. In their relationships with their fathers and later with their boy friends or husbands, girls do not threaten the important and frequently precarious heterosexual sources of love. Instead, aggression is more safely directed toward other women with whom they covertly compete for love. In relationships between men, aggression is overt and the powerful relationships are clear; female aggression is covert, the power relationships rarely admitted. With the denial of disguise of anger, a kind of dishonesty, a pervasive uncertainty, necessarily creeps into each of a woman's relationships, creating further anxiety and continued or increased efforts to secure affection.

The absence of objective success in work makes girls invest in, and be unendingly anxious about, their interpersonal worth. Women use interpersonal success as a route to self-esteem since that is how they have defined their major task. If they fail to establish a meaningful, rewarding, unambivalent love relationship, they remain cued into the response of others and suffer from a fragile or vulnerable sense of self. Those who are secure enough, who have evolved an identity and feeling of worth in love relationships, may gamble and pursue atypical, nontraditional, competitive, masculine achievements.

According to Erik Erikson, the most important task in adolescence is the establishment of a sense of identity. This is more difficult for girls than for boys. Because her sexuality is internal, inaccessible, and diffuse, because she feels ambivalent toward the functions of her mature reproductive system, because she is not punished for her impulsivity, because she is encouraged to remain dependent, a girl's search for her feminine identity is both complex and delayed. To add to her problems, she is aware both of the culture's preference for masculine achievements and of the fact that there is no longer a single certain route for achieving successful femininity. The problem grows ever more complex, ever more subtle. . . .

It is probably not accidental, therefore, that women dominate professions that utilize skills of nurturance, empathy, and competence, where aggressiveness and competitiveness are largely dysfunctional.[14] These professions, notably teaching, nursing, and secretarial work, are low in pay and status. The routes to occupational success for women are either atypical and hazardous or typical, safe, and low in the occupational hierarchy. (It is interesting to note that in the USSR where over 70 percent of the physicians are women, medicine is a low-status occupation.)

In spite of an egalitarian ideal in which the roles and contributions of the sexes are declared to be equal and complementary, both men and women esteem masculine qualities and achievements. Too many women evaluate their bodies, personality qualities, and roles as second-rate. When male criteria are the norms against which female performance, qualities, or goals are measured, then women are not equal. It is not only that the culture values masculine productivity more than feminine productivity. The essence of the derogation lies in the evolution of

Does this represent sex-role-appropriate behavior?

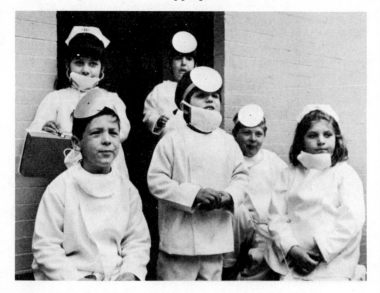

the masculine as the yardstick against which everything is measured. Since the sexes are different, women are defined as not-men and that means not good, inferior. It is important to understand that women in this culture, as members of the culture, have internalized these self-destructive values. . . . [15]

The culture generally rewards masculine endeavors and those males who succeed—who acquire money, power, and status, who enjoy an easy and free sexuality, who acquire and produce things, who achieve in competition, who produce, who innovate and create. By these criteria, women have not produced equally. The contributions that most women make in enhancement and stabilization of relationships, their competence and self-discipline, their creation of life are less esteemed by men and women alike. It is disturbing to review the extent to which women perceive their responsibilities, goals, their very capacities, as inferior to males; it is similarly distressing to perceive how widespread this self-destructive self-concept is. Society values masculinity; when it is achieved it is rewarded. Society does not value femininity as highly; when it is achieved it is not as highly rewarded. . . .

Very few young women understand the very real limits upon achieving imposed by maternity, because they traditionally have had little experience with traditional role responsibilities before they marry. Typically, girls do not ask why there are so few female role models around who succeed in work while they have young children. While children are a real achievement, a source of joy and fulfillment, they are also time-consuming and energy-depleting, a major source of responsibility and anxiety. In today's child-centered milieu, with the decline of the extended family and the dearth of adequate child-care facilities, the responsibility for childrearing falls directly on the mother alone.

Success in the traditional tasks is the usual means by which girls achieve feelings of esteem about themselves, confidence, and identity. [16] In general they have continued, even as adults, to esteem themselves as they are valued by others; that source of esteem is interpersonal, best earned within the noncompetitive, nonaggressive traditional role. Without independent, objective competitive achievements, confidence is best secured within the traditional role—in spite of the priority given to masculine achievements. Whether or not the woman is achievement-oriented, her years of major childrearing responsibilities result in a decline in old work skills, a loss of confidence that she can work, a fear of failing within a competitive milieu that she has left. In other words, not only have specific techniques been lost or new data become unfamiliar, withdrawal from a competitive-achievement situation for a significant length of time creates the conviction that she is not able.

The very characteristics that make a woman most successful in family roles—the capacity to take pleasure in family-centered, repetitive activities, to sustain and support members of the family rather than pursuing her own goals, to enhance relationships through boundaryless empathy—these are all antithetical to success in the bounded, manipulative, competitive, rational, and egocentric world of work. [17] Because they are not highly motivated and because they are uncertain about what is normal or desirable, many women do not work. Even those who do continue to feel psychologically responsible for the maintenance of the family and are unwilling to jeopardize family relationships. Most work at jobs that contribute to family vacations, college fees, or the general family budget. [18] Even women who pursue a career or profession, rather than merely holding a meaningless job, assume the responsibility for two major, demanding roles. Rather than make this commitment, many women professionalize their voluntary or club activities, bringing qualities of aggression, competitiveness, and organizing skills to these "safer" activities.

Women tend not to participate in roles, or seek goals that threaten their important affiliative relationships because in those relationships they find most of their feelings of esteem and identity. This perpetuates psychological dependency which may be functional in the relationships but injurious to the self-concept of those who have internalized the values of the culture. Undeniably, it is destructive to feelings of esteem to know that you are capable and to be aware that you are not utilizing much of your potential. [19] The question of whether nontraditional success jeopardizes feelings of femininity has not yet been answered. Most women today would not be willing to achieve a greater success than their husbands. In this tradition-bound, sex-stereotyped culture, even though millions of women are employed, old values are internalized and serve as criteria for self-evaluation.

Neither men nor women entering marriage expect the sexes to share equally in privileges and responsibilities. Very few couples could honestly accept the wife's having the major economic responsibility for the family while the husband deferred to the demands of her work. Few individuals could reverse roles without feeling that he is not "masculine," and she is not "feminine."[20] Masculinity and feminity are aspects of the self that are clearly tied to roles—which role, how typical or deviant, how well accomplished, the extent of the commitment.

Yet a new reality is emerging today, for this is an era of changing norms. Although the unidimensional stereotype still persists and remains partially viable, it is also simplistic and inaccurate. Both men and women are rejecting the old role allocations which are exaggerated and costly because they push men and women into limited slots solely on the basis of sex. But an era of change results in new uncertainties and the need to evolve new clear criteria of masculinity and femininity, which can be earned and can offer feelings of self-esteem to both sexes.

The socialization model is no longer clear; in its pure form it exists primarily in media, less in life. Since almost half of American women work, the percentage rising with the rising level of education, it is clear that, at least for educated middle-class women, the simplistic stereotype is no longer valid. Similarly we find that more men are rejecting success as the sole source of esteem or masculinity. The male turning toward his family reflects his need not to be bound or limited by the unidimensional role model. For both sexes this is a period of change in which both old and new values coexist, though the visible norms derive from the old model. Today's college students seem to be more aware than the generation that preceded them of the consequences of role choice; they seem to be evolving a goal in which men are more nurturant than they were, while females are freer to participate professionally without endangering the male's esteem. . . .

It is easy to be aware of the discrepancy between the stereotyped norm and the reality. People are not simple. Whenever one sees a total investment or role adoption in its stereotyped, unidimensional form, one suspects a flight from uncertainty about masculinity or femininity. During a period of transition one can expect to see increasing numbers of women quelling anxiety by fleeing into a unidimensional, stereotyped femininity. As new norms gain clarity and force, more flexible roles, personalities, and behaviors will evolve. Role freedom is a burden when choice is available but criteria are unclear; under these circumstances it is very difficult to know whether one has achieved womanhood or has dangerously jeopardized it.

Notes

[1] J. Silerman, "Attentional Styles and the Study of Sex Differences," in D. Mostofsky, ed., *Attention: Contemporary Theory and Analysis* (New York: Appleton-Century Crofts, 1970): H. A. Witkin et al., *Personality through Perception: An Experimental and Clinical Study* (New York: Harper, 1954); J. Kagan, "Acquisition and Significance of Sex Typing and Sex Role Identity," in M. L. Hoffman and L. W. Hoffman, eds., *Review of Child Development Research* (New York: Russel Sage Foundation, 1964), 1:137–167; L. M. Terman and L. E. Tyler, "Psychological Sex Differences," in L. Carmichael, ed., *A Manual of Child Psychology,* 2nd ed. (New York: John Wiley, 1954), ch. 19; E. Douvan and J. Adelson, *The Adolescent Experience* (New York: John Wiley, 1966).

[2] Helene Deutsch, *Psychology of Women* (New York: Grune & Stratton, 1944), vol. 1: K. Horney, "On the Genesis of the Castration Complex in Women," *International Journal of Psychoanalysis 5* (1924): 50–65.

[3]Douvan and Adelson, *op. cit.*

[4]H. S. Becker, "Social Class Variations in One Teacher-Pupil Relationship," *Journal of Educational Sociology* 25 (1952): 451–465.

[5]E. Maccoby, ed., *The Development of Sex Differences* (Stanford: Stanford University Press, 1966).

[6]M. S. Horner, "Fail: Bright Women," *Psychology Today* 3 (November 1969): 36.

[7]J. M. Bardwick, *The Psychology of Women* (New York: Harper & Row, 1971.); E. Douvan, "New Sources of Conflict at Adolescence and Early Adulthood," in Judith M. Bardwick et al., *Feminine Personality and Conflict* (Belmont, Calif.: Brooks/Cole, 1970.

[8]M. E. Ivey and J. M. Bardwick, "Patterns of Affective Fluctuation in the Menstrual Cycle," *Psychosomatic Medicine* 30 (1968): 336–345.

[9]Douvan, *op. cit.*

[10]J. G. Coleman, *The Adolescent Society* (New York: Free Press, 1961).

[11]Horner, *op. cit.*

[12]Deutsch, *op cit.;* Douvan and Adelson, *op. cit.*

[13]J. Bardwick and J. Zweben, "A Predictive Study of Psychological and Psychosomatic Changes Associated with Oral Contraceptives," mimeograph, 1970.

[14]M. Mead, *Male and Female* (New York: William Morrow, 1949).

[15]Bardwick, *op cit.;* Mead, *op. cit.*

[16]Douvan and Adelson, *op. cit.*

[17]D. L. Gutmann, "Woman and Their Conception of Ego Strength," *Merrill-Palmer Quarterly* 11 (1965): 29–240.

[18]F. I. Nye and L. W. Hoffman, *The Employed Mother in America* (Chicago: Rand-McNally, 1963.)

[19]G. Gurin, J. Veroff, and S. Feld, *Americans View Their Mental Health* (New York: Basic Books, 1960).

[20]D. J. Bem and S. L. Bem, "Training the Woman to Know Her Place," based on a lecture delivered at Carnegie Institute of Technology, October 21, 1966, revised 1967.

★Probe Questions

Judith Bardwick states that "too many women evaluate their bodies, personality qualities, and roles as second-rate. When male criteria are the norms against which female performance, qualities, or goals are measured, then women are not equal." There are insights to be gained, however, by reversing that statement to read, "Too many men evaluate their bodies, personality qualities, and roles as second-rate. When female criteria are the norms against which male performance, qualities, or goals are measured, then men are not equal."

Do you think it is possible to accept the first statement and reject the other? Can women achieve liberation without a concomitant liberation of men?

Current literature abounds with the high psychological costs of growing up female. But what are the psychological costs of being a male in our society? What are the benefits that men can derive from women's liberation?

Masculinity and femininity are aspects of self–concept that are clearly tied to roles. What cultural values do Miss or Mr. America contests represent?

Self-Concept Through Communication

Today, psychologists know that a strong sense of identity is critical for mental well-being. As we have seen thus far in our discussion of socialization, our ideas of self are significantly affected by how people respond to us and what we imagine they think of us. Thus, through interpersonal communication we develop an understanding of what we are like and come to form a concept of self.

For example, in 1960 Richard Videbeck conducted a study in which thirty students in an introductory speech class read aloud six poems in the presence of a "visiting expert" in oral communication. Of course the "visiting expert" was a confederate of the experimenter's and randomly and without regard to actual performance gave half the students a positive appraisal—calling attention to their superiority in controlling voice and conveying meaning— and gave the other half of the class a negative, critical appraisal of the same qualities.

Before and after the performance the students rated themselves on the same qualities appraised by the "expert"—their adequacy in controlling voice and conveying meaning. They were also asked to rate themselves in areas related to those appraised but not specifically considered by the expert, as well as in abilities wholly unrelated to those considered by the expert, such as their adequacy in social conversation. Figure 4.4 indicates the amount of change in the self-ratings that took place after the expert evaluation in each of the content areas. The students who received a positive appraisal showed a general increase in their feelings of self-adequacy, an increase that was strongest for attributes directly appraised and weakest for unrelated aspects. Students who received a negative appraisal revised their self-estimates in a negative direction, with the impact varying directly with the relevance of the content to the appraisals. Videbeck's study clearly demonstrates that appraisal from others strongly influences one's conception of self.[15]

It is interesting to note that one survey of 150 college-aged students who were asked to describe the two most negative experiences in their lives revealed that most negative experiences involved interpersonal relations and that most of those involved interactions with teachers! Individual situations of negative experiences with teachers involved humiliation in front of a class, unfairness in evaluation, destroying self-confidence, personality conflicts, and embarrassment.[16]

Robert Rosenthal's experiment conducted in a lower socio-economic neighborhood on the West Coast provides additional evidence of the importance of teachers' appraisals on self-concept. In classes for children of high, low, and average ability, Rosenthal randomly picked 20 percent of the children in each classroom and identified them to their teacher as having scored high on a test for intellectual abilities and who would show remarkable gains in intellec-

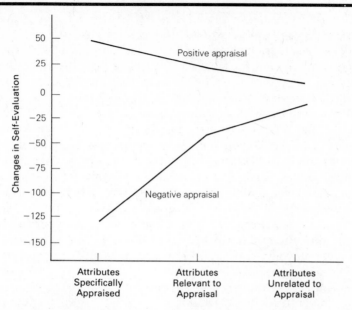

SOURCE: R. Videbeck, "Self-conception and the Reaction of Others," *Sociometry*, 1960, 23, 43.

FIGURE 4.4 One study demonstrated the extent to which self-evaluation increases or decreases in response to positive or negative appraisal. The appraisal even affects self-evaluation in unrelated areas.

tual development during the next eight months. Thus, the only difference between these children and their classmates was what their teacher had been told about them. At the end of the year the students in randomly formed group showed more intellectual gains than their counterparts. It was concluded that the single factor contributing to the students' success was the expectation in the minds of the teachers.[17]

Dean Barnlund has described how two communicators can construct six "persons," each of whom is involved in the communication transaction. For example, in a communication between Al and Marge, Al's image of himself is one "person." In addition, there is Al's image of Marge, Al's image of the way Marge sees him, Marge's image of herself, Marge's image of Al, and Marge's image of how Al sees her. Human communication, then, is not simply a matter of the action-reaction patterns of static beings. Rather, each of us constructs the other and is in turn constructed by the other in every transaction.[18]

Labeling: Words Used to Describe Us

Another important factor that affects self-concept is labeling—the words that we use to describe ourselves and others. Individuals learn to label their dominant behavior patterns in socially prescribed ways. For instance, one might learn that certain behavior is generally classified as "antisocial" and other behavior as "prosocial." One then observes that one's own behavior falls largely into the former category and applies the label accordingly. If that label is confirmed on enough occasions by enough people, the concept of "antisocial" could come to play a dominant role in one's view of self.

Perhaps at the beginning of your course your instructor used an activity called "Who Are You?" by asking you to list ten words or phrases that describe yourself. For example, former President Lyndon Johnson once described himself as "a free man, an American, a United States Senator, a Democrat, a liberal, a conservative, a Texan, a taxpayer, a rancher,and not as young as I used to be nor as old as I expect to be." Answer the question now on a piece of paper. The first few descriptive terms may come easily, but you may have to give some thought to the later ones. Examine your answers. The words you have used are labels that you have given to yourself.

Perhaps you used such terms as "aggressive," "need for achievement," "dominant," "submissive," "liberal," "conservative," "adventuresome," "cautious," "open," "rigid," "authoritarian," and so on. These trait names are useful in describing an individual's behavior, but they should not be regarded as *causes* of that behavior.[19] It is true, though, that once a label has been applied to a person, he may start to behave in ways that justify or reinforce it; also, others may judge *all* his behaviors in terms of the label—remember our discussion of the "halo effect" in Chapter 2?

The single best indicator of the way in which an individual sees the world is the way in which he organizes his experience through language. There is, then, a relationship between one's self-concept and one's communicative behavior. Self-concept is formed through interaction, and behavior is labeled by self-concept.

For example, I once conducted a study involving two experimental groups, one of each sex, and each group composed of two subjects with a self-concept expressing high acceptance of other people and two subjects with a self-concept expressing low acceptance of others. The groups were given no problem to solve; they were just told to spend time talking. The most significant result was the identification of a behavior pattern in subjects expressing high acceptance of others that indicated they received more satisfaction from the discussion, were able to make more group-maintaining types of communications, and that they received more communications directed to them.[20] This study shows that self-concept and communication behavior are related—one can be predicted from the other.

Figure 4.5 shows how self-concept is a function of interpersonal communication and of intrapersonal communication within a given context or culture.

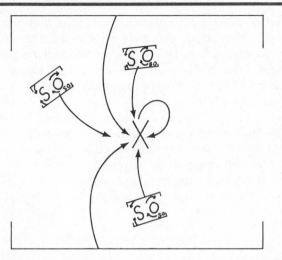

FIGURE 4.5 In the model, "X" represents the self which receives an identity from information from the surrounding context or culture (represented by brackets), from information received through intrapersonal communication, and from socializers or significant others (S.O.) through interpersonal communication.

How is this information related to your present course? Is there a relationship between your self-concept, for example, and the grade you are likely to receive in a communication course? Within the discipline of speech communication, researchers have primarily been concerned with improving the student's concept of self or with decreasing the discrepancy between the student's *ideal* self-concept and his *real* self-concept. The researchers' concern with self-concept is based on the assumption that improved speaking ability is related to a high degree of congruence between real self-concept and ideal self-concept.[21] Thus, by helping the student realize a better self-concept, they can help him to improve his public speaking ability.

More recently, researchers have been concerned with the self-concept, or the label, that best describes the behaviors most likely to receive high grades in an interpersonal communication course. The trait most often investigated—the Machiavellian personality—has been described as one that views others as objects to be manipulated; shows a lack of concern with conventional morality, has a utilitarian view of interactions with others, lacks gross psychopathology (meaning that contact with at least the more objective aspects of reality is within normal range); and has low ideological commitments, as evidenced by a belief that the end justifies the means. The Machiavellian personality is most effective in situations that provide face to face contact. In such circumstances they manipulate more, win more, are persuaded less, and persuade others more. They are also very effective in situations that provide latitude for improvisation and when they must initiate responses as they can or will. In situations in which others may become distracted by irrelevant details, they are able to concentrate single-mindedly on the objective of winning.[22]

Researcher Michael Burgoon demonstrated that Machiavellianism was a predictor of success in communication courses in which small-group or one-to-one communication activities constitute most of the performance experience.[23] Eugene Weinstein has pointed out that the more the Machiavellian embraces manipulative techniques as an orientation toward interaction, suspects that others are also manipulative, and conceals his willingness to exploit, then the more competent and successful he will be in controlling others.[24]

★Probe Questions

If the willingness to manipulate others is the "best" predictor of a student's success in an interpersonal or small group communication course, what is the best predictor of the success of a teacher of those courses? Would it be useful for you to know the "Mach scores" of your teachers so you could (a) know which teacher was the easiest to exploit? (b) know which teacher was most likely to maintain control of the class?

The point is that these questions, from a personal perspective, cannot remain open either for teachers or students, even though they might remain open for the social scientist. Teachers and students have to cope with one another, whereas the social scientist presumably can remain aloof and somewhat removed from such interpersonal relationships.

As a student, and as a reader of this textbook, you do have some choice in the matter. You can ignore these questions, dismiss them as irrelevant, or you can accept them and consider it important to find answers for them by making your own personal decisions about teaching and learning objectives and the problems of exploiting and being exploited.

Therapeutic Communication

As we have seen, the socialization process serves the function of training us to fit into the age, sex, and occupational roles of our society, and as a result of the roles we play, we form a self-concept. And because adolescence is the period in which the most choices have to be made, it is also the time in which the problem of identity is most acute.[25] One's earlier ways of defining self in relation to body, parents, and the opposite sex may become inappropriate during adolescence. To develop a sense of identity, the individual must be able to summarize observations about himself in a conceptual form. In adulthood, placement in almost any formal organization, whether religious or military, social service or business, depends on this capacity to conceptualize self. If we play these roles suitably, we are regarded as normal, but normal individuals are not necessarily healthy individuals. For example, if normal is what most people do, then abnormal is any deviation from the majority. Given this definition, consider a famous study conducted in Manhattan in the early 1960s in which it was reported that a full 81.5 percent of the population that was studied was "less than well."

Healthy individuals are those who play their roles satisfactorily and at the same time derive satisfaction from their roles. Many of us at some time in our lives have either had difficulty in learning a particular role or have been able to play a particular role well but have suffered boredom, frustration, and anxiety. When we are dissatisfied with our roles, we feel a need for change. But the question is, "How does one change one's self-concept or one's typical behavior patterns?"

One way to help oneself change is to seek professional counseling. Professional counseling and therapy involve a series of interviews between a trained therapist and a client. The focus of the interviews is on the person seeking help and on his problems. And the aim of counseling and therapy is to effect change in the client's work or social relationships by bringing about a change in his perspective.

We all spend the greater part of our lives trying to discover who we are and trying to make our roles congruent with our self-images. Because this is a difficult task, feelings of alienation from one's self and from society is probably the most widespread affliction of modern man. One factor that contributes significantly to feelings of alienation is a lack of close friends or relations with whom to share one's inner struggle. Confidants cannot solve one's conflicts, but they can make the struggle for identity easier to bear. There are some who struggle actively to avoid becoming known by anyone. Others, who are healthier, seek to make themselves fully known to at least one other human being.[26]

Freud discovered that the neurotic people whom he treated were struggling to avoid being known, and he found that when people actively evade self-knowledge they get sick. Freud believed that people could become well and stay relatively well if they come to know themselves through self-disclosure to another person.

Therapeutic communication, then, does not have to be restricted to the interaction between a therapist and a client. Any interpersonal communication—so long as it is honest and intent on self-understanding—can be therapeutic. And it is well to remember that therapeutic communication, regardless of the context, does not necessarily result in dramatic personality changes. Jurgen Ruesch has described therapeutic communication as

". . . not confined to an appointed hour in the doctor's office. On the contrary, it occurs almost anywhere—on the playfield, in battle, on the ward, at home, or at work. Neither is it bound to the use of certain props such as couch, or chair, nor does it run off according to a special formula. Generally, therapeutic communication involves more than just the therapist and the patient. A child can be therapeutic for the mother and a boss can be therapeutic for his employee; therapy is done all day long by many people who do not know that they act as therapists, and many people benefit from such experiences without knowing it. Therapeutic communication is not a method invented by physicians to combat illness; it is simply something that occurs spontaneously everywhere in daily life. . . ."[27]

One major difference between formal therapy and therapeutic interpersonal communication is one of *intent*; in the former, the therapist deliberately creates a relationship that he believes will help his client; whereas in the latter, one person spontaneously responds to another in such ways that facilitate greater self-awareness. It seems evident—based on the preponderance of feelings of alienation—that there is not enough therapeutic interpersonal communication in contemporary society.

It is useful to examine the formal therapeutic relationship more closely in order to be able to identify some of the underlying principles of interpersonal communication. One such relationship is provided in Adapted Reading No. 11. It is a transcript of a therapeutic encounter between the well-known psychologist Carl Rogers and a female client. The excerpt from the therapy session was staged for a film, however it is a quite accurate representation of what actually does happen. Rogers originated a style of therapy known as *client-centered therapy*, which assumes that the client and therapist maintain a relationship of equals and the therapist's primary function is to reflect back what he or she thinks the client is feeling.[28] As you read the excerpt try to characterize Rogers' style of therapy. Rogers has said of that experience that a deeply communicative contact was established and that the client kept in contact with him for eight years, primarily, he felt, in appreciation for the closeness they achieved.[29]

Carl Rogers Conducts a Therapy Session

Carl Rogers has said that psychotherapy is good communication within and between humans and that good communication within or between humans is always therapeutic. From this segment of a therapeutic interview conducted by Rogers, try to determine what he meant by "good communication." With what "good communicators" or "good listeners" do you feel free to discuss your problems? What about them makes you feel free to speak with them about personal problems?

R*ogers:* From my own years of therapeutic experience I have come to feel that if I can create the proper climate, the proper relationships and conditions, a process of therapeutic movement will almost inevitably occur in my client. You may ask, "What is this climate? What are these conditions? Will they exist in the interview of the woman I'm about to talk with and whom I've never seen before?" Let me try to describe very briefly what these conditions are as I see them. First of all, one question is: Can I be real in the relationship? This has come to have an increasing amount of importance to me over the years. I feel that genuineness is another way of describing the quality I would like to have. I like the term congruence by which I mean what I'm experiencing inside is present in my awareness and comes out through my communications. In a sense, when I have this quality I am all in one piece in the relationship. I would like to have a transparency. I would be quite willing for my client to see all the way through me. That there would be nothing left being hidden. And when I'm real in this sense that I'm trying to describe, then I know that my own feelings will often bubble up into awareness and be expressed in ways that won't impose themselves on my client. Then the second question I would have is: Will I find myself praising this person? Caring for this person? I certainly don't want to pretend a caring that I don't feel. In fact, if I

Adapted from "Client-Centered Therapy," Film No. 1, in E. Shostrom (ed.), Three Approaches to Psychotherapy, *1965, Psychological Films, Inc., 189 North Wheeler Street, Orange, California 92669. Used by permission from Carl R. Rogers and Psychological Films, Inc.*

dislike my client persistently, I feel it's better that I should express it. But I know that the process of therapy is much more likely to occur and constructive change is much more likely if I feel a real spontaneous praising of this individual with whom I am working. Praising of this person or this separate individual. You can call that quality acceptance; you can call it caring; you can call it a non-possessive love, if you wish. I think any of these terms tend to describe it. I know that the relationship will prove more constructive if it's present. Then the third quality, Will I be able to understand the inner world of this individual from the inside? Will I be able to see it through her eyes? Will I be able to be sufficiently sensitive to move around inside the world of her feelings so that I know what it feels like to be her? So that I can see not only the surface meanings but some of the meanings that lie somewhat underneath the surface. I know that if I can let myself sensitively and accurately enter into her world of experience, then change and therapeutic movement are much more likely. But suppose I am fortunate and that I do experience some of these attitudes in the relationship, what then? Well then a variety of things are likely to happen. Both from my clinical experience and from our research investigations we find that if attitudes of the sort that I'm describing are present, then quite a number of things will happen. She'll explore some of her feelings and attitudes quite deeply. She's likely to discover some hidden aspects of herself that she wasn't aware of previously. Feeling herself prized by me, it's quite possible she'll come to prize herself more. Feeling that some of meanings are understood by me, then she can more readily perhaps listen to herself. Listen to someone whose meanings she hasn't been able to catch before. Perhaps if she senses a realness in me she'll be able to be a little more real within herself. I suspect that there will be a change in the manner of her expression; at least, this has been my experience in other instances. From being remote from her experiencing, remote from what's going on within her, it's possible that she'll move toward more immediacy of experiencing; that she will be able to sense and express what's going on within her in the immediate moment, from being disapproving of herself it's quite possible she will move towards a greater degree of acceptance of herself. From somewhat of a fear of relating she may move towards being able to relate more directly and to encounter more directly. From construing life and somewhat rigid black and white patterns she may move toward more tentative ways of construing her experience and of seeing the meanings in it. From a locus of evaluation which is outside of herself it's quite possible she will move toward recognizing a greater capacity within herself for making judgments and drawing conclusions. So those are some of the changes that we have tended to find and I think that they are all of them changes that are characteristic of the process of therapy, or therapeutic movement. If I have any success in creating the kind of conditions that I described initially then we may be able to see some of these changes in the client even though I know in advance that our contact is going to be very brief.

Good morning. I'm Dr. Rogers. You must be Gloria.

Gloria: Yes, I am.

Rogers: We have a half hour together and I really don't know what we'll be able to make of it, but I hope we can make something of it. I'll be glad to know whatever concerns you.

Gloria: Well, I'm nervous, but I feel more comfortable the way you're talking in a low voice and I don't feel like you're being so harsh on me.

Rogers: I hear the trembling in your voice, you are nervous.

Gloria: Well the main thing I want to talk to you about is I'm just newly divorced. I had some insanity before, and I felt comfortable before, and I felt comfortable when I left, and all of a sudden, now the biggest change is adjusting to my single life. One of the things that bother me the most is especially men, and having men in the house, and how it affects the children. The thing that keeps coming to my mind I want to tell you about is I have a daughter, 9, who at one time I felt had a lot of emotional problems. And I wish I could stop shaking. I'm real conscious of things affecting her. I don't want her to get upset. I don't want to shock her. I want so bad for her to accept me. And to level with each other, especially about sex. The other day she saw a woman that was single and pregnant and she asked me all about if women can get pregnant if they're single. And at first I was fine. I wasn't ill at ease at all with her until she asked me if I ever made love to a man before, since I left her daddy, and I lied to her. And ever since that it keeps coming to my mind because I feel so guilty. I never lie and I want her to trust me. And I almost want an answer from you. I want you to tell me if it will affect her wrong if I tell her the truth.

Rogers: And you're concerned about her and the fact that this open relationship that has existed being ruined.

Gloria: Yes, but I have to be on guard about that because I remember when I found out my mother and father made love. It was terrible and I didn't like her anymore, for a while. And I don't want to lie to Pam either and I don't know.

Rogers: And you sure wish I could give you the answer to this as to what to tell her, because what you really want is for me to give you the answer.

Gloria: I want to especially know if it would affect her if I was completely honest and open with her, or if it would affect her if I lied. I feel like it's bound to make a strain because I lied to her. And also I thought, well gee, what about when she gets a little older and if I make up a touchy situation, she probably wouldn't want to because she thinks I'm so good and so clean. And yet I'm so afraid she could think I'm really a devil and I want so bad for her to accept me. And I don't know how much a nine year old can take.

Rogers: And really both alternatives concern you. But she may think you're too good or better than you really are. She may think that you're worse than you are.

Gloria: Not worse than I really am. I don't know if she can accept me the way I am. I think I painted a picture that I'm all sweet and motherly and I'm a little ashamed of my shady side too.

Rogers: That cuts a little deeper. If she had been near you, would she, could she accept you?

Gloria: That is what I don't know. I don't even know how I feel about it, because there are times when I feel so guilty, like when I have a man over, I even try to make a special set-up, so that if I were ever alone, the children would never catch me in that sort of thing. And yet I also know I have these desires.

Rogers: It isn't only her problem or the relationship with her, it's in you as well.

Gloria: In my guilt, I feel guilty.

Rogers: What can I accept myself as doing? And you realize that you set up subterfuges so as to make sure that you don't get caught or something. You realize that you are acting from guilt.

Gloria: I would like to feel comfortable with whatever I do. If I choose not to tell Pam the truth I can't feel if she can't handle, and I don't. I want to be honest and yet there are things I don't even accept.

Rogers: If you aren't comfortable, how can you possibly be comfortable in telling her? And yet, as you say, you do have these desires, you do have your feelings, but you don't feel good about them.

Gloria: Right. I suppose you'll let me just sit here and stew it over. I want you to help me get rid of my guilt. If I can get rid of my guilt feeling about lying or going to bed with a single man, any of that, just so I can feel more comfortable.

Rogers: And I guess really I can say no, don't want to let you stew over in your feelings, but on the other hand I also feel that this is the kind of very private thing I couldn't possibly answer for you, but I certainly will try to help you work towards dealing with it. I don't know if that makes any sense to you, but I mean it.

Gloria: I appreciate your saying that, I think you really mean it.

Certainly there are many different styles of therapy, but whatever the approaches they all have the same purpose of helping the client, or patient, to lead a more satisfying and fulfilling life. Studies conducted by Fred Fiedler that compared three styles of therapy showed more differences between skilled and unskilled therapists using the same therapeutic style than between skilled therapists using different therapeutic styles. Fiedler concluded that "a good therapeutic relationship is very much like any good interpersonal relationship."[30] Along the same line, Rogers contends that, "We may say then that psychotherapy is good communication within and between men. We may also turn that statement around and it will still be true. Good communication, free communication, within or between men, is always therapeutic."

In line with this thinking is the approach to psychological disturbance taken by Thomas Szasz—a well-known and controversial psychologist. Szasz argues that disturbed individuals should not be considered as having an "illness," but rather as persons who have problems in living. He believes that when a person is labeled "mentally ill," he comes to see himself as helpless and ineffectual in effecting change. Szasz does not believe in the therapeutic process as it is currently conceived, and maintains that whatever "sickness" exists is in the society that has labeled these persons as sick.[31]

Interpersonal Attraction

We may love or hate one another for a variety of reasons, but fundamental to the feelings we have for others are the feelings we have for ourselves. The psychologist Erich Fromm was one of the first to observe the close connection between a person's evaluations of self and his feelings for others.[32] Years later, Carl Rogers noted a similar phenomenon in many of his patients: Those who felt least capable of reaching their own goals found it hardest to accept the people around them.[33]

What do we need to know about the process of interpersonal attraction as it applies to interpersonal communication? Why do we choose to communicate with the people that we do? The research literature is complex and contradictory, so for this summary I am relying on the recent work of Steven Duck. What follows is a brief overview of some of the studies done in recent years that have tried to answer the above questions, as compiled by Duck.[34]

Festinger, Schachter, and Back studied the effects of *proximity* in determining an individual's choices. (Remember, from our discussion in Chapter 3, that friendship groups were often composed of next-door neighbors.) Similarly, G. C. Homans suggested that frequency of interaction plays a part in friendship formation.[35] Although proximity may be necessary, it may not, by itself, explain friendship formation. P. B. Warr, for example, has shown that proximity can result in either positive or negative feelings.[36] In other words, proximity does not in itself guarantee positive feelings; other factors are also required.

Some people have suggested that *physical attractiveness* is an important factor.[37] Indeed there is evidence to suggest that physical characteristics and attractiveness serve a filtering function for individuals in the selection of friends of both sexes.[38] The child development specialist James Dobson contends that even by the age of three or four, children can tell whether other people think they are beautiful or ugly. Physical attractiveness is a potent factor. In fact, there is reason to believe that in the presidential campaign of 1960, Richard Nixon lost many votes as a result of his unfavorable physical appearance in a televised debate with John Kennedy.

Another factor that influences one's choice of friends may be *reciprocity-of-liking*, which stems from Heider's balance theory. In other words, the people we like may be those who like us, or who like the same things we do. In fact, it has been found that most marriage partners are from the same religious, economic, and educational backgrounds.

One, rather complex, factor may be derived from the *level-of-aspiration* theory.[39] The assumption here is that one's aspiration to achieve realistic goals depends not only on the desirability of the goal but also on the perceived likelihood of its being achieved. In other words, one might choose a lover or a marriage partner based on that person's availability. If we perceive that a person is unlikely to ever reciprocate our feelings of liking or loving, we will likely switch our affection to someone else.

B. I. Murstein has suggested the *stimulus-value* theory as another factor.[40] According to Murstein, physical attractiveness plays an initial part in the search for a marital partner in that individuals will tend to choose partners who embody a level of attractiveness similar to their own. Subsequently, however, one also attempts to find a partner who has stimulation value; that is, one who is interesting and whose religious outlook, professional aspiration, political attitudes and so on are like one's own. According to this view, attraction is determined by the extent to which homogeneity of values is apparent and also by the degree of role compatibility that exists between individuals.

R. F. Winch has suggested *complementarity of needs* as a factor.[41] This hypothesis suggests that persons who are, for example, low on dominance would tend to choose a partner who is high on dominance. In other words, it is claimed that individuals might seek as marital partners some person who possesses the very qualities that they lack in order that one might complement the other. This hypothesis is summed up in the old adage "opposites attract."

But in contrast to the above hypothesis, is the notion of *similarity*. It argues that individuals look for similarities between themselves and others. Two of the major areas that have been investigated are similarity of attitudes and similarity of personalities. H. C. Triandis, for example, has shown that similarity in categorizing and structuring the relationships between particular jobs (similarity of attitudes) aided communication effectiveness between supervisors and subordinates in a factory (interpersonal attraction).[42] Although research on personality similarity has not yet been particularly convincing, C. E. Izard, using the Edwards Personal Preference Schedule, has succeeded in giving some support to the suggestion that mutual friends have similar personality profiles.[43]

Another explanation, which is more consistent with the previous material on interpersonal communication, is George Kelly's theory of *personal constructs*. This theory offers us the means to understand communication with others and permits us to relate interpersonal attraction to interpersonal communication as we have studied it.[44] Kelly's position is that a person's main concern is to interpret and understand his own experience. In order to do this, the individual develops concepts (or, according to Kelly, personal constructs) with which to categorize and interpret his experience. Evidence is provided for the value of one's own constructs by comparison with the constructs of others. Thus, a kind of social reality for one's constructs can be gained by associating with others.

Because everyone's experiences are different, people develop constructs that differ from other people's constructs. Nevertheless, Kelly argues that some overlap in personal constructs is inevitable and also necessary in order to avoid complete isolation and feelings of alienation. Kelly also advanced two corollaries. The *commonality* corollary states that to the extent that one person employs a personal construct that is similar to one employed by someone else, his processes are psychologically similar to those of the other person. Kelly does not argue that similar individuals will have had similar experiences, but that they will have similar construction processes. The *sociality* corollary states that to the extent that one person can interpret the construction process of another he plays a role in the social processes that involve the other person. Thus, the extent of our meaningful and productive relations with another is limited by the extent to which we can understand what the other is up to. It follows, then, that a mutual commonality of construction processes will facilitate the likelihood that two people will understand each other. And, in turn, such an understanding will enhance the value of the interaction. In other words, a similarity in construing processes will facilitate the formation of friendships. Friendship follows from similarity of construing processes because it eases communication. The more constructs one shares with others the more one's own constructs will seem to be well-formed and justified. Similarity provides a measure of social reality, objectifies subjective interpretations and categorizations of that which is outside, and reinforces one's established way of structuring experience.

★Probe Questions

Does the theory of personal constructs provide a clear solution to the problems of interpersonal communication? Probably not. The differences between two people's sets of constructs (their psychological orientations) may be as much of a key to solving problems of communication as the similarities between their constructs. The personal construct theory does not say whether communication is facilitated by the similarities or differences between people. In other words, people may communicate about their differences and become more similar as a result—as the following example demonstrates.

Consider that two mentally disturbed persons with highly similar sets of constructs would presumably provide "therapeutic" support through communication. The two would find mutual emotional satisfaction, a strengthening of their self-concepts, and additional security through the confirmation of their beliefs. Thus, through their interpersonal relationship, the two would become more and more disturbed.

Does Kelly's hypothesis suggest that a psychologist has to be somewhat disturbed in order to understand the constructs of his client? Who gains the most therapeutic support in the client-therapist relationship?

Functional personal constructs (that is, constructs that do not create problems in living) may come from interpersonal relationships in which differences in personal constructs lead to change. That is, one may have to seek out people who use different constructs, even with the knowledge that those differences may cause losses in emotional satisfaction, strength of purpose, and belief in one's own processes in order to achieve a desired change.

Which type of person are you: one who restricts your relationships to a few people who support you, or one who tries to interact with many different types of people, some of whom may sometimes put you down?

Alienation

All of us have had experience with some feelings of alienation. If not from society in general, then at least from another person—perhaps a parent, a brother or sister, or a close friend. It is unlikely that one is able to sustain satisfying and meaningful relationships at all times with all the people one cares for.

It must be understood, though, that it is impossible *not* to communicate. In an interpersonal relationship, the refusal of one person to interact with the other person is itself a form of communication. When a father refuses to communicate with his son, the son clearly understands the message that his father does not want to talk with him. In such a situation, what kinds of communicative behavior should the son expect from his father? In a close relationship, such as that between a parent and a child, one important function of communication is to test or confirm the relationship. In an argument, a response of either agreement or disagreement is also a response that confirms and continues the existence of the relationship. But a refusal to interact at all is a denial both of the relationship and even of the existence of the person. Thus, the son quite clearly understands his father's refusal to communicate as a denial of the importance of the father-son relationship and as a statement of the lack of the son's importance to the father.

How could the son respond to his father's denial? According to Kim Giffin he could respond in one of four possible ways: First, the son can repeat his initial communication attempt, which in effect is a repetition of his testing of the relationship. If he is now successful, the effect of the initial denial is insignificant. (We've all recovered from a minor rejection.) Second, the son can initiate overt communication about the denial. He can ask his father why he won't talk to him. Third, the son can make a more overt demand for recognition from his father; that is, the son can shout, or demonstrate, or otherwise violate his father's expectations. Four, the son can accept the denial. If the son has correctly perceived his father's denial, the son's withdrawal behavior is an intelligent and normal response. He has correctly perceived the status of the relationship and has responded normally. When the son accepts the conclusion that he cannot communicate with his father—that it is pointless to try further—social alienation has occurred. From the son's perspective, it is not worthwhile to communicate with his father at any time, under any circumstances.[45]

When social alienation has occurred—that is, when an interpersonal relationship has been denied—then by definition each person cannot observe or be aware of the other person's feelings and perceptions. It is no wonder then that the father ascribes "no feelings" to his now alienated son, or denies the son's true feelings of affection. Social alienation, then, refers to an interpersonal relationship in which one person withdraws from or avoids interaction with another, and becomes increasingly unaware of the other person's feelings.

Summary

Socialization is a continuous, life-long process that enables us to fit into society and through which a self-concept is formed. Stories of children nourished by wolves support the theory that "human-ness" is learned through interpersonal interactions. One's earliest socializing agents are parents, and it is within the family that one's self-concept begins to be formed. Socialization continues in the school, which provides opportunities for peer-group relationships, and, later, within the work environment. The acquisition of sex roles has been described in terms of social-learning theory and cognitive-developmental theory. Sex-role stereotyping is prevalent in Western society and leads to the formation of false and often destructive differences between male and female roles. Our self-concept is significantly affected by other people's responses to us and what we imagine they think of us. The labels we and others use to describe ourselves really describe our behavior, and our be-havior, in turn, helps define our self-concept. The best indicator of the way in which an individual sees the world is that individual's way of organizing experience through language. If one desires to change, one could seek out therapeutic communication. Thera-peutic communication is not restricted to the relationship between a therapist and a client; rather, it is any communication that pro-motes greater understanding of self and greater understanding of one's effect upon others.

Factors that contribute to interpersonal attraction include prox-imity, physical attractiveness, similarity, and so on. The personal construct theory argues that we are attracted to those who employ a construction of experience similar to our own. Friendship follows from a similarity of construing processes because it eases communication. Alienation is the result of a total breakdown in communication within an interpersonal relationship.

Footnotes

[1]Paul F. Pfuetze, *Self, Society, Existence,* New York: Harper & Row, Publishers, 1961, p. 302.

[2]Frank E. X. Dance and Carl Larson, *Speech Communication: Concepts and Behavior,* New York: Holt, Rinehart and Winston, Inc., 1972, pp. 64–73.

[3]J. A. L. Singh and Robert M. Zingg, *Wolf-Children and Feral Man,* New York: Harper & Row, Publishers, 1939.

[4]Kingsley Davis, *Human Society,* New York: Macmillan, 1949, pp. 204–208.

[5]Robert Hopper and Rita C. Naremore, *Children's Speech: A Practical Introduction to Communication Develop-* *ment,* New York: Harper & Row, Publishers, 1973.

[6]Joyce Maynard, *Looking Back: A Chronicle of Growing Old in the Sixties,* New York: Doubleday & Company, Inc., 1973.

[7]Group for the Advancement of Psychiatry, *Normal Adolescence,* New York: Charles Scribners & Sons, 1968, pp. 55–56.

[8]Timothy Dickinson, "Wrap-around," Harper's Magazine, July 1975, p. 5.

[9]Paul H. Mussen, "Early Sex Role Development," in David A. Goslin, *Handbook of Socialization Theory and Re-*

search, Chicago: Rand McNally, 1969, pp. 707–731.

[10]Mussen, p. 720.

[11]L. A. Kohlberg, "A Cognitive-Developmental Analysis of Children's Sex-Role Concepts and Attitudes," in Eleanor Maccoby, ed., *The Development of Sex Differences*, Stanford, California: Stanford University Press, 1966, p. 82.

[12]C. Brindley, *et al.*, "Sex Differences in the Activities and Social Interactions of Nursery School Children," in R. D. Michael and J. H. Crook, eds., *Comparative Ecology and Behavior of Primates*, New York: Academic Press, 1973.

[13]Dorothea M. Ross and Shelia A. Ross, "Resistance by Pre-school Boys to Sex-Inappropriate Behavior," *Journal of Educational Psychology*, 1972, 63, 342–346.

[14]Richard Green *et al.*, "Playroom Toy Preferences of Fifteen Masculine and Fifteen Feminine Boys," *Behavior Therapy*, 1972, 3, 425–429.

[15]R. Videbeck, "Self-Conception and the Reaction of Others," *Sociometry*, 1960, 23, 351–362.

[16]John M. Branan, "Negative Human Interaction," *Journal of Counseling Psychology*, 1972, 19, 81–82.

[17]Robert Rosenthal and Lenore Jacobson, *Pygmalion in the Classroom*, New York: Holt, Rinehart and Winston, 1968.

[18]Dean C. Barnlund, "Toward a Meaning-Centered Philosophy of Communication," *Journal of Communication*, 1962, 12, 197–211.

[19]Robert L. Ebel, "And Still the Dryads Linger," *American Psychologist*, 1974, 29, 485–492.

[20]Fred E. Jandt and Delmer M. Hilyard, "An Experimental Study of Self-Concept and Satisfactions," *Today's Speech*, 1975, 23:4, 39–44.

[21]Carolyn B. Smith and Larry R. Judd, "A Study of Variables Influencing Self-Concept and Ideal Self-Concept Among Students in the Basic Speech Course," *Speech Teacher*, 1974, 23, 215–221.

[22]Richard Christie and Florence L. Geis, *Studies in Machiavellianism*, New York: Academic Press, 1970.

[23]Michael Burgoon, "The Relationship Between Willingness to Manipulate Others and Success in Two Different Types of Basic Speech Communication Courses," *The Speech Teacher*, 1971, 20, 178–183.

[24]Eugene A. Weinstein, "The Development of Interpersonal Competence," in David A. Goslin, *Handbook of Socialization Theory and Research*, Chicago: Rand McNally, 1969.

[25]E. H. Erikson, "The Problem of Ego Identity," *Psychological Issues*, 1959, 1, 101–166.

[26]Sidney M. Jourard, *Personal Adjustment: An Approach Through the Study of Healthy Personality*, New York: Macmillan, 1958.

[27]Jurgen Ruesch, *Therapeutic Communication*, New York: W. W. Norton, 1961.

[28]Carl R. Rogers, *Client-Centered Therapy*, Boston: Houghton Mifflin, 1951.

[29]Carl R. Rogers, "In Retrospect: Forty-Six Years," *American Psychologist*, 1974, 29, 115–123.

[30]Fred E. Fiedler, "The Concept of an Ideal Therapeutic Relationship," *Journal of Consulting Psychology*, 1950, 14, 239–245.

[31]T. S. Szasz, *The Myth of Mental Illness*, New York: Hoeber-Harper, 1961.

[32]E. Fromm, "Selfishness and Self Love," *Psychiatry*, 1939, 2, 507–523.

[33]C. Rogers, "Therapy, Personality and Interpersonal Relationships," in S. Koch, ed., *Psychology: A Study of a Science*, vol. III, New York: McGraw-Hill, 1959.

[34]Steven W. Duck, *Personal Relationships and Personal Constructs: A Study of Friendship Formation*, London: John Wiley & Sons, 1973.

[35]G. C. Homans, *The Human Group*, New York: Harcourt, Brace and World, 1950.

[36]P. B. Warr, "Proximity as a Determinant of Positive and Negative Sociometric Choice," *British Journal of Social and Clinical Psychology*, 1965, 4, 104–109.

[37]E. Berscheid, K. Dion, E. H. Walster, and G. M. Walster, "Physical Attractiveness and Dating Choice: A Test of the Matching Hypothesis," *Journal of Experimental Social Psychology*, 1971, 7, 173–190.

[38]D. Byrne, O. London, and K. Reeves, "The Effects of Physical Attractiveness, Sex and Attitude Similarity on Interpersonal Attraction," *Journal of Personality*, 1968, 36, 259–271.

[39]K. Lewin, T. Dembo, L. Festinger, and P. Sears, "Level of Aspiration," in J. McV. Hunt, ed., *Personality and the Behavior Disorders*, vol. I, New York: Ronald Press, 1944, pp. 333–378.

[40]B. I. Murstein, "Stimulus-

Value-Role: A Theory of Marital Choice," *Journal of Marriage and the Family*, 1970, 32, 465–481, and "Physical Attractiveness and Marital Choice," *Journal of Personality and Social Psychology*, 1972, 22, 8–12.

[41]R. F. Winch, *Mate Selection: A Study of Complementary Needs*, New York: Harper & Row Publishers, 1958.

[42]H. C. Triandis, "Cognitive Complexity and Interpersonal Communication in Industry," *Journal of Applied Psychology*, 1959, 43, 321–326.

[43]C. E. Izard, "Personality Similarity and Friendship, *Journal of Abnormal and Social Psychology*, 1960, 61, 47–51, and "Personality Similarity, Positive Affect and Interpersonal Attraction," *Journal of Abnormal and Social Psychology*, 1960, 61, 484–485.

[44]G. A. Kelly, *The Psychology of Personal Constructs*, New York: Norton, 1955, and "Behavior is an Experiment," in D. Bannister, ed., *Perspectives in Personal Construct Theory*, London: Academic Press, 1970.

[45]Kim Giffin, "Social Alienation by Communication Denial," *Quarterly Journal of Speech*, 1970, 56, 347–357.

Chapter

After reading this chapter, you should be able to:

ꟷ Participate in a discussion while being aware of group processes.

ꟷ Recognize and define the functions of group leadership.

ꟷ Distinguish between training or sensitivity groups and consciousness-raising groups.

ꟷ Discuss the causes and resolutions of interpersonal conflict.

SMALL-GROUP COMMUNICATION AND INTERPERSONAL CONFLICT

¶ In a recent study of leisure activity, Serena E. Wade, an associate professor of speech communication, surveyed several hundred tenth-grade students from four high schools in Santa Clara County, California. The results indicated that interpersonal discussion was a major component of almost all teen-age leisure behavior.[1] The speech communication discipline has for several decades concentrated on problem solving in group discussions, and traditionally group discussions were seen as a cornerstone of a democratic society in which citizens cooperatively resolved mutual concerns.[2] Today, our perspective is broader, and we know that group discussions serve many other purposes in addition to problem solving. All of us are members of many groups for many different reasons; we belong to religious organizations, social clubs or cliques, community organizations, sports teams, and so on. At times these groups are problem-solving groups; at times they are not. Thus, group discussion can serve any one of numerous purposes, including the purpose of a productive use of leisure time.

Bernard Berelson and Gary Steiner have developed a useful definition of the term *small group:* it can be taken to mean an aggregate of people, from two up to an unspecified, but not too large, number of people, who associate together in face-to-face relations over an extended period of time; who differentiate themselves in

All of us are members of many different small groups. Can you identify several small groups you belong to?

some regard from others around them; who are mutually aware of their membership in the group; and whose personal relations are taken as an end in itself. If the aggregate of people gets much larger than fifteen to twenty, the group loses some of the small-group qualities, and begins to break up into smaller subgroups. In sum, the essential elements in the definition are small size, personal relations, some duration, mutual identification with the group and hence some solidarity, differentiation from non-group members, shared goals, common symbols, and autonomy in setting up procedures. As this definition suggests, society is full of small groups and each of us spends a great deal of our life in them.[3]

The theories and research pertaining to small-group communication are of such quantity and scope that no comprehensive survey is possible in one chapter of an introductory text. The intent of this chapter is to focus on some basic concepts related to developing skills in communicating in small groups.

Participation-Observation Skills

Basically, one must learn to be both a participant and an observer in group discussions. We all have the tendency to get so involved with

what is happening in the group—with what is being discussed—
that we lose some objectivity in evaluating the *process* of the discussion. In a heated argument, for instance, we are more likely to remember the *content* or the issues that were raised than the actual
process of the communication, such as the number of times each
person spoke, who spoke to whom, who attempted to compromise,
who initiated a personal attack, and the like. In order to become an
effective communicator, it is just as important to be aware of the
process of the discussion as it is to actively participate in the
conversation.

But awareness itself is not enough. After one develops skills in
observing and understanding the group process, he must then
make judgments, based on what he knows about group functioning, as to what is lacking or what group functions are not being
adequately performed. Individuals must then either provide these
functions themselves or attempt to encourage another group
member to do so. For example, after reading this chapter you will
know that to efficiently solve a problem, a group requires information. As a skilled participant-observer you might diagnose your
group's problem as a lack of information, and then act upon this
observation by suggesting that you or the other members seek out
and supply the needed information before proceeding.

This combination of participant-observer skills can be developed with practice. You can begin, for example, by becoming more
aware of the number of times each participant in one of your groups
speaks; as well as such patterns of communication as who speaks to
whom. Figure 5.1, for example, shows the distribution of all interaction in eighteen sessions of a six-member group in an experimental situation. The findings indicate that if participants in a small

Person origi- nating act	To individuals						Total to in- divid- uals	To group as a whole	Total initi- ated
	1	2	3	4	5	6			
1		1238	961	545	445	317	3506	5661	9167
2	1748		443	310	175	102	2278	1211	3989
3	1371	415		305	125	69	2285	742	3027
4	952	310	282		83	49	1676	676	2352
5	662	224	144	83		28	1141	443	1584
6	470	126	114	65	44		819	373	1192
Total received	5203	2313	1944	1308	872	565	12205	9106	21311

Source: Robert F. Bales, Fred L. Strodtbeck, Theodore M. Mills, and Mary E. Roseborough, "Channels of Communication in Small Groups," *American Sociological Review*, 1951, 16, 463.

Figure 5.1 Much can be learned about a group by counting the number of times a
person speaks to each other member and to the group as a whole and the number of
times a person is spoken to.

group are ranked by the total number of acts they initiate, they will also tend to be ranked (1) by the number of acts they receive, (2) by the number of acts they address to specific other individuals, and (3) by the number of acts they address to the group as a whole.[4]

Categorizing Communication Acts

Another way to become more sensitive to the process of group communication is to learn to categorize communication acts as being either *task* or *socioemotional* in purpose. Generally, *task* communication acts are those verbal and nonverbal communication behaviors directed toward solving the group's problem or toward the substance of the discussion. *Socioemotional* communication acts are those verbal and nonverbal communication behaviors directed toward maintaining the group as a functioning whole.

Robert Freed Bales and his associates at Harvard University developed a set of twelve categories to provide an even more accurate systematic classification of task and socioemotional acts.[5] By studying Figure 5.2 you will see that six of the categories further define task acts and the other six further define socioemotional acts.

Bales' category system is of particular value in the tabulation of the relative frequencies of the types of interaction in a given group. In observations of twenty-four different groups, ranging in size from two to seven members, working on a standard task, Bales noted the following relative percentages:[6]

1.	Shows solidarity	3.4 percent
2.	Shows tension release	6.0 percent
3.	Shows agreement	16.5 percent
4.	Gives suggestions	8.0 percent
5.	Gives opinions	30.1 percent
6.	Gives information	17.9 percent
7.	Asks for information	3.5 percent
8.	Asks for opinion	2.4 percent
9.	Asks for suggestion	1.1 percent
10.	Shows disagreement	7.8 percent
11.	Shows tension	2.7 percent
12.	Shows antagonism	0.7 percent

Bales pointed out that different groups will yield different profiles. Thus, it might be illuminating to compare these percentages with those obtained from groups in which you participate.

Another example of a process observation is to categorize the communication climate as either threatening or nonthreatening; in other words, as defensive or supportive. Jack Gibb studied this phenomenon for eight years and has enumerated certain behaviors that contribute to defensiveness:

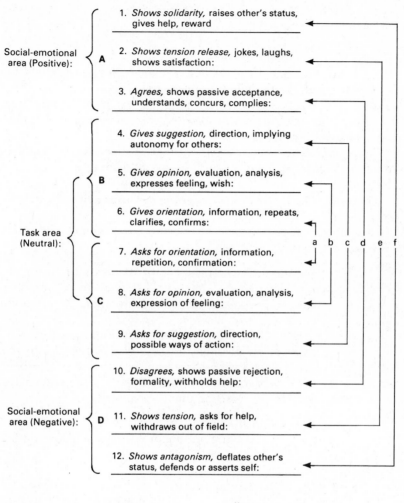

Social-emotional area (Positive):

A

1. *Shows solidarity,* raises other's status, gives help, reward

2. *Shows tension release,* jokes, laughs, shows satisfaction:

3. *Agrees,* shows passive acceptance, understands, concurs, complies:

Task area (Neutral):

B

4. *Gives suggestion,* direction, implying autonomy for others:

5. *Gives opinion,* evaluation, analysis, expresses feeling, wish:

6. *Gives orientation,* information, repeats, clarifies, confirms:

C

7. *Asks for orientation,* information, repetition, confirmation:

8. *Asks for opinion,* evaluation, analysis, expression of feeling:

9. *Asks for suggestion,* direction, possible ways of action:

Social-emotional area (Negative):

D

10. *Disagrees,* shows passive rejection, formality, withholds help:

11. *Shows tension,* asks for help, withdraws out of field:

12. *Shows antagonism,* deflates other's status, defends or asserts self:

a   b   c   d   e   f

A. Positive reactions
B. Attempted answers
C. Questions
D. Negative reactions

Key

a. Problems of orientation
b. Problems of evaluation
c. Problems of control
d. Problems of decision
e. Problems of tension management
f. Problems of integration

SOURCE: R. F. Bales, *Interaction Process Analysis,* Reading, Mass.: Addison-Wesley, 1950, p. 59. Two decades later Bales slightly revised the system of categories. This revision is shown in R. F. Bales, *Personality and Interpersonal Behavior,* New York: Holt, Rinehart & Winston, 1970, p. 92.

FIGURE 5.2 Bales' twelve category system is used to describe communications in groups.

1. *Evaluation* by expression, manner of speech, tone of voice, or verbal content, perceived by the listener as criticism or judgment, will produce defensive behavior.

2. Communication perceived as an attempt to *control* the listener will produce defensiveness.

3. *Stratagems* that are perceived as "clever" devices produce defensiveness; that is, partially hidden motives breed suspicion. Persons seen as "playing a game," feigning emotion, withholding information, or having private access to sources of data will stimulate defensive responses.

4. An appearance of *neutrality* or lack of concern will heighten an attitude of defensiveness. An impersonal manner is feared and resented.

5. Conveying an attitude of *superiority* arouses defensive behavior.

6. *Dogmatism,* or arrogance in asserting one's opinions, is a final stimulus of defensive behavior.[7]

If an individual perceives a personal threat in a group, he or she is likely to behave defensively. Defensive behavior by one member of a group is likely to provoke defensiveness in others; hence, a vicious circle begins.

The reverse is also true, however. In a supportive, nonthreatening climate, receivers of messages are less likely to read into the messages distorted meanings arising from projections of personal anxieties, motives, and concerns. According to Gibb, defensive behavior is reduced by interaction that is perceived as:

1. Descriptive rather than evaluative or critical.

2. Oriented toward solving mutual problems instead of toward personal control.

3. Spontaneous rather than strategic.

4. Empathic rather than neutral.

5. Indicative of an attitude of equality instead of superiority.

6. Expressive of provisionally held viewpoints instead of dogmatic certainties.

The Problem-Solving Process

Another way to observe group processes is to follow the group's problem-solving progress. Bales attempted to describe that process by observing groups under controlled laboratory conditions. He was able to identify three problem-solving phases:

1. *Orientation.* The group as a whole has some degree of ignorance and uncertainty about the relevant facts, but individual members may possess facts relevant to the decision. The group's problem of arriving at a common cognitive orientation to, or definition of, the situation must be solved, if at all, through interaction.

2. *Evaluation.* The members of the group ordinarily possess somewhat different values or interests. The task, then, is to evaluate the group's problem in terms of each of the members' criteria in order to ascertain a proposed course of action.

3. *Control.* Members attempt to directly influence the action of one another in order to arrive at a concrete plan. The acceptance of the task sets up, in most instances, a moderately strong pressure for group decision, with the expectation that the excellence of the decision can and will be evaluated by each member.[8]

Although Bales' three phases reveal that groups concentrate on different kinds of problems over time, it does not reveal the interaction process that groups use to solve those problems.

B. Aubrey Fisher has attempted to describe the nature of the interaction process over time. Fisher's observations led him to devise a four-phase pattern based on the proportional fluctuation of interaction units, favorable, unfavorable, or ambiguous, toward the decision proposals. In the early stage of a discussion, favorable and ambiguous attitudes are expressed with greater frequency than are unfavorable attitudes. Fisher labels this stage as *orientation.* Then, in the second phase, labeled as the *conflict* stage, ambiguity decreases and unfavorable attitudes are expressed more often as members become increasingly aware of the group's alternatives. Conflict dissipates during the third phase, *emergence,* and disfavor dissipates to ambiguity, but not to favor. In the final phase, *reinforcement,* the members acknowledge the final decision and accept it favorably as the only alternative.[9]

Based on your own experiences in groups, you may wonder if there are not more efficient ways to go about solving problems in small groups. Group problem–solving can be both frustrating and time-consuming. One major hindrance to efficient group problem solving has been called *hidden agendas.* According to L. P. Bradford, hidden agendas include all the conflicting motives, desires, aspirations, and emotional reactions held by the group members or by the group as a whole that cannot be fitted legitimately into the accepted group task, in other words, the problems that cannot be laid on top of the table.[10] Sometimes it is desirable to get the hidden agenda out in the open; at other times the hidden agenda is best ignored. For example, one group member may have another appointment and is trying to rush the group to complete its agenda. The group could discuss this situation in a positive fashion if rushing may hurt the group's goals. In a business organization, when meetings are used to reinforce status positions, such a hidden agenda is best left ignored.

A recent study by Carl E. Larson compared three group problem-solving plans, reproduced here as Figure 5.3. Larson was able to demonstrate that a successful group outcome can be facili-

Single Question Form

1. What is the single question, the answer to which is all the group needs to know to accomplish its purpose?
2. What sub-questions must be answered before we can answer the single question we have formulated?
3. Do we have sufficient information to answer confidently the sub-questions? (If yes, answer them. If no, continue below.)
4. What are the most reasonable answers to the sub-questions?

Ideal Solution Form

1. Are we all agreed on the nature of the problem?
2. What would be the ideal solution from the point-of-view of all parties involved in the problem?
3. What conditions within the problem could be changed so that the ideal solution might be achieved?
4. Of the solutions available to us, which one best approximates the ideal solutions?

Reflective Thinking Form

1. What are the limits and specific nature of the problem?
2. What are the causes and consequences of the problem?
3. What things must an acceptable solution to the problem accomplish?
4. What solutions are available to us?
5. What is the best solution?

SOURCE: Carl E. Larson, "Forms of Analysis and Small Group Problem-Solving," *Speech Monographs*, 1969, 36, 452–455.

FIGURE 5.3 These three problem-solving plans were used on a study. What advantages does a small group gain using such a plan?

tated by the "Single Question Form," which emerged from descriptive investigations of the reasoning characteristics of successful problem–solvers, and the "Ideal Solution Form," which resulted from extensive practical experience with managerial groups. Larson suggests that even more effective forms may yet be developed.[11]

A final example of process observation is the observation of leadership in the group. In many cases there is no question about who the leader is. Frequently, groups are called together or formed by specific individuals, as often happens in business and industry. In such cases, the person who initiates the group is designated as the leader, and typically this person assumes the *responsibility* for the functioning of the group. When a leader is not designated either by himself or by tacit approval, all members share part of the responsibility for the functioning of the group. Such an arrangement is called *shared leadership.*

But how does one learn to fulfill the responsibility of group leadership? By becoming an aware and informed participant-observer, one can learn to diagnose group processes and then attempt to provide the communication behaviors that the group requires to function more efficiently. One means of doing this is to learn to recognize the functions of leadership. Figure 5.4 describes various leadership

What skills in interpersonal communication will help one participate successfully in a problem-solving group discussion?

functions necessary for the efficient functioning of a small group and some of the self-oriented functions that can hinder group progress. Become familiar enough with these various roles so that you can notice their absence. The next step is to become familiar with the behaviors that these leadership functions suggest so that you will be able to perform them when necessary. Skillful small-group communication requires behavioral flexibility.

Relationships in Groups

One early form of small-group research was *sociometry*, which was developed by Jacob L. Moreno stemming from his work in Germany with spontaneity theater.[12] Sociometry emphasizes the importance of "liking" relationships and of informal structure in groups. One way to analyze the group structure, then, is to ask group members to indicate their interpersonal choices by rating other group members. For example, members might be asked to name the person they would most like to go to a movie with, the member they would most like to study with, and so on. From this data a *sociogram* is prepared, which depicts the patterns of interpersonal choices. Sample sociograms are shown in Figure 5.5. The sociogram is useful for identifying the position of each group member in the informal structure of the group. If ratings on several criteria are combined, individuals may be identified as "over-chosen" or "under-chosen" in the informal structure, regardless of the particular position they occupy in the group. Although the "over-chosen" members tend to be those

A. GROUP-ORIENTED FUNCTIONS

1. Building and Maintaining Interpersonal Relations (Social-Emotional Functions)

(a). Participation/Interaction:

   1. *Gate-Keeping:* communication expediting: attempting to keep communication channels open; being sensitive to others' desires to participate; helping others to contribute by expressing interest in their views.
   2. *Encouraging:* overtly demonstrating recognition and approval of the useful contributions of other members; reacting to others' contributions in ways that encourage the communicator to talk again later; demonstrating pleasure when others excel; indicating an understanding, or at least an interest in understanding the ideas of others.
   3. *Following:* attentive listening to others' contributions; passively agreeing, accepting, approving of others' contributions.

(b). Climate-Making:

   1. *Mediating:* focusing attention on issues rather than on personalities during a conflict or disagreement between others; putting a tense situation into a wider context.
   2. *Compromising:* offering to temporarily give up some personally desirable idea or status for the attainment of a group-desired objective; "coming half-way" in moving along with the group.
   3. *Tension-releasing:* relieving tensions by jesting or with constructive humor.

2. Helping the Group Accomplish its Job (Task Functions)

(a). Ideation:

   1. *Initiating activity:* starting the discussion; proposing tasks, goals, solutions; suggesting new ideas or a changed way of regarding the group problem or goal; following up procedural suggestions with information and facts.
   2. *Seeking information:* requesting needed facts; asking for authoritative information pertinent to the problem being discussed; asking for a clarification of comments made.
   3. *Giving information:* offering facts, generalizations, specific illustrations, or other forms of evidence; reporting related personal experience.

Source: Adapted by Nelson R. Ober from Kenneth D. Benne, and Paul Sheats, "Functional roles of group members," *Journal of Social Issues*, 1948, 4(2), 41–49; David Potter, and Martin P. Andersen, *Discussion*, Belmont, California, Wadsworth Publishing Company, 1963; and Adult Education Assn. *Adult Leadership*, Chicago, January 1953, pp. 17–18.

Figure 5.4 This chart outlines the concepts of tasks and of socioemotional functions into specific member roles. It also lists some self-oriented functions which can be disfunctional for a small group.

(b). Critical Thinking:

1. *Seeking opinion:* asking not primarily for the facts of the case, but for a judgment of the value of an idea, suggestion, or other contribution.
2. *Giving opinion:* interpreting or evaluating the significance of ideas and suggestions; stating one's opinion of an idea or suggestion which has been made or one's opinion of alternative suggestions.
3. *Logical reasoning:* testing evidence and opinions; questioning inferences and generalizations; revealing fallacies in reasoning; showing causes and/or effects; making analogies.
4. *Elaborating:* clarifying words or concepts suggesting implications of proposals; showing relationships; paraphrasing; developing meanings; indicating issues and alternatives.

(c). Procedure Setting:

1. *Organizing:* planning or proposing problem-solving procedures; reminding others of problem-solving agenda; raising questions about the direction which the discussion is taking; pointing to departures from agreed upon directions or goals; initiating transitions to new phases of the problem.
2. *Goal focusing:* encouraging the group to define its problem and explicitly formulate its goal; orientating the group by seeking consensus on the objectives sought.
3. *Summarizing:* defining the position of the group with respect to its goals by reviewing what has occurred; making a brief general statement of what has been said about some aspect of the problem so as to test for consensus.

B. INDIVIDUAL OR SELF-ORIENTED FUNCTIONS

1. *Playboy-ing:* making a display of lack of involvement in the group's functioning by being cynical, nonchalant, engaging in excessive horse-play, or other more or less studied forms of "out of field" behavior.
2. *Aggressing:* deflating the status of others; expressing tactless disapproval of the values, acts, or feelings of others; attacking the group, particular members, or the problem the group is working on; joking aggressively; showing envy toward another's contributions by trying to take credit for them.
3. *Dominating:* trying to assert authority or superiority by manipulating the group or certain members of the group through flattery, asserting a superior status or right to attention, giving directions in an authoritative manner, or interrupting the contributions of others.
4. *Blocking:* negative and stubborn resistance; disagreeing and opposing without reason or beyond reason; attempting to maintain or bring back an issue after the group has rejected or by-passed it.
5. *Recognition-seeking:* working to call attention to oneself, whether through boasting, reporting on personal achievements, acting in unusual ways, or struggling to prevent being placed in an "inferior" status or position.

NOTE: In using classifications like those above, group members must guard against the tendency to blame any person (whether themselves or another) who falls into such "non-functional" behavior. It probably is more useful to regard such behavior as a symptom that all is not well with the group's ability to satisfy individual needs through group-centered activity. Further, members need to be alert that what appears as, for example, "blocking" to one person may appear to another as a needed effort to "clarify" or "mediate."

FIGURE 5.4 (cont'd)

FIGURE 5.5 A casual participant or observer may notice some of the relationships and may sense the "tone" of relations within a small group. If, however, the group exceeds a few members, it is unlikely that even an astute and experienced observer will have a thorough grasp of the basic relationships without prolonged observation or the aid of objective measures. One technique for the objective presentation and interpretation of relations within groups is called the *sociogram*. It is a diagram of the informal relations within a group. A sociogram shows the informal group structure, such as subgroup and friendship patterns, and the position of each individual among his fellows. A sociogram is a preliminary step in understanding group action or individual action in a group setting. It may be used to summarize verbal choices, written choices, or direct observations of a competent observer.

To prepare a sociogram, the student should gather data from a small group, preferably 12 or fewer in number, and follow through the basic steps outlined below. He may wish to ask questions regarding leadership or some characteristic other than friendship. The questions depend entirely upon the problem being investigated, but they must be phrased clearly and unambiguously. It is usually advisable to pretest the questions to ensure that they ask what is intended. Students may measure their degree of insight into group relations by predicting the choices the members of the group will make and comparing them with the actual choices.

As an exercise, a third-grade teacher asked his class of 15 boys and 15 girls to "Write the name of the child you like best in class," and then "the name of the child you like second best." For simplicity we shall explain the processing of the boys' choices only. It is not necessary to show the whole sociogram because only three boys chose or were chosen by girls. Figure 5.5 continues on page 152.

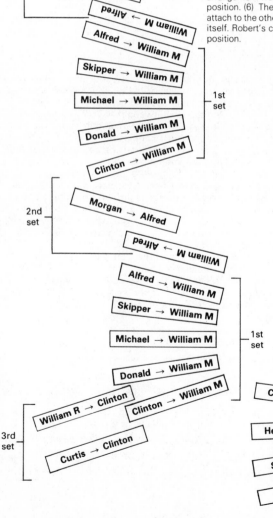

Procedure

(1) We wrote each chooser's name on the left-hand side of a slip of paper with an arrow pointing to the name of his first choice, which was written on the right-hand side. (2) After a slip had been made for each choice, we sorted the slips of those who had named the same person as best friend. We found four subgroups, called sets, in which the same person had been named as best friend by several persons: William M, chosen by Donald, Skipper, Michael, Clinton, and Alfred; Alfred, chosen by William M and Morgan; Clinton, chosen by William R and Curtis; Robert, chosen by Charles, Herbert (and Sally). (3) The set with the most slips (William M's) was arranged to converge on his name. (4) William M chose Alfred, who was a member of another set. Because William M's and Alfred's choices were mutual, their slips were placed parallel to each other. The other choice in the second set (in this case Morgan's choice of Alfred) was placed in position with the first set. (5) Another set which could be attached to the arrangement was Clinton's, and it was put in position. (6) The fourth set (Robert's) did not attach to the other sets, and it was arranged by itself. Robert's choice was then placed in position.

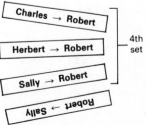

Sociogram of first choices

(7) The remaining individual slips were fitted into the arrangement, and the sociogram of first choices was completed by sketching the arrangement as a diagram. (Second choices not shown in this figure.)

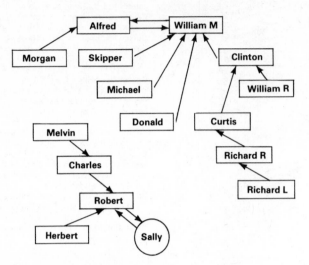

Interpretation   1. The outstanding finding of the first choices is William M's position as the *star*. He received five first choices from the other 14 boys and two second choices. Clinton received two first choices and five second choices, making him a strong runner-up to William M. Between them they received 14 choices, and their choice of Alfred created a *triangle,* which dominates the sociogram. The three boys combined received 19 choices.

2. In the first-choice sociogram, there is one *mutual choice,* or *pair,* between boys—William M and Alfred—and one between a boy and a girl—Robert and Sally. Additional pairs show when the second choices are counted.

3. There is an *island* consisting of Melvin, Charles, Herbert, Robert (and Sally) on the first choices. In the second choices a bridge is thrown from the island to the main group of boys by Melvin's choice of Clinton, and there are additional ties between this group and the girls. The island has other girls who do not appear in the figure, and it is interesting that the girls in this group are only weakly integrated with the main group of girls.

4. There are seven *isolates:* Skipper, Michael, Herbert, Donald, Morgan, Richard L, and William R. These boys received no choices.

5. One *error* appears in Richard L's failure to make a second choice.
Note that such errors reduce the *total* number of choices made by the group.

Applications and limitations: Like any other research technique, the sociogram has its limitations.

FIGURE 5.5 (cont'd)

who prefer close personal relationships with others, they are not necessarily the tacitly approved group leaders.

Several research studies have been conducted to determine the type of formal communication network (that is, who says what to whom, and how often) that would result in better performance. One such study was conducted by Alex Bavelas and his associates.

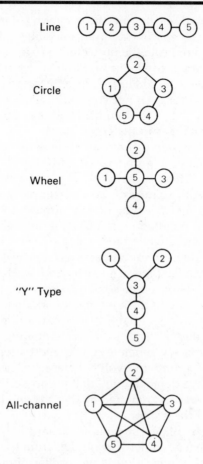

FIGURE 5.6 The connecting lines between group members (represented by numbers) represent an open communication channel, which the group members may use. For example, in the Line structure group member 1 may communicate only with group member 2, but in the All-channel structure, group member 1 may communicate with all other members. It is not possible to catagorize all networks as either centralized or decentralized simply according to their structure. The wheel, for instance, is highly structured by its structure. The All-channel, on the other hand, which by its structure appears to be decentralized, may become a centralized network if the group members decide to not use some of the channels.

The study was conducted by setting up the types of communication networks shown in Figure 5.6.

Each network (composed of five members) was first given a simple task to complete and then a more complex task. In the first experiment, each of the members of each network received six colored marbles, of which only one color was common to all the members.

The task assigned was to find the common color. In the second experiment, the approach was the same, but multicolored marbles were used to complicate the problem. Certain rules were laid down for the participants. In attempting to find the answer, each participant was allowed to communicate only according to the channel lines established for each network. For instance, in the case of the wheel network, the outer members had only one-way communication with the member in the center, while each of the members in the circle had two-way communication with members on either side. The results of this study showed the *wheel* to be faster for the simple task, and the *circle* network for the complex task. The general finding was that the nature of the task (simple or complex) to be performed determined the type of communication network required. Easier tasks are handled more efficiently by centralized networks, (such as the *wheel*), while more complex tasks lend themselves to decentralized communication patterns (such as the *circle*).

Two other researchers, Faucheux and MacKenzie, also studied the relationship between task complexity and networks. However, they were interested in the kind of network that would evolve if the group was left free to establish its own communication pattern. The results of their research were similar to those found by Bavelas: simple tasks typically generate centralized patterns, while complex tasks force the group to evolve a decentralized network. Other experiments have demonstrated that group performance is affected both by the interaction required by the task and by the communication network of the group.

At Michigan State University, Richard V. Farace and his associates have extended network studies from the five-person group to large organizations. They have used communication network analysis to define a set of groups in a large organization. Their research studies the actual communication network in organizations—who talks to whom—which is never fully represented by the formal organization chart.

Sensitivity Training

One question that I am frequently asked about the field of interpersonal communication is, "Isn't a course in interpersonal communication really a form of sensitivity training?" When I explain that we are studying the theory and process of interpersonal communication, I'm asked to explain just what a sensitivity group does that is different from what is done in a communication course.

More than two decades ago Leland Bradford, director of the Adult Education Division of the National Education Association, and his associates, drawing on the work of the social psychologist Kurt Lewin, established the first center of sensitivity training at Bethel, Maine. Thus was founded the National Training

Laboratories, abbreviated as NTL, associated with the National Education Association. Against initially strong opposition, the training group, or T-group, gained acceptance from industry, social scientists, and educators.

The typical T-group consists of a small group of people, usually under twenty, who meet in a comfortable, isolated setting, called "the laboratory" for approximately two weeks. As T-groups were first conducted, the emphasis was primarily on the achievement of prescribed tasks and on the sociology of the group itself, rather than on its psychology. In other words, the focus was on the roles and functions of leadership and group membership, rather than on the individual member's personality and personal development.

Training groups for improving communication within organizations were a later development. Business and industry would and do continue to pay for training-group experiences for executives, middle management, and supervisory and production personnel. Similar training groups are organized for the hard-core unemployed in which the focus of the group experience is on vocational and organizational skill-learning, rather than on personal exploration.

The growing interest in training groups and the trend toward the psychological emphasis on the individual member's personality and personal development led to the creation of a different, but related, kind of group—variously called encounter groups, confrontation sessions, marathon labs, or more generally, human growth sessions; these sensitivity groups are short-term—twenty-four hours or a weekend—and emphasize the exposure of beliefs and feelings that usually are not put on public display by individuals. Perhaps the most widely known setting for these growth experiences is the Esalen Institute, which offers a wide variety of programs. For example, one weekend seminar at Esalen, with B. F. Skinner, the developer of operant conditioning, was followed by groups conducted by a Protestant theologian, an advocate of LSD, a Carmelite monk, an existential psychotherapist, the president of the American Psychological Association, an historian, an authority on ESP, a Zen scholar, an architect, and a Hindu mystic. These are some of the people who have served as trainers at Esalen.

A trainer is the individual who conducts the group. The trainer has a thorough understanding of group and individual behavior, and skill in using training technology. The trainer may open the group in a variety of ways. The following statement is an example:

This group will meet for many hours and will serve as a kind of laboratory where each individual can increase his understanding of the forces which influence individual behavior and the performance of groups and organizations. The data for learning will be our own behavior, feelings, and reactions. We begin with no definite structure or organization, no agreed-upon procedures and no specific agenda. It will be up to us to fill the vacuum created by the lack of these familiar elements and to study our group as we evolve. My role will be to help the group to learn from its own experience, but not to act as a traditional chairman nor to suggest how we should organize, what our procedure should be, or exactly what our agenda will include. With these few comments, I think we are ready to begin in whatever way you feel will be most helpful.

Typically some members may attempt to organize the group by promoting an election of a chairman or the selection of a discussion topic. Other members may withdraw in silence. Usually, members attempt to get the trainer to play a more directive role, like that of the typical chairman. Whatever a member does, he also is observing and reacting to the behavior of the other members and having an impact on them. These perceptions and reactions are the data for group discussion and learning.

Trainers and group members are using increasingly more non-verbal exercises in order to help create a climate of openness and trust within the group. The techniques employed range from exercises with a minimum of body contact to exercises that are physically intimate and that provoke deep emotional responses, a major contribution of Esalen. Although these exercises can provoke powerful feelings, this need not be a frightening experience. In police-community relations training sessions, for example, even seemingly simple physical contact—a hand shake or a hug—can evoke unknown feelings. Often, police officers and community residents have never thought of one another beyond certain stereotypical roles, and a simple, human act may be all that is needed to establish a bond of brotherhood. The experiences may be multidimensional—

How do the nonverbal exercises employed by this group affect the climate of openness and trust within the group?

sculpture, painting, music, dance, and movement—all designed to direct the participants' attention to the myriad ways in which meaningful experiences can be achieved.

Carl Rogers' style of training, which he labels the *basic encounter group*, encourages group members to explore their own and others' feelings and emotions. Rogers has spoken of a filmed group session with people who were "involved in the drug scene, including straight individuals, such as a narcotics agent, and 'stoned' individuals, including a convicted drug pusher. There were blacks and whites, the young and middle-aged, ghetto products and members of the middle class. The group process by which communication and closeness became a living part of this diverse group is an experience I shall never forget."[13] Part of the transcript of that filmed experience is reproduced as Adapted Reading No. 12.

It should be emphasized that sensitivity groups are *not* therapy groups. A therapy group places more emphasis on the inner life of the group member; such things as dreams, childhood recollections, sexual material, and the like are considered. The sensitivity group focuses on the group member's behavior in that immediate group setting. Let's look at some of the studies of sensitivity groups.

In studies of courses using sensitivity-training techniques at the University of Kansas, Cal Downs concluded that sensitivity training as a teaching technique does have an impact on participants but that this impact is primarily on how the participant understands the role of leadership in the small group. Sensitivity training did not produce vast changes in the participants' values or self-concepts, and the types of changes that did occur were not very different from those produced by a more traditional type of course. In fact, Downs found indications that students selected courses using sensitivity training as a teaching technique because such courses were in accord with the values or self-images that they already held.[14]

Carl Rogers Conducts an Encounter Group

In an encounter group, the communication behavior of the trainer is a critical factor, and the communication behavior of the group members may be different from how they might communicate in a problem-solving group. Nonetheless, the same types of process observations can be made for encounter groups as was described in this chapter for problem-solving groups. From this transcript of a portion of an encounter group conducted by Carl Rogers, determine what leadership functions Rogers provides for the group. Prepare a diagram for this segment showing the number of times each person spoke and to whom (if possible). Use Bales or Gibb to categorize the interaction. What conclusions can you draw from your data?

Rogers: This is almost the first thing you've said from yourself, you make a pretty good observer, you make observations about other people, ask questions of other people, but this time you're saying something from yourself. I enjoy that.

Male #1 (George): But I'm still going back to the fact that here right now, at this moment, sure this is real, and if you consider life as just a continuation of presences, a continuation of moments, and everything that's real is a succession of moments. OK that's all well and good. But yet if you're going to take what this "here" knowledge gives us, and go out into tomorrow's here and now, then for us to really apply this to our life in the future. For us to really apply this to our life, like this is beautiful here. And for us to make tomorrow or next week as beautiful as today is, we're going to have to tear down society. Society is saying "You gotta go do the job."

Adapted from "Because That's My Way," a 60 minute color film. Used by permission from Carl R. Rogers and WQED, Metropolitan Pittsburgh Public Broadcasting Inc.

Rogers: I feel that there are quiet revolutionaries and there are violent ones. I think most of my life I've been a quiet revolutionary.

Male #1 (George): We don't have the channel open to us that you have open to yourself. To be a quiet revolutionary. Like we tried, the hippie movement tried to be quiet revolutionaries. We tried to be so quiet that the way we tried to spread the revolution was to just do it by example. We tried to just live together, to love each other. It was the flower children, the love generation. Now these very same kids, and it just makes me all the more bitter and cynical. I was one of them, I was a flower child, and I'm not ashamed to admit it, but Haight-Ashbury was exploited, we got our heads beat in trying to get McCarthy elected. I'm really bitter about that. The only way I can deal with that rage is to be violent. I can't be a quiet revolutionary. They won't let me. You can sit over there sanctimoniously and say "I'm a quiet revolutionary." They won't let me.

Male #2: Actually just what he said, you know, he finally thought it out—you know, you can't know anything about this until it's been done to you or perpetrated against you . . . so I can understand his bitterness. He wasn't in the dungeons like I was, but he's seen his friends get knocked around, he's seen their heads get busted. I don't know the circumstances, but I can tell just by his conversation, just by the way he expressed himself now, that he witnessed this.

Male #1 (George): And I don't want anybody to think that I don't like being a revolutionary or that I'm going to build all my rage against the police, since that's too easy (laughter).

I have to, and I don't mean to offend you, I have to sort of pity you, because of the fact you're a tool for those people that don't, won't let change become about.

Male #3 (a policeman): Well, that may be so but you still need law and order, no matter what.

Male #1 (George): Those two words have a definition but law and order doesn't mean law and order anymore. (George exits.)

Female #1: Children at the age of 5 reach out for assistance, a mommy or a daddy or brother or sister, and sure enough there's mommy to hold their hand. And suddenly that child grows up and nobody's going to reach out. Are we building false hopes in these little children? Some of you can reach out.

Rogers: Could I interrupt for just a minute, because a lot has been going on in Russ and he's just been sitting quietly here weeping, and I would really like to know what the score is.

Male #4 (Russ): I've had this shit . . . this plain hell . . . My mother reached out for me, and I enjoyed it, but my dad didn't. He never showed one lousy stinking bit of compassion for me. I got more out of my mother with all that compassion she gave me than with that non-compassion my father gave me. He never held me, he never cried with me, and that made it worse for me to face life than if somebody would hold me. It's a lot worse when you have nobody than when you have somebody. One person to hold you, at least you have that one person at least if it's nobody else, and you only have that moment of compassion between each other, that's a hell of a lot, and it sticks in your mind a hell of a long time. I just couldn't talk with him, George he's wrong, but I couldn't talk to George, and I hate to talk when he's left and he's gone now, but he was just like my dad, sitting there telling me this is the right way. Get your hair cut, because this is the right way . . . and he was sitting there saying . . . Be violent with me because this is the right way, this is it. And he says I did this before . . . give me the chance to sit around and try to do it this time. Maybe he failed but maybe I'll succeed in a non-violent way. Look at Ghandi, he succeeded. Just because George failed doesn't mean I'm gonna fail. I don't have to start out violent and I hope to God I never have to be violent. He only knows how to hit and be violent. I can't hit because I know how a heel feels when it's crushed into your face, how it feels to be kicked in the side, how it feels when you're hit in the throat and you're choking, and I don't want anyone to feel that stinking, lousy, shit, pain, and I just can't be violent, and I hope that I never am . . . .

Rogers: I sure heard your need for a Father and I sure heard your dislike for violence.

Male #2: I want to say something about these two young people here. This is what society has done to them, this is why they are so confused and not only them, but millions, thousands of others, they're just confused like these two.

Male #4 (Russ): I can't go up to George and hold his hand and cry on his shoulder because just like he did to her. He just shot it right down afterwards. He just said this is just one second, one thing. It was just shot right down all the way.

Rogers: For me, it was very true that just to be held for one minute by your father would have made a hell of a lot of difference.

Male #4 (Russ): And when he shook my hand the other day it meant more in the world than any time he screamed and hollered at me, he shook my hand, he showed me he was proud that I passed my license the first time when he failed and had to go for a second try. When he shook my hand he showed me that he had some kind of pride for me.

Rogers: These moments make a difference.

Male #4 (Russ): I'd rather be loved all my life and showed it rather than pushed aside and yelled at all the time. It made me face the world better, it made me hate . . . not hate . . . but that hiding and concealing of compassion, I just couldn't take it . . . Like, when this started, I thought I was really closer to George than anyone else here. And as it's gone on, and I thought I wasn't even close to that . . . cop, (laughter) George couldn't let go, couldn't feel what it was like to be ashamed and let yourself go and he (cop) let himself go. George, I think he let go once, it was short and it was like he was scared to let go all the way. But he (cop) let go many times, and I think all the way when he was talking about his father, and I could talk to her because she let go . . . all the time and all the way, and I'm closer to him because I can see a lot of things that he went through, and he lets go in a different way now. (laughter)

Female #1: Russ, and you don't condemn George either.

Male #4 (Russ): No, I don't condemn George.

Female #1: You've got to have that compassion for him because he has the inability to let go.

Male #4 (Russ): I agree, I don't hate the guy, he's just uptight.

Female #1: George may be the one person out of the whole group who needs us.

Perhaps the most complete study of sensitivity-training groups was conducted by Lieberman, Yalom, and Miles at Stanford University. They established eighteen groups totaling 210 students enrolled in a course on race and prejudice.

Each group used one of ten different sensitivity-training devices. Indices of change were based on self-ratings, observer ratings, other group member ratings, and non-participant peer ratings of member behavior. The areas that were measured included attitudes toward encounter groups, personal anticipations, racial attitudes, personal dilemmas, and self-characterization. The results do not provide an impressive amount of support for the hypothesis that sensitivity training has substantially positive effects. Some groups had almost totally positive effects on their members, while others had almost totally negative effects. Overall, the results revealed that approximately one third of the group members experienced positive change, another third no change, and the final third negative change.[15] In the control group, nearly 15 percent experienced positive change.

Under *qualified* leadership, sensitivity training is generally a positive experience; for most people the experience probably causes no more emotional strain than what one feels on the day of an examination. Probably the experience is not desirable for individuals who are highly defensive or for those who continually distort interpersonal feedback. Unfortunately, not all who claim to be trainers are qualified; some trainers lack experience but have good intentions—others have neither qualifications or good intentions.

Consciousness-Raising Groups

A relatively new use of the small group—consciousness raising—deserves study. James Chesebro, John Cragan, and Patricia McCullough studied three consciousness-raising groups composed of a total of fifteen members who were all active and militant members of Gay Liberation. Consciousness raising is a new phenomenon first employed in 1966–1967. According to Chesebro, Cragan, and McCullough, consciousness raising is a personal, face-to-face interaction that appears to create new psychological orientations for the group members. Participants may develop new group identities, often forming "new minorities," which focus on such sociocultural divisions as sex, age, sexual preference, education, wealth, power, or prestige. As a result, members often perceive each other as "brothers" and "sisters" in a new "community."

The small-group face-to-face interaction is consistent with the belief that shared personal experience can generate political theory and action. The primary task of the small consciousness-raising group is to determine the nature and causes of the group's oppression and to provide a foundation for initiating change. The researchers identified four stages in consciousness raising: In moving through the four-stage process, participants created a new identity for themselves (Stage One), perceived themselves as pitted against agents of the establishment (Stage Two), denied establishment values and advocated newly created ones (Stage Three), and, finally, agreed to support the liberation efforts of unrecognized oppressed groups, hence broadening the revolution (Stage Four).[16]

In a related essay, Louise McPherson examined consciousness-raising women's groups. Consciousness raising among people involved in the women's movement is designed to change women's attitudes about themselves, working from the premise that women must first learn to overcome belief in their sex-role stereotypes. Women's liberation consciousness-raising groups are frequently leaderless in order to develop each member's self-reliance. Without leadership, the women must speak for themselves and thereby develop confidence in their own abilities. Self-disclosure is stressed as members are encouraged to relate experiences from their own lives that delineate a pattern of oppression of women in general. Finally, members devote much time to reading and discussing the current movement literature. The overall effect of women's liberation is one of self-redefinition.[17]

Intimacy

It is a popular criticism of all non-problem-solving groups that they deal in "touchy-feely" rather than in any legitimate interpersonal communication. Although this criticism may be true of some groups, it certainly is not true of the majority of them. Thus, it is legitimate to examine non-problem-solving groups as one means of attaining interpersonal intimacy.

Erik Erikson's theory of personality sets out eight psychosocial stages of development that confront all of us as growing individuals. Erikson contends that each developmental stage contains a task, or crisis, that must be resolved. How one resolves the crisis of one stage will have consequences on the next, and so on. At some time between adolescence and middle age, we must face the crisis of "intimacy versus isolation"; that is, after we have completed the task of adolescence, which is to resolve the identity crisis, we must either form close relationships with others or develop a sense of isolation, a feeling that there is no one other to depend on in the world.[18] Murray Davis describes four different "others" with whom we may become intimate: friends, lovers, spouses, and siblings. Friends may be intimates insofar as they engage in all intimate behaviors except sexually related ones. Lovers are intimates insofar as they engage in sexually related intimate behavior (and, usually, other intimate behavior as well). Spouses are intimates insofar as they, by becoming officially related share a common future of potential inti-

What can you say about the degree of intimacy represented here? Why is nonverbal communication used to communicate feelings?

mate behavior, though they may not be currently engaging in any intimate behaviors. Siblings are intimates insofar as they, by being officially related, share a common past of intimate behavior, though they too may not be currently engaging in many intimate behaviors.[19]

Alan Dahms describes intimacy on three related levels: intellectual, physical, and emotional, as shown in Figure 5.7.

According to Dahms, all levels are of equal importance; none should be omitted and none should be emphasized to the exclusion of others.

Intellectual relationships may reflect game-playing. Notice that Dahms includes "words" as characteristic of an intellectual relationship. Ask your instructor to describe "game-playing" at professional conventions; for instance, how in cocktail lounges and meetings it often becomes more important for some to communicate to others how successful they have been in obtaining grants and consulting with major corporations. Dahms contends that although we like to think that speech is one of the important ways in which people set up in-depth communication processes, it is also possible that speech is most often used to keep others *away* by relating to one another solely in terms of the roles we play. Speech may be one of the most popular distance tools.

The next level of intimacy is physical. The touch of a friendly hand, a warm hug or badly needed caress can brighten up the glummest day or erase feelings of loneliness and uncertainty.

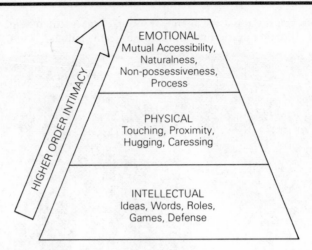

EMOTIONAL
Mutual Accessibility,
Naturalness,
Non-possessiveness,
Process

PHYSICAL
Touching, Proximity,
Hugging, Caressing

INTELLECTUAL
Ideas, Words, Roles,
Games, Defense

HIGHER ORDER INTIMACY

SOURCE: Alan M. Dahms, *Emotional Intimacy: Overlooked Requirement for Survival,*
Boulder, Colorado: Pruett Publishing Company, 1972, p. 20.

FIGURE 5.7 Dahms shows three different kinds of intimacy. While they are shown as a
hierarchy, it is incorrect to assume that a relationship proceeds through each kind.

Touching satisfies the need for that close, nonsexual intimacy that
we all miss from early childhood. (Refer back to the section on Ashley Montague's writings and thoughts on touching in Chapter 3.)

Dahm's final level of intimacy, emotional, has four characteristics: mutual accessibility, naturalness, nonpossessiveness, and process. People enjoying an emotionally intimate relationship as a
couple or in a group tend to see each other as mutually accessible.
Each person feels he or she has complete access to the other that is
free of criticism. Accessibility enhances a feeling of naturalness. A
relationship is considered natural in the sense that persons are accepted as they are, not for their ability to change themselves to meet
another's requirements or to play a role assigned to them by others.
In natural relationships, feelings are important and are respected.
The third characteristic of emotional intimacy is nonpossessiveness.
Caring on the highest level does not mean smothering the other
with possessiveness or ownership. The attainment and maintenance of emotional intimacy is a process that requires constant
attention. When time and energy are not expended to maintain the
process, the relationship deteriorates.[20]

Of course, no one advocates that we strive for an intimate
relationship with everyone else in the groups to which we belong.
Alan Sillars has written in a thoughtful analysis of human
communication that self-disclosure should be subject to regulation
by the situation and goals of an interaction; that is, certain social
realities may render self-disclosure neither effective nor desirable

and might reduce rather than promote understanding.[21] In other words, one needs to develop a sense of appropriateness.

★Probe Questions

This chapter began by referring to a study that indicated that participating in small groups is an important use of leisure time. What groups do you seek out? What groups seek you out?

We know that a group exerts pressure on its members to conform. What do your various group memberships reveal about who you are?

Can group membership be a means of seeking identity, of discovering and intensifying elements of a shared self-concept? If there are women's consciousness-raising groups, should there also be men's consciousness-raising groups? How would they operate?

Can group membership be a means of seeking intimacy? Are sensitivity-training groups a means of seeking interpersonal intimacy? If intimacy is found within the group, what happens when the group stops and its members go their separate ways?

Interpersonal Conflict

If we were to survey people's attitudes toward interpersonal conflict, we might find that it is a popularly held belief that conflict—quarreling, arguing, fighting—is disruptive and should be avoided. However, we must also keep in mind that while conflict may be inevitable, it is through conflict that existing norms and practices are challenged and changed, and through conflict that we are frequently our most creative and innovative. Since conflict can be either destructive or productive, how to *avoid* conflict is not the issue. Rather, managing interpersonal conflict for maximum benefits and minimum costs is the skill to be developed.

The academic study of social conflict can be traced to the German philosopher Georg Simmel.[22] Some say Simmel was the founder of modern sociology. Others say he made no contribution. But regardless of who is right, Simmel introduced many ideas about conflict, calling it one of the most vivid interactions among humans and labeling it positive in contrast to interactions of indifference or the termination of interaction.

By definition, then, interpersonal conflict involves two or more people who can only be in conflict through communication, either verbal or nonverbal. People not communicating with one another cannot be in conflict. Thus, social conflict refers to a particular set of human communicative behaviors.

It then becomes critical to be able to label certain communicative behaviors as conflict behaviors. Conflict behaviors abound in contemporary society: verbal abuse, separation, fights, divorce, delin-

Should conflict—quarreling, arguing, fighting—always be avoided?

quency, strikes, campus and ghetto riots, and so forth. On an interpersonal level, certainly some communication behaviors signal a
high probability of conflict. It would seem that conflict behaviors
could be easily labeled. However upon closer examination, it becomes apparent that commonly labeled conflict behaviors are not
always perceived as such by the people involved. For example, my
shouting a series of obscenities at a person with whom I am in frequent and willing contact, while easily being labeled by an observer
as "conflict behavior," may in fact, be an attempt on my part to
communicate intimacy and, thus, be labeled by me and my friend as
affective or supportive behavior. The point is that behaviors commonly assumed to be conflict behaviors cannot be labeled as such
unless the communicators themselves perceive those behaviors as
conflict behaviors. If one person perceives certain communicative
behaviors as conflict behaviors and the other partner in the interaction does not perceive them as such, then a "misunderstanding"
or a "communication breakdown" is said to have occurred. By this
view, conflict about whether or not there is conflict would also be
labeled as a problem of "misunderstanding" or as a "communication breakdown." In a very real way, then, social conflict is not an
external reality; conflict behaviors are associated with the attitudes
held by the people in a relationship, which determine their perceptions of that relationship as well as their communicative behaviors
with each other.

Generally, Simmel argued that both harmony and disharmony,
association and competition, or favorable and unfavorable tenden-

cies must exist together in a society, and that conflict with "outsiders" helps to unify groups.

One question Simmel raised concerned human hostility. Are we born aggressive? If so, it would explain most conflicts among humans. Several authors, such as Robert Ardrey, Konrad Lorenz, and Anthony Starr, all writing in the 1960s, suggested that because instinctive aggression could be demonstrated in animals, humans too are programmed by evolution to be aggressive. Evolution suggests that a species must be aggressive to survive. Animal studies also have demonstrated claims to territory resulting in aggressive acts when that territory is invaded. Erich Fromm argues, on the other hand, that primitive man was peace-loving, and that cooperation and sharing were necessary for survival.[23]

Clearly, we do not know the answer. We do, however, have some clues as to how society contributes to aggressiveness. For example, although aggression is not a necessary concomitant of competition, any examination of American society vividly illustrates the extent to which we are taught aggressiveness in competitive behaviors—and it begins very early, with children's television programs that emphasize good guy/bad guy violence and Little League baseball games that often place youngsters under enormous parental pressure to win. In fact, winning per se seems to be a favorite American pastime.

In 1956, Lewis Coser's book *The Functions of Social Conflict* offered a definition of conflict as "a struggle over values and claims to scarce status, power and resources in which the aims of the opponents are to neutralize, injure, or eliminate their rivals."[24] Coser's definition reflects a sociopolitical view of social conflict in that it focuses one's perspective on the assumption that the conflicting parties have well-defined goals or interests, and that there are only two possible behaviors: struggling with rivals in order to obtain (or keep) resources or not struggling, and therefore not obtaining or retaining the resources.

Coser's definition explicitly suggests that parties view their relationship as being in conflict when they are both pursuing the same objective. Further, this definition implies that both parties are "playing by the rules" of a zero-sum game; that is, one in which only one party can successfully obtain the objective that is desired and valued by each.

For example, two female roommates may both be actively dating. Together they have a seemingly endless set of alternatives (men) from which to choose. In some sense they may be in competition, but they are not in conflict because neither perceives the behaviors associated with dating as conflicting with their relationship. However, when one of the two attempts to date the man the other is seriously involved with, the alternatives become radically

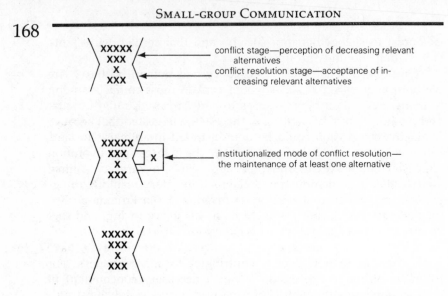

FIGURE 5.8 If status, power, and resources are thought of as "relevant alternatives" (shown as Xs), then conflict increases as these decrease.

reduced. There is now only one man for two friends, and each probably now perceives the other's attempts to date him as conflict behaviors. Conflict exists because only one of the friends can "win"; hence, their relationship with each other becomes an issue.

In some sense, then, conflict is the process of perceiving fewer and fewer relevant alternatives by the parties in a relationship, and the process of conflict resolution is the process by which the parties introduce and accept an increasing number of perceived relevant alternatives. This model of conflict and conflict resolution is shown in Figure 5.8. In this model, the establishment of institutionalized modes of conflict resolution, such as collective bargaining and grievance procedures, may be considered as a way of maintaining at least one alternative as a mode of conflict resolution.

A classic series of studies of conflict were conducted by Muzafer Sherif and his associates with preadolescent boys at a summer camp in Robbers Cave, Oklahoma, in 1954. The experiment had three stages. In the first stage, two groups of boys were brought to the camp and kept isolated from each other while each solidified themselves as a group. The groups became known as the Rattlers and the Eagles. In the second stage, the two groups were brought into contact in a series of competitive group activities and mutually frustrating situations that produced a high level of intergroup hostility. During this stage, the experimenters arranged for the groups to come into contact in pleasurable settings, such as attending a movie together and eating in the same mess hall. Such contact produced jeers, catcalls, insults, and food-throwing fights. Stage three was dedicated to the reduction of intergroup hostility. They staged a series of "emergencies," designed so that the boys would have to work together to remedy them in order to get something they all wanted. The "emergencies" included such things as "the drinking-water problem" in which they were told that a water line had broken and the help of all the boys was required in order to find the damage and repair it, and "the camp-out problem" in which a truck stalled requiring mutual effort to restart. Stage three was successful in reducing the existing tensions between the groups. In fact, through mutual cooperation, friendships began to develop between members of opposing groups. The researchers attributed the reduction in hostilities to the interpersonal experiences generated by cooperation.[25]

More recently, a most significant book, sections of which are reprinted as Adapted Reading No. 13, by Irving L. Janis on "groupthink," suggests that when concurrence-seeking (the avoidance of conflict) is the group's norm, independent critical thinking (the challenging of existing norms and practices, creativity, innovativeness) is less likely to occur.

Remember our discussion in the previous chapter on interpersonal attraction? Have you ever been in a group in which just being with the people in that group was so attractive to you that you felt you had to go along with everything that was done? This is what Janis is discussing when he points out that the avoidance of conflict can become a group norm; that is, people may be under subtle pressure not to stand up and object to the group's thinking even when they feel it is wrong, and when this happens, the group's ability to think critically suffers.

Adapted Reading No. 13

Victims of Groupthink

Group decision-making can counteract the limitations of individuals' decision-making, but groups too are subject to shortcomings. One of these is a tendency for independent critical thinking to be replaced by "groupthink." What encourages the development of groupthink? How can it be avoided?

Year after year newscasts and newspapers inform us of collective miscalculations—companies that have unexpectedly gone bankrupt because of misjudging their market, federal agencies that have mistakenly authorized the use of chemical insecticides that poison our environment, and White House executive committees that have made ill-conceived foreign policy decisions that inadvertently bring the major powers to the brink of war. Most people, when they hear about such fiascoes, simply remind themselves that, after all, "organizations are run by human beings," "to err is human," and "nobody is perfect." But platitudinous thoughts about human nature do not help us to understand how and why avoidable miscalculations are made.

Fiasco watchers who are unwilling to set the problem aside in this easy fashion will find that contemporary psychology has something to say (unfortunately not very much) about distortions of thinking and other sources of human error. The deficiencies about which we know the most pertain to disturbances in the behavior of each individual in a decision-making group—temporary states of elation, fear, or anger that reduce a person's mental efficiency; chronic blind spots arising from a person's social prejudices; shortcomings in information-processing that prevent a person from comprehending the complex consequences of a seemingly simple policy decision. One psychologist has suggested that because the information-processing capabilities of every individual are limited, no responsible leader of a large organization ought to make a policy decision without using a computer that is programmed to spell out

Adapted from Irving L. Janis, "Introduction: Why So Many Miscalculations?" Victims of Groupthink, *Boston: Houghton Mifflin Company, 1972, pp. 2–13. Used by permission of the publisher.*

all the probable benefits and costs of each alternative under consideration. The usual way of trying to counteract the limitations of individuals' mental functioning, however, is to relegate important decisions to groups.

Imperfections of Group Decisions

Groups, like individuals, have shortcomings. Groups can bring out the worst as well as the best in man. Nietzsche went so far as to say that madness is the exception in individuals but the rule in groups. A considerable amount of social science literature shows that in circumstances of extreme crisis, group contagion occasionally gives rise to collective panic, violent acts of scapegoating, and other forms of what could be called group madness. Much more frequent, however, are instances of mindless conformity and collective misjudgment of serious risks, which are collectively laughed off in a clubby atmosphere of relaxed conviviality. Consider what happened a few days before disaster struck the small mining town of Pitcher, Oklahoma, in 1950. The local mining engineer had warned the inhabitants to leave at once because the town had been accidentally undermined and might cave in at any moment. At a Lion's Club meeting of leading citizens, the day after the warning was issued, the members joked about the warning and laughed uproariously when someone arrived wearing a parachute. What the club members were communicating to each other by their collective laughter was that "sensible people like us know better than to take seriously those disaster warnings; we know it can't happen here, to our fine little town." Within a few days, this collective complacency cost some of these men and their families their lives.

Lack of vigilance and excessive risk-taking are forms of temporary group derangement to which decision-making groups made up of responsible executives are not at all immune. Sometimes the main trouble is that the chief executive manipulates his advisers to rubber-stamp his own ill-conceived proposals. . . . During the group's deliberations, the leader does not deliberately try to get the group to tell him what he wants to hear but is quite sincere in asking for honest opinions. The group members are not transformed into sycophants. They are not afraid to speak their minds. Nevertheless, subtle constraints, which the leader may reinforce inadvertently, prevent a member from fully exercising his critical powers and from openly expressing doubts when most others in the group appear to have reached a consensus. In order to take account of what is known about the causes and consequences of such constraints we must briefly review some of the main findings of research on group dynamics.

Effects of Group Cohesiveness

. . . The power of a face-to-face group to set norms that influence members was emphasized by two leading sociologists early in the twentieth century—Charles Horton Cooley and George Herbert Mead. During that same period, William Graham Summer postulated that in-group solidarity increases when clashes arise with out-groups.

Kurt Lewin, the social psychologist who began using empirical methods to study group dynamics during the 1940s, called attention to the prerequisites for effective group decisions. He described the typical dilemmas faced by executive committees, including wartime groups of military planners who select bomb targets and peacetime groups of policy-makers who try to improve relations between nations. Lewin emphasized the need for fact-finding and objective appraisal of alternatives to determine whether the chosen means will achieve a group's goals. He warned that the lack of objective standards for evaluating goal achievement allows many opportunities for errors of judgment and faulty decisions. Lewin's analysis of the behavior of small groups also emphasized the importance of group cohesiveness—that is, members' positive valuation of the group and their motivation to continue to belong to it. When group cohesiveness is high, all the members express solidarity, mutual liking, and positive feelings about attending meetings and carrying out the routine tasks of the group. Lewin was most interested in the positive effects of group cohesiveness and did not investigate instances when members of cohesive groups make gross errors and fail to correct their shared misjudgments.

The potentially detrimental effects of group cohesiveness were emphasized by another theorist, Wilfred Bion, an eminent group therapist. Bion described how the efficiency of all working groups can be adversely affected by the preconscious myths and misconceptions of their mutually dependent members—that is, by shared, basic assumptions that tend to preserve the group without regard for the work at hand.

Under the influence of Kurt Lewin's pioneering work, Leon Festinger, Harold Kelley, Stanley Schachter, and other social psychologists have carried out experiments and field investigations on the consequences of group cohesiveness. Summarizing a large body of research findings that had accumulated during the 1950s and 1960s on the ways members of cohesive groups influence each other, Dorwin Cartwright concluded that the evidence converges on three main types of effects:

Other things being equal, as cohesiveness increases there is an increase in a group's capacity to retain members and in the degree of participation by members in group activities. The greater a group's cohesiveness the more power it has to bring about conformity to its norms and to gain acceptance of its goals and assignment to tasks and roles. Finally, highly cohesive groups provide a source of security for members which serves to reduce anxiety and to heighten self-esteem.

Also under investigation are the causes of group cohesiveness —how and why group identification and feelings of solidarity develop. It has long been known that group solidarity increases markedly whenever a collection of individuals faces a common source of external stress, such as the threat of being injured or killed in military combat. Some researchers are beginning to consider the effects on group solidarity of subtler sources of stress, such as those that beset groups of harried policy-makers in large organizations.

Conformity to Group Norms

In studies of social clubs and other small groups, conformity pressures have frequently been observed. Whenever a member says something that sounds out of line with the group's norms, the other members at first increase their communication with the deviant. Attempts to influence the nonconformist member to revise or tone down his dissident ideas continue as long as most members of the group feel hopeful about talking him into changing his mind. But if they fail after repeated attempts, the amount of communication they direct toward the deviant decreases markedly. The members begin to exclude him, often quite subtly at first and later more obviously, in order to restore the unity of the group. A social psychological experiment conducted by Stanley Schachter with avocational clubs in an American university—and replicated by Schachter and his collaborators in seven European countries—showed that the more cohesive the group and the more relevant the issue to the goals of the group, the greater is the inclination of the members to reject a nonconformist. Just as the members insulate themselves from outside critics who threaten to disrupt the unity and esprit de corps of their group, they take steps, often without being aware of it, to counteract the disruptive influence of inside critics who are attacking the group's norms.

The norms to which the members of a cohesive group adhere, as Bion's analysis implies, do not always have a positive effect on the quality of the group's performance. Studies in industrial organizations indicate that while the norms of some work groups foster conscientiousness and high productivity, the norms of other, similar work groups foster slowdowns and socializing activities that reduce productivity. The same type of variation in norms that facilitate or interfere with the group's work objectives may be found among policy-making groups in large organizations.

Much of the current research on group dynamics is an effort to pinpoint the causes of the crucial differences in group norms that make for good or poor performance on group tasks, especially tasks pertaining to decision-making. Among the phenomena that have been intensively investigated in recent years are two detrimental tendencies arising under certain conditions not yet adequately understood—the tendency of groups to develop stereotyped images that dehumanize out-groups against whom they are engaged in competitive struggles and the tendency for the collective judgments arising out of group discussions to shift toward riskier courses of action than the individual members would otherwise be prepared to take.

What Is Groupthink?

The group dynamics approach is based on the working assumption that the members of policy-making groups, no matter how mindful they may be of their exalted national status and of their heavy responsibilities, are subjected to the pressures widely observed in groups of ordinary citizens. In my earlier research on group dynamics, I was impressed by repeated manifestations of the effects—both unfavorable and favorable—of the social pressures that typically develop in cohesive groups—in infantry platoons, air crews, therapy groups, seminars, and self-study or encounter groups of executives receiving leadership training. In all these groups, just as in the industrial work groups described by other investigators, members tend to evolve informal objectives to preserve friendly intragroup relations and this becomes part of the hidden agenda at their meetings. When conducting research on groups of heavy smokers at a clinic set up to help people stop smoking, I noticed a seemingly irrational tendency for the members to exert pressure on each other to increase their smoking as the time for the final meeting approached. This appeared to be a collusive effort to display mutual dependence and resistance to the termination of the group sessions.

Sometimes, even long before members become concerned about the final separation, clear-cut signs of pressures toward uniformity subvert the fundamental purpose of group meetings. At the second meeting of one group of smokers, consisting of twelve middle-class American men and women, two of the most dominant members took the position that heavy smoking was an almost incurable addiction. The majority of the others soon agreed that no one could be expected to cut down drastically. One heavy smoker, a middle-aged business executive, took issue with this consensus, arguing that by using will power he had stopped smoking since joining the group and that everyone else could do the same. His declaration was followed by a heated discussion, which continued in the halls of the building after the formal meeting adjourned. Most of the others ganged up against the man who was deviating from the group consensus. Then, at the beginning of the next meeting, the deviant announced that he had made an important decision. "When I joined," he said, "I agreed to follow the two main rules required by the clinic—to make a conscientious effort to stop smoking and to attend every meeting. But I have learned from experience in this group that you can only follow one of the rules, you can't follow both. And so, I have decided that I will continue to attend every meeting but I have gone back to smoking two packs a day and I will not make any effort to stop smoking again until after the last meeting." Whereupon, the other members beamed at him and applauded enthusiastically, welcoming him back to the fold. No one commented on the fact that the whole point of the meetings was to help each individual to cut down on smoking as rapidly as possible. As a psychological consultant to the group, I tried to call this to the members' attention, and so did my collaborator, Dr. Michael Kahn. But during that meeting the members managed to ignore our comments and reiterated their consensus that heavy smoking was an addiction from which no one would be cured except by cutting down very gradually over a long period of time.

This episode—an extreme form of groupthink—was only one manifestation of a general pattern that the group displayed. At every meeting, the members were amiable, reasserted their warm feelings of solidarity, and sought complete concurrence on every important topic, with no reappearance of the unpleasant bickering that would spoil the cozy atmosphere. The concurrence-seeking tendency could be maintained, however, only at the expense of ignoring realistic challenges (like those posed by the psychological consultants) and distorting members' observations of individual differences that would call into question the shared assumption that everyone in the group had the same type of addiction problem. It seemed that in this smoking group I was observing another instance of the groupthink pattern I had encountered in observations of widely contrasting groups whose members came from diverse sectors of society and were meeting together for social, educational, vocational, or other purposes. Just like the group in the smoking clinic, all these different types of groups had shown signs of high cohesiveness and of an accompanying concurrence-seeking tendency that interfered with critical thinking—the central features of groupthink.

I use the term "groupthink" as a quick and easy way to refer to a mode of thinking that people engage in when they are deeply involved in a cohesive in-group, when the members' strivings for unanimity override their motivation to realistically appraise alternative courses of action. "Groupthink" is a term of the same order as the words in the newspeak vocabulary George Orwell presents in his dismaying *1984*—a vocabulary with terms such as "doublethink" and "crimethink." By putting groupthink with those Orwellian words, I realize that groupthink takes on an invidious connotation. The invidiousness in intentional: Groupthink refers to a deterioration of mental efficiency, reality testing, and moral judgment that results from in-group pressures.

Selection of the Fiascoes

When I began to investigate the Bay of Pigs invasion, the decision to escalate the Korean War, and other fiascoes, for purposes of studying sources of error in foreign policy decision-making, I was initially surprised to discover the pervasiveness of symptoms of groupthink. Although the symptoms that could be discerned from published accounts of the deliberations did not seem as obtrusive as in the face-to-face groups I had observed directly, nevertheless signs of poor decision-making as a result of concurrence-seeking were unmistakable. . . .

At least six major defects in decision-making contribute to failures to solve problems adequately. First, the group's discussions are limited to a few alternative courses of action (often only two) without a survey of the full range of alternatives. Second, the group fails to reexamine the course of action initially preferred by the majority of members from the standpoint of nonobvious risks and drawbacks that had not been considered when it was originally evaluated. Third, the members neglect courses of action initially evaluated as unsatisfactory by the majority of the group: They spend little or no time discussing whether they have overlooked nonobvious gains or whether there are ways of reducing the seemingly prohibitive costs that had made the alternatives seem undesirable. Fourth, members make little or no attempt to obtain information from experts who can supply sound estimates of losses and gains to be expected from alternative courses of actions. Fifth, selective bias is shown in the way the group reacts to factual information and relevant judgments from experts, the mass media, and outside critics. The members show interest in facts and opinions that support their initially preferred policy and take up time in their meetings to discuss them, but they tend to ignore facts and opinions that do not support their initially preferred policy. Sixth, the members spend little time deliberating about how the chosen policy might be hindered by bureaucratic inertia, sabotaged by political opponents, or temporarily derailed by the common accidents that happen to the best of well-laid plans. Consequently, they fail to work out contingency plans to cope with foreseeable setbacks that could endanger the overall success of the chosen course of action.

I assume that these six defects and some related features of inadequate decision-making result from groupthink. But, of course, each of the six can arise from other common causes of human stupidity as well—erroneous intelligence, information overload, fatigue, blinding prejudice, and ignorance. Whether produced by groupthink or by other causes, a decision suffering from most of these defects has relatively little chance of success.

The . . . foreign policy fiascoes I have selected for intensive case studies are the ones of greatest historical importance among the defective decisions by the United States government I have examined. Each clearly meets two important criteria for classifying a decision as a candidate for psychological analysis in terms of group dynamics: Each presents numerous indications that (1) the decision-making group was cohesive and that (2) decision-making was extremely defective. . . .

When the conditions specified by these two criteria are met, according to the groupthink hypothesis there is a better-than-chance likelihood that one of the causes of the defective decision was a strong concurrence-seeking tendency, which is the motivation that gives rise to all the symptoms of groupthink.

The Imperfect Link Between Groupthink and Fiascoes

Simply because the outcome of a group decision has turned out to be a fiasco, I do not assume that it must have been the result of groupthink or even that it was the result of defective decision-making. Nor do I expect that every defective decision, whether arising from groupthink or from other causes, will produce a fiasco. Defective decisions based on misinformation and poor judgment sometimes lead to successful outcomes. We do not necessarily have to accept at face value the well-known thesis—eloquently put forth by Leo Tolstoy in *War and Peace* and elaborated by Norman Mailer in *The Naked and the Dead*—that the decisions made by military commanders have nothing to do with military success. But we must acknowledge that chance and the stupidity of the enemy can sometimes give a silk-purse ending to a command decision worth less than a sow's ear. At the outset of World War I, the French high command made incredible errors, repeatedly ignoring warnings from their military intelligence officers about the Schlieffen plan. But the German high command made even grosser errors while executing the plan, preventing the Germans from capitalizing on the French rout and depriving them of the quick victory that was within their grasp.

Groupthink is conducive to errors in decision-making, and such errors increase the likelihood of a poor outcome. Often the result is a fiasco, but not always. Suppose that because of lucky accidents fostered by absurd command decisions by the Cuban military leaders, the Kennedy administration's Bay of Pigs invasion had been successful in provoking a civil war in Cuba and led to the overthrow of the Castro regime. Analysis of the decision to invade Cuba would still support the groupthink hypothesis, for the evidence shows that Kennedy's White House group was highly cohesive, clearly displayed symptoms of defective decision-making, and exhibited all the major symptoms of groupthink. Thus, even if the Bay of Pigs decision had produced a triumph rather than a defeat, it would still be an example of the potentially adverse effects of groupthink (even though the invasion would not, in that case, be classified as a fiasco).

Hardhearted Actions by Softheaded Groups

At first I was surprised by the extent to which the groups in the fiascoes I have examined adhered to group norms and pressures toward uniformity. Just as in groups of ordinary citizens, a dominant characteristic appears to be remaining loyal to the group by sticking with the decisions to which the group has committed itself, even when the policy is working badly and has unintended consequences that disturb the conscience of the members. In a sense, members consider loyalty to the group the highest form of morality. That loyalty requires each member to avoid raising controversial issues, questioning weak arguments, or calling a halt to softheaded thinking.

Paradoxically, softheaded groups are likely to be extremely hardhearted toward out-groups and enemies. In dealing with a rival nation, policymakers comprising an amiable group find it relatively easy to authorize dehumanizing solutions such as large-scale bombings. An affable group of government officials is unlikely to pursue the difficult and controversial issues that arise when alternatives to a harsh military solution come up for discussion. Nor are the members inclined to raise ethical issues that imply that this "fine group of ours, with its humanitarianism and its high-minded principles, might be capable of adopting a course of action that is inhumane and immoral."

Many other sources of human error can prevent government leaders from arriving at well worked out decisions, resulting in failures to achieve their practical objectives and violations of their own standards of ethical conduct. But, unlike groupthink, these other sources of error do not typically entail increases in hardheartedness along with softheadedness. Some errors involve blind spots that stem from the personality of the decisionmakers. Special circumstances produce unusual fatigue and emotional stresses that interfere with efficient decision-making. Numerous institutional features of the social structure in which the group is located may also cause inefficiency and prevent adequate communication with experts. In addition, well-known interferences with sound thinking arise when the decision-makers comprise a noncohesive group. For example, when the members have no sense of loyalty to the group and regard themselves merely as representatives of different departments, with clashing interests, the meetings may become bitter power struggles, at the expense of effective decisionmaking.

The concept of groupthink pinpoints an entirely different source of trouble, residing neither in the individual nor in the organizational setting. Over and beyond all the familiar sources of human error is a powerful source of defective judgment that arises in cohesive groups—the concurrence-seeking tendency, which fosters overoptimism, lack of vigilance, and sloganistic thinking about the weakness and immorality of out-groups. This tendency can take its toll even when the decision-makers are conscientious statesmen trying to make the best possible decisions for their country and for all mankind.

I do not mean to imply that all cohesive groups suffer from groupthink, though all may display its symptoms from time to time. Nor should we infer from the term "groupthink" that group decisions are typically inefficient or harmful. On the contrary, a group whose members have properly defined roles, with traditions and standard operating procedures that facilitate critical inquiry, is probably capable of making better decisions than any individual in the group who works on the problem alone. And yet the advantages of having decisions made by groups are often lost because of psychological pressures that arise when the members work closely together, share the same values, and above all face a crisis situation in which everyone is subjected to stresses that generate a strong need for affiliation. In these circumstances, as conformity pressures begin to dominate, groupthink and the attendant deterioration of decision-making set in.

The central theme of my analysis can be summarized in this generalization, which I offer in the spirit of Parkinson's laws: *The more amiability and esprit de corps among the members of a policy-making in-group, the greater is the danger that independent critical thinking will be replaced by groupthink, which is likely to result in irrational and dehumanizing actions directed against outgroups.*

Summary

One approach to improving small-group communication skills is that of participation-observation, that is learning to participate in the *content* of the discussion while also learning to be aware of the *process* of the discussion. In this way it is possible to provide the communication behaviors necessary for the efficient functioning of the group. Some of the means of process observation are: classifying communication acts either as task or socioemotional in function; using Bales' category system; using Gibb's descriptions of group climate; observing the group's developmental problem-solving phases and use of problem-solving plans; and watching for the occurrence and absence of leadership functions. Relationships within groups can be determined by developing sociograms and by studying communication networks. The effectiveness of a network is dependent on the type of task that is being handled.

Sensitivity-training groups are designed to improve small-group communication with the intention either of improving task-related problem-solving abilities or of enhancing self-awareness. Consciousness-raising groups are primarily for the purpose of determining the factors that create oppression and initiating change—both personal and social. Intimacy is a developmental task of young adulthood and must be achieved to avoid isolation. Three levels of intimacy are intellectual, physical, and emotional.

Conflict is a form of interpersonal communication which, if properly managed, may be productive rather than destructive. Conflict behaviors exist only when they are recognized as such by the parties involved. Competition becomes conflict when one party attempts to injure or eliminate the other. Conflict can be reduced by increasing the number of alternatives and by working cooperatively to achieve shared goals. When the avoidance of conflict is the group's norm, "groupthink" may develop and create a loss of independent, critical thinking.

Footnotes

[1]Serena E. Wade, "Interpersonal Discussion: A Critical Predictor of Leisure Activity," *Journal of Communication,* 1973, 23, 426–445.

[2]Dean C. Barnlund and Franklyn S. Haiman, *The Dynamics of Discussion,* Boston: Houghton Mifflin Company, 1960.

[3]Bernard Berelson and Gary A. Steiner, *Human Behavior: An Inventory of Scientific Findings,* New York: Harcourt Brace Jovanovich, 1964, pp. 325–326.

[4]Robert F. Bales, Fred L. Strodtbeck, Theodore M. Mills, and Mary E. Roseborough, "Channels of Communication in Small Groups," *American Sociological Review,* 1951, 16, 461–468.

[5]R. F. Bales, *Interaction Process Analysis: A Method for the Study of Small Groups,* Reading, Mass.: Addison-Wesley, 1950.

[6]R. F. Bales and E. F. Borgatta, "Size of Group as a Factor in the Interaction Profile," in H. P. Hare, E. F. Borgatta, and R. F. Bales, eds., *Small Groups,* New York: Knopf, 1955, pp. 396–413.

[7]J. Gibb, "Defensive Communication," *Journal of Communication,* 1961, 11, 141–148.

[8]R. F. Bales, "The Equilibrium

Problem in Small Groups," in Hare, Borgatta, and Bales, *Small Groups*.

[9]B. Aubrey Fisher, "Decision Emergence: Phases in Group Decision-Making," *Speech Monographs*, 1970, 37, 53–66.

[10]L. P. Bradford, "The Case of the Hidden Agenda," in *Group Development*, Selected Reading Series One, Washington, D.C.: National Training Laboratories and National Education Association, 1961.

[11]Carl E. Larson, "Forms of Analysis and Small Group Problem-Solving," *Speech Monographs*, 1969, 36, 452–455.

[12]J. L. Moreno, *Who Shall Survive?* rev. ed., Beacon, N.Y.: Beacon House, 1953.

[13]Carl R. Rogers, "In Retrospect: Forty-Six Years," *American Psychologist*, 1974, 29, 121.

[14]Cal W. Downs, "The Impact of Laboratory Training on Leadership Orientation, Values, and Self-Image," *Speech Teacher*, 1974, 23, 197–205.

[15]Morton A. Lieberman, Irvin D. Yalom, and Matthew B. Miles, *Encounter Groups: First Facts*, New York: Basic Books, Inc., 1973.

[16]James W. Chesebro, John F. Cragan, and Patricia McCullough, "The Small Group Technique of the Radical Revolutionary: A Synthetic Study of Consciousness Raising," *Speech Monographs*, 1973, 40, 136–146.

[17]Louise McPherson, "Communication Techniques of the Women's Liberation Front," *Today's Speech*, 1973, 21(2), 33–38.

[18]E. H. Erikson, *Childhood and Society*, New York: Norton, 1963.

[19]Murray Davis, *Intimate Relations*, New York: The Free Press, 1973.

[20]Alan M. Dahms, *Emotional Intimacy: Overlooked Requirement for Survival*, Boulder, Colorado: Pruett Publishing Company, 1972.

[21]Alan L. Sillars, "Expression and Control in Human Interaction: Perspective On Humanistic Psychology," *Western Speech*, 1974, 38, 269–277.

[22]Georg Simmel, *Conflict* and *The Web of Group Affiliations*, Kurt H. Wolff and Reinhard Bendix, trans., New York: The Free Press, 1955.

[23]Erich Fromm, *The Anatomy of Human Destructiveness*, New York: Holt, Rinehart and Winston, 1973.

[24]Lewis Coser, *The Functions of Social Conflict*, New York: The Free Press, 1956.

[25]M. Sherif, O. J. Harvey, B. J. White, W. E. Hood, and C. W. Sherif, *Intergroup Conflict and Cooperation: The Robber's Cave Experiment*, Norman, Okla: University of Oklahoma Book Exchange, 1961.

Chapter

After reading this chapter, you should be able to:

¶ Discuss the factors that contribute to cross-cultural differences and give examples of how these differences are manifested.

¶ Compare and contrast North American culture with several other cultures.

¶ Explain the importance of understanding cultural differences.

CROSS-CULTURAL
COMMUNICATION

¶ No two people are exactly the same—not even identical twins. But people are not altogether different, either. We all share certain things in common with at least some other people. For instance, we are all members of the human race, and thus share the characteristics and qualities that differentiate us from other species. So, humans, are different from one another and alike one another. Our differences are a result both of our heredity, or biological make-up, and of our environment—particularly the culture that we are part of. People who grow up in the same culture are more alike than people who grow up in different cultures. This chapter is about the ways in which similarities are created within cultures and differences created across cultures through the phenomenon of interpersonal communication.

The Concept of Culture

Ward H. Goodenough, a cultural anthropologist, has quite simply defined *culture* as whatever it is one has to know or believe in order to behave in a manner acceptable to the members of that culture.[1] Goodenough's concept of culture is one that focuses on the continuous interpersonal communication process that transmits from generation to generation those learned values and behaviors that distinguish one social group from another. We learn from our parents, other family members, friends, and political and social leaders how to behave like those around us—*how not to be different.*

The interaction that takes place within a culture for the purpose of perpetuating that culture is all-pervasive. And, generally, we are so much a part of the process that we are not even aware of having been socialized until by some chance we have significant contact with someone from another culture whose values and behaviors are quite different. A characteristic response to such contact reflects the overwhelming identification we have with our culture—we assume our own values and behaviors are somehow naturally true, correct, valid, and logical and that what is different is somehow improper.

In the early 1960s, the movie *Mondo Cane* electrified American audiences by graphically depicting some of the more bizarre practices of cultures around the world. In one sequence, gourmets in a Formosan restaurant are shown selecting live young puppies which are then prepared to order; in contrast, a Pasadena animal cemetary is shown with its floral tributes, luxurious caskets, and elaborate tombstones for pet dogs. It is important to emphasize, however, that the extreme and often grotesque examples of cultural differences portrayed in the film are the exception rather than the rule. And the cultural differences among people that are of concern to us in this chapter are likely to be much more subtle than the extreme differences emphasized in *Mondo Cane.* It is also important to keep in mind that the overwhelming majority of the world's population never travel more than a few miles from the place of their birth.[2] Each of us is a member of a comparatively small number of possible, different proximate, or physically close, groups from which we learn our identity. To become more aware of our cultural learning within these groups is to become more aware of ourselves.

Differences in Perceiving

If we assume that humans are most like other humans at the time of birth, an understanding of cultural differences in perception can be more easily understood. At birth we are literally bombarded with a multitude of stimuli. Eventually we learn to attach meaning to these stimuli, and these meanings are the results of what we have learned to name them, or how we have learned to categorize them. Part of this categorizing is affective and/or evaluative. But whereas the words we learn to assign to categories of perception may be translated from one language to another, the perception of these categories probably cannot be translated from culture to culture. For example, it was pointed out in Chapter 2 that we are physiologically capable of perceiving 7,500,000 different, distinguishable colors.[3] Yet, you and I do not have names for each one of these 7,500,000 colors. We have learned within our culture to group certain of these colors together and label them as a category. How did we learn this? Probably because as children we were taught to name the colors contained in a box of crayons. As a result, most people in this culture probably have a closely shared perception of the category of colors we label "red," for example. But what happens if the crayons in another culture only come in two, three, or four colors? Most likely the culture's categories would be larger.

Figure 6.1 shows a comparison of words used to refer to colors by speakers of English, Shona (spoken in Rhodesia), and Bass (spoken in Liberia). The different words clearly refer to different categories of color perceptions.

Another perceptual difference has been pointed out by Marshall Segall and his associates, who found that people who live in forests or in rural areas can perceive crooked and slanted lines more accurately than can people who live in urban areas.[4] Recall from our discussion in Chapter 2 that perception is a transaction between the perceiver and the perceived; that is, the perceiver interprets what he receives in light of his or her experiences. Therefore, the above example seems to demonstrate that the two regional groups perceived the same event differently as a result of their different cultural learnings.

Differences in Thinking

Just as we learn to interpret the perceptual world through our culture, we also learn to think in ways that are prescribed by the culture. Edward C. Stewart has described American thinking in terms of "facts" rather than "ideas," and has characterized North American thinking as being generally *inductive* rather than *deductive*, which means that *generalizations* are made based on observations and experiences.[5] By contrast, Eastern thought processes are gener-

English

red	orange	yellow	green	blue	purple

Shona

cipsuka		cicena	citenia	cipsuka

Bassa

ziza	hui

SOURCE: Peter Farb, *Word Play: What Happens When People Talk*, New York: Alfred A. Knopf, 1974, p. 172.

FIGURE 6.1 In some languages, the principal color words divide the spectrum quite differently from the way the English color vocabulary does.

ally deductive. Stewart points out, however, that Americans also seem to have a need to relate theory to practice, to demonstrate the utility of their ideas and theories, and to apply concepts to the real world. Thus, according to Stewart, although American thought patterns may be described as inductive, moving from the concrete to the abstract, they seem to require that ideas be tested and validated through application to the "real" world.

Further, Stewart sees Americans as drawing a clear distinction between the subjective and objective, or between subject and predicate in the English language. Stewart interprets this distinction as reflecting the typical thought patterns that require a cause or agent for events or actions. Americans are not comfortable with the idea of a "natural" or "unexplained" occurrence or with a statement of fact without knowing who was responsible, that is, who did it or who caused it to be done.

These patterns of thought do seem completely natural, until they are contrasted with other thought patterns. For example, the idea of a natural occurrence is familiar and acceptable to the Chinese. The Chinese pattern of thought may be described as relational, which rests on experience and does not separate the experiencing person from objective facts, figures, or concepts. The Chinese do not analyze a topic divisively by breaking it down into parts. Chinese thinking is based on concrete conceptions weighted with judgment and lacking the precision and abstraction of Western concepts. These conceptions lack the power of analysis and classification, but excel in identification because they evoke concreteness, emotion, and commitment to action. Chinese thought strives for unity between events or objects and their given symbols. An event may be explained by reference to another event that occurred at the same time. This movement from event to event has been referred to as correlational logic. In contrast, in Western thought, events must be related in some causal, subject-predicate way.[6]

Such patterns of thinking, although considered definitely foreign by many Americans, have fascinated those who have seen them portrayed by the mass media in such television series as "Kung Fu."

Consider, for example, the American pattern of thought that justified the Vietnam War (as explained by the "domino theory," perhaps) and then consider an Eastern interpretation of America's involvement (perhaps in terms of Western imperialism).

Differences in Language

Many academic disciplines refer to the Sapir-Whorf hypothesis when accounting for the differences in languages across cultures. A relatively simple idea, the Sapir-Whorf hypothesis has nevertheless generated some confusion. We hope not to add to that confusion here.

Benjamin L. Whorf, a successful fire prevention engineer at the Hartford Fire Insurance Company, came into contact with the noted linguistic-anthropologist Edward Sapir through a course that Sapir was teaching at Yale. Largely self-taught, Whorf had studied ancient Hebraic, Aztec, and Mayan cultures, and developed the idea that reality for a culture is discoverable in its language. Although this notion was not entirely original, Whorf's papers written in the 1930s discussing the Hopi language produced exact and documented expression of the Sapir-Whorf hypothesis.

This hypothesis may be expressed by saying that "language is culture and that culture is controlled by and controls language," which implies much more than simply that one cannot be understood without the other. Goodenough's definition of language, a parallel to his definition of culture, shows language to have a relation to culture in the same sense that a part has a relation to the whole. Thus, language is all the things that one has to know and believe in order to adequately and effectively communicate with the members of a culture.[7]

The Sapir-Whorf hypothesis points out that each of us lives *not* in the midst of the whole world but only in that part of the world that our language permits us to know. Thus, the real world as each of us knows it is to a large extent predetermined by the language habits of our culture. Therefore, the differences between languages represents basic differences in the "world view" of the people of various cultures and in what persons perceive about their environment.

Do these signs give evidence of intercultural, interracial, or contracultural communication?

In English, H_2O in the liquid state is signified by the symbol "water," which implies no meanings for what this substance may be used for or for its specific quantity. The Hopi, however, use the symbol *pahe* to refer to large amounts of H_2O, such as natural lakes and rivers, and the symbol *keyi* to refer to small amounts of H_2O, such as is contained in domestic jugs and canteens. English, however, distinguishes between lakes, streams, waterfalls, geysers, and the like. But *pahe* implies no such distinction. A speaker of Hopi does not "know" these distinctions, since, as the Sapir-Whorf hypothesis argues, language and thought are synonymous. Similarly, speakers of English "know" that there is some difference between water in a river and water in a canteen. The point of this comparison is that neither English nor Hopi have a language to describe all the possible states, quantities, forms, and functions of water. Languages would be unbearably complicated and unmanageable if they contained words for every possibility. Thus, each culture develops words, and hence creates a language, according to its needs. In English, for instance, it was found useful to be able to speak of differences between water in lakes, streams, waterfalls, and geysers, but not important to distinguish between water in a canteen, water in a boat, and water underneath the same boat.

Because snow is an important feature of Eskimo life, the Eskimo language contains many words for different kinds of snow.[8] For example,

qana	falling snow; snowflakes
akilukak	fluffy fallen snow
aput	snow on the ground
piqsirpoq	drifting snow
kaguklaich	snow drifted in rows
qimuqsuq	snowdrift

Notice that the English translations of each of the different Eskimo words all contain the word "snow"—our only word for that phenomenon. Similarly, to us a seal, such as we might see in a zoo, is a seal. To the Eskimo there are many categories of seals: "a young swimming seal," "a male harbor seal," and the like. In English there are many words by which to refer to horses: "bronco," "pony," "mare," "gelding," "stallion," and so forth. But for the Eskimo, living in a horseless culture, such a variety of categories does not exist.

According to the Sapir-Whorf hypothesis, these differences *begin* to explain or reflect the culture of a people. In other words, language directs the perceptions of its speakers to certain things by providing perceptual and experiential categories that are accepted unconsciously; that is, they are outside the control and unnoticed by the speaker of the language.[9]

The verbal code is, of course, only a portion of communicative behavior. Nonverbal communication, as a language code, is also learned within the culture and is a part of the culture. For example, to nonverbally communicate the message "Everything is O.K.," an American might first wink and then make a ring of his thumb and index finger and hold it up in the air. However, in India this gesture would be interpreted differently because in many Indian cultures these two signs represent an obscene invitation to bed. [10]

The writings of Edward T. Hall are fully illustrated with examples of nonverbal cultural differences. Appointment time is an example. We learn in our culture to be punctual—particularly with appointments with people of higher status. If you had an appointment with the dean of your college at 10:00 A.M., you probably would show up in plenty of time for the appointment, and would probably not have to wait more than five or ten minutes before the dean could see you. However, as Hall points out, in Latin American cultures, for example, a forty-five minute wait in an outer office is not at all unusual—no more so than a five minute wait would be in American culture. We are not upset by a five minute wait; the Latin American is not upset by a forty-five minute wait. [11] Time is understood and used differently in different cultures.

Differences in Communication Habits

Just as we have explored differences in perceiving, thinking, and language, we can also examine differences in a culture's preferred mode of communication. Marshall McLuhan's work most aptly argues that our society has changed from a print-dominated society to one in which different modes of expression (film, television, etc.) are preferred. [12]

It can be argued then that at a given time different cultures have different preferred modes of expression. Even a few years ago, audience surveys indicated that about fifty million people in the United States (and presumably a comparable proportion in Canada) spent *five or more hours a day* watching television. More recently, surveys indicate that that figure may be six hours a day. Assuming a normal life expectancy, the average North American could conceivably spend eighteen years in front of a television set and witness, in addition to other things, some five million minutes of commercials.

Other statistics could be gathered to demonstrate our current preference for this mode of communication. But in other cultures television is not important, and other modes of communication are preferred.

For example, in the United States, the emphasis on technology (especially in electronics and in the automobile industry) has created a society that is more private than public. In this country, most communication occurs within the home, with a limited number of individuals. But in other cultures, such as in Europe and

Latin America, people have ready access to a larger segment of society as a result of their reliance on public transportation and the establishment of public meeting places, such as cafes, town squares, plazas, and so on. Thus, in other cultures it may be said that communication takes a more active form and is conducted among a greater number of people than in the United States.

Differences in Values

Stewart has strikingly described the North American value system in regard to nature. That is, North Americans tend to think of themselves apart from other forms of life in that they view humans as the only possessors of a soul, or whatever elusive term might be used, and, as such, distinct from other animals, plants, and objects.[13] In other cultures, however, humans conceive of themselves as a form of life differing from other forms only in degree. In the non-Western world, animals and inanimate objects have their own essence.

The American cultural separation of humankind and nature has "allowed" us to exploit nature for our own material richness. And our assumption of absolute supremacy over nonhuman life forms permits us to not have to think in terms of exploitation. Trees were destroyed to manufacture the paper for this textbook. This one example illustrates our cultural value of the dissemination of "knowledge" to mass numbers of people by the printed page. Of course, the benefits of print are not being questioned here, but our values regarding nature may have to change. If not, our arrogant attitude toward nature may kill us all.

These values are reflected on television. The program "Wild Kingdom," for instance, features Marlin Perkins who may be seen rounding up a herd of zebras or capturing a tiger to be transferred to another, safer area. The program regularly deals with the capture of animals, usually for the purpose of shipping them to a secure area for preservation. The broader problem of what kind of environment this concept of conservation is creating, i.e., using wildlife for entertainment, is not considered. It is interesting to note how Perkins refers to nature while introducing his sponsor: "Man protects threatened animals . . . Mutual of Omaha can protect your security."[14]

Another example of the cultural separation of humans and nature, which allows humans to exploit nature, was revealed on the CBS program "60 minutes," broadcast in February, 1973. CBS newsman Morley Safer reported that the United States Navy had deployed a dolphin to plant and retrieve from a foreign harbor a device used to detect the type of atomic fuel used in Russian nuclear-powered submarines. Our Navy has reportedly trained dolphins to plant and retrieve intelligence devices, attack enemy divers, and place explosives as part of a top secret $30 million "biological weapons system."

Can you imagine how people would communicate differently in each of these structures? Environment and architectural style are nonverbal elements that do affect interpersonal communication.

Alternatives to American assumptions about the relationship between humans and the environment can be found in other societies. One view prevalent in much of the Far East stresses unity among all forms of life and inanimate objects. Humans are considered to be integrated into nature, and this relationship is expressed in the whole fabric of Oriental life styles. In Japanese architecture, for example, man-made and natural environments are integrated in the forms and lines of temples and gardens. The feeling is quite different from that of a typical North American building, which towers over and dominates its surroundings.[15] A striking example of this difference in architecture is the East-West Center in Honolulu, Hawaii. One enters the East-West Center on the University of Hawaii campus from a busy street much as one would enter a building in Washington, D.C. The structure is large and imposing; the ceiling is high with great open spaces. On a visit there, I felt the structure to convey power, importance, dominance. However, there is a level of the building that is underneath the street-level entrance. This level, which cannot be entered from the street, houses the student snack areas and opens onto a quiet, green garden in the rear of the building. To me, the garden and the building in this particular spot seemed integrated. This combination of architecture of the East-West Center is striking in its reflection of different cultural values as expressed through architecture.

As an experiment, stop reading this text for a moment and explore your immediate environment in terms of how it reflects American cultural values. If you are in a classroom in North

America, you probably find yourself in a relatively structured physical environment: perhaps many chairs facing one common direction—one desk facing back at you, a clock, a chalkboard, audio-visual equipment, and so on—all in a rectangular room in a relatively sterile building. What assumptions can you make about how American culture values education?

Linguistic studies of the Navaho reveal cultural values far different from, and perhaps long misunderstood by, white Americans. Navahos view themselves as living in an eternal and unchanging universe made up of physical, social, and supernatural forces. And the Navaho's obligation is to maintain a balance among these forces. Any failure to observe rules or rituals can upset this balance resulting in some misfortune. Sandpainting and other Navaho ceremonies are conducted to put humans back into harmony with the universe. To the Navaho, the good life consists of maintaining intact all the complex relationships of the universe.[16] Thus, a recent television public service announcement that shows a native American crying about the pollution of the environment is especially poignant.

Differences in Self-Concepts

One's self-concept may be thought of as being an answer to the question "Who am I?" Generally, as North Americans we answer this question in terms of gender identification, specific roles (such as a student, a teacher, and so on), nationality, ethnic group, and the like. And, generally, the self is thought to be indistinct from the person.[17]

The concept that the self may not be located in the individual is somewhat difficult for us to understand. Yet the Japanese tend to identify self in a network of obligations among members of a group. For example, the traditional Japanese man would not directly ask a woman to marry him: His family would employ a "marriage broker," or go-between, to act as an intermediary with the woman's family. As a consequence of this kind of understanding of self, congeniality in social interaction becomes the predominant value. This stress on the *relations* among individuals rather than on the individual himself is the concept of "face." Concomitant with the concept of "face" are the ideas of "dignity," "prestige," and "respect." In contrast with our understanding of self, Eastern attitudes and courses of action are only secondarily intended to achieve certain personal goals. Instead, attitudes and actions are primarily intended to preserve affiliations in groups and to maintain congenial social relations.[18]

The Japanese concept of "face" is concerned with the *status* of self. It should be noted that the Chinese concept of "face" is different from the Japanese concept in that the Chinese includes much more concern about the feelings of the other person.[19]

Differences in Interpersonal Relationships

It should be obvious by now that there exist many other forms of interpersonal relationships than what is typical in North America. Let's compare some of the differences between the United States and other cultures. Here, our interpersonal relationships tend to be numerous, friendly, and informal—we rarely form deep and lasting relationships. As Alvin Toffler in his book *Future Shock* has pointed out, we easily change friends and membership groups.[20] And although we are social, we avoid personal commitment—we don't want to get involved.

Characteristic of our social relationships is the theme of equality. Even in interaction with someone on a different hierarchical level, whether it be our employee or employer, we attempt to establish a relationship of equality. For example, it appears to be characteristic of many interpersonal communication instructors to insist that their students use their first name, whether or not the student feels comfortable doing so.

Further, our "friends"—a term which we use to refer to anyone from a passing acquaintance to a life-time intimate—tend to be kept separate from one another. Thus, our friends seem to be centered around certain activities, such as friends from work; recreational friends, i.e. people with whom we play volleyball or go swimming; drinking buddies; and the like. This specialization of friends signifies our reluctance to become deeply and totally involved with

Navaho sandpainting is a ceremony conducted to put humans back into harmony with the universe. What role does art play in other cultures?

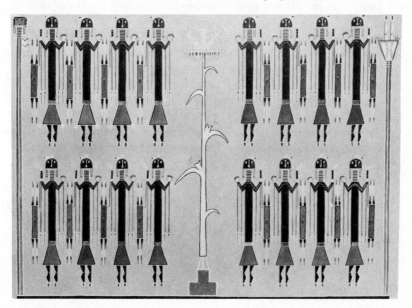

other people, as does our tendency to turn to professionals when in need rather than to our friends.[21]

An interesting contrast is the Russian, who tends to form deep interpersonal relationships with other people. Notice how this fact may contradict the predominant North American cultural stereo–type of the Russian. The Russian tends to assume almost total, constant companionship, which excludes any reticence or secre-tiveness. Whereas we tend to specialize our friends with common interests, the Russian tends to accept the "whole" person.[22]

An Applied Study of Differences

In the previous sections, we have examined differences in per-ceiving, in thinking, in language, in communication habits, and in values. A complete comparison between two cultures would help to complete our stated objective for this chapter of becoming more aware of our cultural learning and, by extension, becoming more aware of ourselves.

Gary L. Althen and Josephine Jaime have presented an outline that compares the value systems of North American and Philippine cultures.[23] The comments on Philippine culture were prepared by a sociologist from the Philippines. The analysis is, of course, com-posed of generalizations, but it is believed that it reflects the promi-nent or most widespread attitudes and behaviors in both cultures. Study and react to Figure 6.2 (see pages 196–197) as an applied study of differences.

What Differences Do Differences Make?

Throughout this chapter, we have spoken about differences. It is a legitimate question to ask what real difference do these differ-ences make. Perhaps the following story will supply the answer.

As a graduate student, I participated with my adviser and other graduate students in a Mexican-American Leadership Training pro-gram sponsored by a university, the Catholic Diocese of Toledo, Ohio, and federal funds. As "enlightened" consultants we worked with the participants and eventually identified the problem in northwestern Ohio as a lack of cultural awareness.

The participants determined that part of the solution might be to provide school teachers with information on the Mexican-American cultural heritage. This solution was implemented through a half-day workshop to which teachers were invited. Nearing the conclusion of the workshop, a large North American white teacher rose to ask a question. He asked whether by presenting material on the Mexican-American's cultural heritage we were not in fact en-couraging separation, that people could never get together if such an emphasis was placed on learning the differences between people. My colleagues and I were quite nervous and silent at this point because "our" project was threatened by this teacher's statement. Then a slightly built priest, a resident of Mexico, rose to speak in halting English. He built an elaborate analogy in which he compared the races of man to the colors of the rainbow. Together, the differences of man create a beautiful image only because of their differences, as do the colors of the rainbow. There would be no rainbow, and hence no beauty, without these differences.

I remember now being struck by the poetry of the priest's analogy. I feel it contains a legitimate perspective for studying cross-cultural communication.

Contact Between Cultures

Of course, a more obvious reason for studying cross-cultural differences is that much can be learned from other cultures. Adapted Reading No. 14 from Ralph Linton's *The Study of Man* speaks of the process of diffusion between cultures—the spreading of new ideas from the source of invention, or creation, to their users, or adopters.

Andrea L. Rich and Dennis M. Ogawa have presented an analysis of intercultural, interracial, and contracultural communication that presents *one* perspective of the possible outcomes of contact between cultures.[24] They view intercultural communication as represented by Figure 6.3. The circles *A* and *B* represent two cultures, which do not and have not existed in a colonial relationship in which one of the cultures took over or dominated the other. The *X* in the figure refers to the shared or improvised communication code. The important defining characteristic of intercultural communication shown here is that individuals from each of the cultures interact with one another as equals.

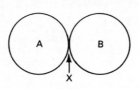

SOURCE: Rich and Ogawa

FIGURE 6.3 Intercultural communication is communication between two cultures as equals.

Assumptions and Values in Philippine and American Cultures

		North American	Filipino
I. Perception of the Self and the Individual			
A.	General perception of self	human being of a particular sex	self perceived in context of family
B.	Self as point of reference	autonomy encouraged; solve own problems, develop own opinions	dependence encouraged; point of reference is authority, older members of family
C.	Nature of man	evil but perfectable; notion of progress: man can change and improve self and it is his responsibility to do so	evil but there is not too much that can be done "ganyan talaga ang buhay" (such is life)
D.	Cultural variation of self-concept	self is identified with individual; behavior aimed at individual goals	point of reference is network of obligations among members of a group summarized in concept of "face"; behavior aimed at preserving group affiliations and maintaining smooth interpersonal relationships
E.	Self-reliance	old self-reliance value still believed upheld (although American often now functions best as member of organization)	dependence not deplored because it strengthens relationships among people
II. Perception of the World			
A.	Man's relation to nature	man is separate from nature	man is separate from nature
B.	Materialism and property	clear distinction between public and private property; materialism is big value	public property divertible to private hands with little guilt; spiritual, religious things are more important than material things
C.	Progress related to concept of time	time moves fast, from past, to present, to future; one must keep up with it, use it to change and master environment	time moves slowly; man must integrate himself with the environment, and adapt to it rather than change it
D.	Progress and optimism in contrast to limited good	optimism exists that there is enough for everybody; economics is final arbiter	[peasants only]: there exists a finite amount of good that can be divided and redivided but not augmented; therefore phenomenon of sociostat: if one member of a community increases in wealth, he is seen as a threat because of the concomitant loss to other members; tendency for community to pull him down to old level by temporary ostracism

FIGURE 6.2 Two cultures can perceive self, world, and others quite differently.

	North American	Filipino
E. Quantification	stress on measurement and concreteness	stress on qualitative feeling
F. Comparative judgments	what is not American is bad	what is not Filipino is different or American; moral judgments not as easily made

III. Motivation

	North American	Filipino
A. Achievement as self-motivation	fulfillment in personal achievement; status is achieved	fulfillment in smooth interpersonal relationships; status is ascribed
B. Fragmentation and totality of personality	personalities can be fragmented; totality of other person does not need to be accepted in order to be able to work with him	personalities reacted to in their entirety; tendency to accept or reject person completely
C. Competition and affiliation	competition is primary method of motivation	communal feeling towards one another excludes the incentive to excel others
D. The limits of achievement: the individual	expansive view of achievement: "Where there's a will, there's a way"	achievement is a matter of fate

IV. Form of Relations to Others

	North American	Filipino
A. Characteristics of personal relations	friendships are numerous but not deep or permanent; social obligations avoided	social obligation network: "utang na loob"
B. Equality	equality is mode of interaction	continual shift from high to low status depending on other person
C. Confrontation	face-to-face confrontation	confrontation through an intermediary to avoid "losing face"
D. Informality and formality	informal and direct	more formal; social interactions more structured
E. Specialization of roles	specialized roles distributed among members of group	all functions vested in leader

V. Form of Activity

	North American	Filipino
A. Doing	"doing" and being active are highly valued	"doing" not emphasized as much, especially in rural areas; it is just as important to "take it easy"
B. Decision-making	decisions made by individual; every member feels responsible for group decisions	decisions made by authority or group; group decisions are usually product of key group members even if they are apparently made by all
C. Work and play	dichotomy of work and play	work and social life are not separated
D. Temporal orientation	stress on future	stress on present and past; life is lived from day to day

What is Truly American?

One result of contact between cultures is that through interaction one culture may learn and adopt certain practices of the other culture. Is there such a thing as a "100 percent American?"

The service of diffusion in enriching the content of individual cultures has been of the utmost importance. There is probably no culture extant today which owes more than 10 per cent of its total elements to inventions made by members of its own society. Because we live in a period of rapid invention we are apt to think of our own culture as largely self-created, but the role which diffusion has played in its growth may be brought home to us if we consider the beginning of the average man's day. The locations listed in the following paragraphs refer only to the origin points of various culture elements, not to regions from which we now obtain materials or objects through trade.

Our solid American citizen awakens in a bed built on a pattern which originated in the Near East but which was modified in Northern Europe before it was transmitted to America. He throws back covers made from cotton, domesticated in India, or linen, domesticated in the Near East, or wool from sheep, also domesticated in the Near East, or silk, the use of which was discovered in China. All of these materials have been spun and woven by processes invented in the Near East. He slips into his moccasins, invented by the Indians of the Eastern woodlands, and goes to the bathroom, whose fixtures are a mixture of European and American inventions, both of recent date. He takes off his pajamas, a garment invented in India, and washes with soap invented by the ancient Gauls. He then shaves, a masochistic rite which seems to have been derived from either Sumer or ancient Egypt.

Adapted from Ralph Linton, The Study of Man: An Introduction, © *1936, Renewed 1964. Reprinted by permission of Prentice-Hall, Inc., Englewood Cliffs, N.J.*

Returning to the bedroom, he removes his clothes from a chair of southern European type and proceeds to dress. He puts on garments whose form originally derived from the skin clothing of the nomads of the Asiatic steppes, puts on shoes made from skins tanned by a process invented in ancient Egypt and cut to a pattern derived from the classical civilizations of the Mediterranean, and ties around his neck a strip of bright-colored cloth which is a vestigial survival of the shoulder shawls worn by the seventeenth-century Croatians. Before going out for breakfast he glances through the window, made of glass invented in Egypt, and if it is raining puts on overshoes made of rubber discovered by the Central American Indians and takes an umbrella, invented in southeastern Asia. Upon his head he puts a hat made of felt, a material invented in the Asiatic steppes.

On his way to breakfast he stops to buy a paper, paying for it with coins, an ancient Lydian invention. At the restaurant a whole new series of borrowed elements confronts him. His plate is made of a form of pottery invented in China. His knife is of steel, an alloy first made in southern India, his fork a medieval Italian invention, and his spoon a derivative of a Roman original. He begins breakfast with an orange, from the eastern Mediterranean, a canteloupe from Persia, or perhaps a piece of African watermelon. With this he has coffee, an Abyssinian plant, with cream and sugar. Both the domestication of cows and the idea of milking them originated in the Near East, while sugar was first made in India. After his fruit and first coffee he goes on to waffles, cakes made by a Scandinavian technique from wheat domesticated in Asia Minor. Over these he pours maple syrup, invented by the Indians of the Eastern woodlands. As a side dish he may have the egg of a species of bird domesticated in Indo-China, or thin strips of the flesh of an animal domesticated in Eastern Asia which have been salted and smoked by a process developed in northern Europe.

When our friend has finished eating he settles back to smoke, an American Indian habit, consuming a plant domesticated in Brazil in either a pipe, derived from the Indians of Virginia, or a cigarette, derived from Mexico. If he is hardy enough he may even attempt a cigar, transmitted to us from the Antilles by way of Spain. While smoking he reads the news of the day, imprinted in characters invented by the ancient Semites upon a material invented in China by a process invented in Germany. As he absorbs the accounts of foreign troubles he will, if he is a good conservative citizen, thank a Hebrew deity in an Indo-European language that he is 100 per cent American.

The foregoing is merely a bit of antiquarian virtuosity made possible by the existence of unusually complete historic records for the Eurasiatic area. There are many other regions for which no such records exist, yet the cultures in these areas bear similar witness to the importance of diffusion in establishing their content. Fairly adequate techniques have been developed for tracing the spread of individual traits and even for establishing their origin points, and there can be no doubt that diffusion has occurred wherever two societies and cultures have been brought into contact.

Figure 6.4 refers to interracial communication such as it occurs in the United States. Circle *A* represents the dominant power structure, or "white America." Circle *B* represents the non-white racial group *as it exists in its purest form uninfluenced by the structure of white America.* For example, this could represent the immigrant before he reached the United States. Circle *C* represents the racial minority in the white-dominated power structure. For example, this could represent the ethnic-American: Black-American, Japanese-American, Mexican-American, etc. Rich and Ogawa hypothesize that several characteristics of interracial communication are represented by Figure 6.4. First, Circle *C* depends both upon the whims of Circle *A* and upon the tenacity of Circle *C* to remain close to *B*. For example, many residents of Mexican-American barrios tend to cling to their "Circle *B*." Further, a member of Circle *C* can never move completely into Circle *A* but he can move back into Circle *B*. Thus, a Japanese immigrant can never become a white American but he is free to return to Japan. Finally, a member of Circle *A* can never become a member of Circle *C*. A white American can never fully understand the experience of being black in white America.

Figure 6.5 refers to what Rich and Ogawa label as contracultural communication. Contracultural communication occurs when intercultural communication is transformed by the imposition of one culture upon the other into interracial communication. The *X* of the intercultural model, the area of shared or improvised communication, becomes the *C* of the interracial model, the area of dominance. When a power relationship exists between cultures, *C* exists.

It is not the intent of this book to develop a political argument for or against American foreign or domestic policies. However, it seems clear that contact between cultures has often been one of domination, often because of a lack of understanding and a lack of respect for cultural differences. Adapted Reading No. 15 from a pamphlet by Benjamin Franklin relates an incident of contact between native Americans and American colonists in which this attitude of domination is evident.

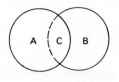

SOURCE: Rich and Ogawa

FIGURE 6.4 Interracial communication is communication between a minority (C) and a dominant culture (A).

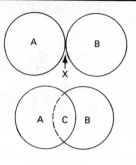

SOURCE: Rich and Ogawa

FIGURE 6.5 Contracultural communication represents intercultural communication becoming interracial communication.

Tomorrow and Beyond

Although there are probably few remaining unknown cultures on earth, it is likely we have not exhausted all the possibilities. There are cultures yet to be found. And, perhaps we will be found by other cultures. It will be interesting to see how we respond to new challenges.

The world was shocked in 1971 to discover the "lost tribe" of the Tasaday cave dwellers in a remote rain forest on the island of Mindanao, about 560 miles south of Manila. In mid-April 1973, a baby girl was born to the Tasaday, and several months later a boy to bring the known number to twenty-nine. The Tasaday are protected by the Panamin Foundation, which protects cultural minorities in the Philippines. The Tasaday have no known enemies, no weapons, and no words in their language for hate, war, or dislike.

The popular television science fiction series *Star Trek*, still popular in reruns, was built on the premise of contact between cultures from different worlds. Whether or not you believe that is possible, the *Star Trek* episodes provide some interesting concepts for study. Adapted Reading No. 16 is an excerpt from one *Star Trek* script. A basic concept of the series was the "prime directive"; that is, that the officers and crew of the spaceship *U.S.S. Enterprise* were to avoid interfering with the natural development of any culture with which they came in contact.

The Savages of North America

*Does the proposal made to the Six
Nations by the Government of
Virginia, as recorded in a pamphlet by
Benjamin Franklin, describe an
example of intercultural, interracial, or
contracultural communication?*

Savages we call them, because their Manners differ from ours,
which we think the Perfection of Civility; they think the same
of theirs.

Perhaps, if we could examine the Manners of different Nations
with Impartiality, we should find no People so rude, as to be
without any Rules of Politeness; nor any so polite, as not to have
some Remains of Rudeness.

The Indian Men, when young, are Hunters and Warriors; when
old, Counsellors; for all their Government is by Counsel of the
Sages; there is no Force, there are no Prisons, no Officers to compel
Obedience, or inflict Punishment. Hence they generally study
Oratory, the best Speaker having the most influence. The Indian
Women till the Ground, dress the Food, nurse and bring up the
Children, and preserve and hand down to Posterity the Memory of
public Transactions. These Employments of Men and Women are
accounted natural and honourable. Having few artificial Wants,
they have an abundance of Leisure for Improvement by
Conversation. Our laborious Manner of Life, compared with
theirs, they esteem slavish and base; and the Learning, on which
we value ourselves, they regard as frivolous and useless. An
Instance of this occurred at the Treaty of Lancaster, in Pennsylvania,
anno 1744, between the Government of Virginia and the Six
Nations. After the principal Business was settled, the

Adapted from Benjamin Franklin, "Remarks Concerning the Savages of North
America," (Date of composition uncertain. Printed as pamphlet in 1784) From Frank
Luther Mott and Chester E. Jorgenson, eds., Benjamin Franklin: Representative
Selections, with Introduction, Bibliography, and Notes, New York: American
Book Company, 1936, pp. 513–519.

Commissioners from Virginia acquainted the Indians by a Speech, that there was at Williamsburg a College, with a Fund for Educating Indian youth; and that, if the Six Nations would send down half a dozen of their young Lads to that College, the Government would take care that they should be well provided for, and instructed in all the Learning of the White People. It is one of the Indian Rules of Politeness not to answer a public Proposition the same day that it is made; they think it would be treating it as a light matter, and that they show it Respect by taking time to consider it, as of a Matter important. They therefore deferr'd their Answer till the Day following; when their Speaker began, by expressing their deep Sense of the kindness of the Virginia Government, in making them that Offer; "for we know," says he, "that you highly esteem the kind of Learning taught in those Colleges, and that the Maintenance of our young Men, while with you, would be very expensive to you. We are convinc'd, therefore, that you mean to do us Good by your Proposal; and we thank you heartily. But you, who are wise, must know that different Nations have different Conceptions of things; and you will therefore not take it amiss, if our Ideas of this kind of Education happen not to be the same with yours. We have had some Experience of it; Several of our young People were formerly brought up at the Colleges of the Northern Provinces; they were instructed in all your Sciences; but, when they came back to us, they were bad Runners, ignorant of every means of living in the Woods, unable to bear either Cold or Hunger, knew neither how to build a Cabin, take a Deer, or kill an Enemy, spoke our language imperfectly, were therefore neither fit for Hunters, Warriors, nor Counsellors; they were totally good for nothing. We are however not the less oblig'd by your kind Offer, tho' we decline accepting it; and, to show our grateful Sense of it, if the Gentlemen of Virginia will send us a Dozen of their Sons, we will take great Care of their Education, instruct them in all we know, and make *Men* of them."

Perhaps other worlds have attempted communication with ours. Erich Von Daniken's popular books, including *Chariots of the Gods*, which has sold some twenty-five million copies, are built on the thesis that space visitors mingled with earth people in biblical times and influenced early human civilization, culture, and genetics. Our own NASA's Pioneer 10 and Pioneer 11 spacecraft, which will break out of our sun's gravitational grasp, have been equipped with a plaque displaying a message for other cultures. Reproduced as Figure 6.6, the plaque shows two humans and gives information about the ship's origin in symbols that NASA hopes are universal.

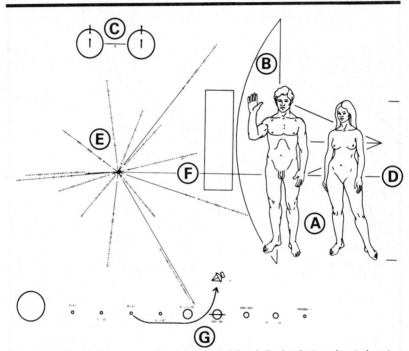

FIGURE 6.6 Cornell astronomers Carl Sagan and Frank Drake designed a six by nine inch aluminum plaque anodized with erosion-resistant gold. In the figure, two representative earthlings are shown at (A). Their height is indicated by the scale drawing of Pioneer in the background (B). The message contains a more subtle dimensional clue (C): An atom of hydrogen is shown undergoing a change of energy state. During this process, the atom gives off a pulse of radiation with a wave length of 21cm, which is also the plaque's basic unit of measure. For example, to the woman's right is the binary symbol for eight (D). Multiplied by 21cm, the figure yields her height, 168cm, or about 5½ feet which can be verified by comparing her size to that of the spacecraft. Fourteen of the lines of the large starburst pattern (E) symbolize specific pulsars, each recognizable by the precise frequency (noted in binary terms) at which they give off radio signals. The fifteenth line (F), extending beyond the humans, indicates the distance of their star to the center of the galaxy. That information should indicate when and where the spacecraft was launched. The representation of the solar system (G), also shows that the Pioneer left from the third planet from the sun, swept past the fifth (Jupiter), and then veered off into interstellar space.

A Piece of the Action, A Star Trek Episode

The television series Star Trek *was built on a basic premise that the officers and crew of the* U.S.S. Enterprise *were to avoid interferring with the natural development of any culture with which they came in contact. The possible results of one culture's imitation of part of another culture provides the basis for this adapted version of a* Star Trek *episode. What can happen in a culture when it adopts parts of other cultures—a technology, a faith, life-preserving medical care?*

It was difficult to explain to Bela Okmyx, who called himself "Boss" of Dana Iotia Two, that though the message from the lost *Horizon* had been sent a hundred years ago, the *Enterprise* had only received it last month. For that matter, he did not seem to know what the "galaxy" meant, either.

Kirk did not know what he expected to find, but he was braced for anything. Subspace radio was not the only thing the *Horizon* had lacked. She had landed before the non-interference directive had come into effect, and while the Iotians were just at the beginnings of industrialization. And the Iotians had been reported to be extremely intelligent—and somewhat imitative. The *Horizon* might have changed their culture drastically before her departure and shipwreck.

Still, the man called Boss seemed friendly enough. He didn't understand what "transported" meant either, in the technical sense, but readily suggested a rendezvous at an intersection marked by a big building with white columns in a public square where, he said, he would provide a reception committee. All quite standard, so far.

Kirk, Spock and McCoy beamed down, leaving Scott at the con. They materialized into a scene which might at first have been taken for an area in any of the older cities of present-day Earth, but with two significant exceptions; no children were visible, and all the adults, male and female alike, were wearing sidearms. Their dress was reminiscent of the United States of the early twentieth century.

This had barely registered when a sharp male voice behind them said, "Okay, you three. Let's see you petrify."

The officers turned to find themselves confronted by two men carrying clumsy two-handed weapons which Kirk recognized as a variant of the old submachine gun.

"Would you mind clarifying your statement, please?" Spock said.

"I want to see you turn to stone. Put your hands up over your head—or you ain't gonna have no head to put your hands over."

The two were standing close enough together so that Kirk could have stunned them both from the hip, but he disliked stopping situations before they had even begun to develop. He obeyed, his officers following suit.

The man who had spoken kept them covered while the other silently relieved them of their phasers and communicators. He seemed momentarily in doubt about McCoy's tricorder, but he took that, too. A few pedestrians stopped to watch; they seemed only mildly curious, and some of them even seemed to approve. Were these men policemen, then? They were dressed no differently from anyone else; perhaps more expensively and with more color, but that was all.

The silent man displayed his harvest to his spokesman. The latter took a phaser and examined it. "What's this?"

"Be very careful with that, please," Kirk said. "It's a weapon."

"A heater, huh? The Boss'll love that."

"A Mr. Bela Okmyx invited us down. He said . . ."

"I know what he said. What he don't tell Kalo ain't worth knowing. He said some boys would meet you. Okay, we're meeting you."

"Those guns aren't necessary," McCoy said.

"You trying to make trouble, bud? Don't give me those baby blue eyes."

"What?"

"I don't buy that innocent routine." Kalo looked at Spock's ears. "You a boxer?"

"No," Spock said. "Why does everybody carry firearms? Are you people at war?"

"I never heard such stupid questions in my life." Kalo jerked his gun muzzle down the street. "Get moving."

As they began to walk, Kirk became aware of a distant but growing thrumming sound. Suddenly a squeal was added to it and it became much larger.

"Get down!" Kalo shouted, throwing himself to the street. The people around him were already dropping, or seeking shelter. Kirk dived for the dirt.

A vehicle that looked like two mismatched black bricks on four wheels bore down on them. Two men leaned out of it with submachine guns, which suddenly produced a terrible, hammering roar. Kalo got off a burst at it, but his angle was bad for accuracy. Luckily, it was not good for the gunners in the car, either.

Then the machine was gone, and the pedestrians picked themselves up. McCoy looked about, then knelt by the silent member of the "reception committee," but he was plainly too late.

Kalo shook his head. "Krako's getting more gall all the time."

"Is this the way you greet all your visitors?" Kirk demanded.

"It happens, pal."

"But this man is dead," McCoy said.

"Yeah? Well, we ain't playing for peanuts. Hey, you dopes, get outta here!" He shouted suddenly to what looked like the beginning of a crowd. "Ain't you never seen a hit before? Get lost!"

He resumed herding his charges, leaving the dead man unconcernedly behind. Kirk kept his face impassive, but his mind was busy. A man had been shot down, and no one had blinked an eye; it seemed as though it were an everyday happening. Was this the cultural contamination they had been looking for? But the crew of the *Horizon* hadn't been made up of coldblooded killers, nor had they reported the Iotian culture in that state.

A young girl, rather pretty, emerged from a store entrance and cut directly across to them, followed by another. "You, Kalo," she said.

"Get lost."

"When's the Boss going to do something about the crummy street lights around here? A girl ain't safe."

"And how about the laundry pickup?" said the second girl. "We ain't had a truck by in three weeks."

"Write him a letter," Kalo said indifferently.

"I did. He sent it back with postage due."

"Listen, we pay our percentages. We're entitled to some service for our money."

"Get *lost*, I said." Kalo shook his head as the girls sullenly fell behind. "Some people got nothing to do but complain."

Kirk stared at him. He was certainly an odd sight—odder than before, now that his pockets were stuffed with all the hand equipment from the *Enterprise* trio, and he had a submachine gun under each arm. But he looked none the less dangerous for that. "Mr. Kalo, is this the way your citizens get things done? Their right of petition?"

"If they pay their percentages, the Boss takes care of them. We go in here."

"In here" was a building bearing a brightly polished brass plaque. It read:

BELA OKMYX
BOSS
NORTHSIDE TERRITORY

The end of the line was an office, large and luxurious, complete with heavy desk, a secretary of sorts and framed pictures—except that one of the frames, Kirk saw, surrounded some kind of pistol instead. A heavy-set, swarthy man sat behind the desk.

"Got 'em, Boss," Kalo said. "No sweat."

The big man smiled and rose. "Well, Captain Kirk. Come in. Sit down. Have a drink. Good stuff—distill it myself."

"No, thank you. You are Mr. Okmyx? This is Mr. Spock, my First Officer. And Dr. McCoy."

"A real pleasure. Sit down. Put down the heater, Kalo. These guys is guests." He turned back to Kirk. "You gotta excuse my boys. You just gotta be careful these days."

"Judging from what we've seen so far, I agree." Kirk said. "They call you the Boss. Boss of what?"

"My territory. Biggest in the world. Trouble with being the biggest is that punks is alla time trying to cut in."

"There is something astonishingly familiar about all this, Captain," Spock said.

"How many other territories are there?"

"Maybe a dozen, not counting the small fry—and they get bumped anyway when I get around to it."

"Do they include, if I may ask," Spock said, "a gentleman named Krako?"

"You know about Krako?"

"He hit us, Boss," Kalo said. "Burned Mirt."

Bela scowled. "I want him hit back."

"I'll take care of it."

Kirk had noticed a huge book on a stand nearby. He rose and moved toward it. Kalo raised his gun muzzle again, but at a quick signal from Bela, dropped it. The book was bound like a Bible, in white leather, with gold lettering reading: *Chicago Mobs of the Twenties.* The imprint was New York, 1993.

"How'd you get this, Mr. Okmyx?" he asked.

"That's the Book. *The* Book. They left it—the men from the *Horizon.*"

"And there is your contamination, Captain," Spock said. "An entire gangster culture. An imitative people, one book, and . . ."

"No cracks about The Book," Bela said harshly. "Look, I didn't bring you here for you to ask questions. You gotta do something for me. Then I tell you anything you want to know."

"Anything we can do," Kirk said, putting the book down, "we will. We have laws of our own we must observe."

"Okay," Bela said. He leaned forward earnestly. "Look, I'm a peaceful man, see? I'm sick and tired of all the hits. Krako hits me, I hit Krako, Tepo hits me, Krako hits Tepo. We ain't getting noplace. There's too many bosses, know what I mean? Now if there was just one, maybe we could get some things done. That's where you come in."

"I don't quite understand," Kirk said.

"You Feds made a lot of improvements since the other ship came here. You probably got all kinds of fancy heaters. So here's the deal. You gimme all the heaters I need—enough tools so I can hit all the punks once and for all—and I take over the whole place. Then all you have to deal with is me."

"Let me get this straight," Kirk said. "You want us to supply you with arms and assistance so you can carry out aggression against other nations?"

"What nations? I got some hits to make. You help me make them."

"Fascinating," Spock said. "But quite impossible."

"I'd call it outrageous," McCoy said.

"Even if we wanted to," Kirk said, "our orders are very . . ."

Bela gestured to Kalo who raised his gun again. Though Kirk did not see any signal given, the door opened and another armed man came in.

"I ain't interested in *your* orders," Bela said. "You got eight hours to gimme what I asked for. If I don't get the tools by then, I'm gonna have your ship pick you up again—in a large number of very small boxes. Know what I mean, pal?"

Kalo belatedly began to unload the captured devices onto the Boss's desk. He pointed to a phaser. "This here's a heater, Boss. I don't know what the other junk is."

"A heater, eh? Let's see how it works." He pointed it at a wall. Kirk jerked forward.

"Don't do that! You'll take out half the wall!"

"That good, eh? Great. Just gimme maybe a hundred of these and we don't have no more trouble."

"Out of the question," Kirk said.

"I get what I want." Bela picked up a communicator. "What are these here?"

Kirk remained silent. Jerking a thumb toward McCoy, Bela said to Kalo, "Burn him."

"All right," Kirk said hastily. "It's a communications device, locked onto my ship."

Bela fiddled with one until it snapped open in his hand. "Hey," he said to it. "In the ship."

"Scott here. Who is this?"

"This here's Bela Okmyx. I got your Captain and his friends down here. You want 'em back alive, send me a hundred of them fancy heaters of yours, and some troops to show us how to use them. You got eight hours. Then I put the hit on your friends. Know what I mean?"

"No," Scott's voice said. "But I'll find out."

Bela closed the communicator. "Okay. Kalo, take 'em over to the warehouse. Put 'em in the bag, and keep an eye on 'em, good. You hear?"

"Sure, boss. Move out, you guys."

The warehouse room had a barred window and was sparsely furnished, but it was equipped with another copy of The Book. Kalo and two henchmen were playing cards at a table, guns handy, their eyes occasionally flicking to Kirk, Spock and McCoy at the other end of the room.

"One book," McCoy said. "And they made it the blueprint for their entire society. Amazing."

"But not unprecedented," Spock said. "At one time, in old Chicago, conventional government nearly broke down. The gangs almost took over."

"This Okmyx must be the worst of the lot."

"Though we may quarrel with his methods, his goal is essentially the correct one," Spock said. "This culture must become united—or it will degenerate into complete anarchy. It is already on the way; you will recall the young women who complained of failing services."

"If this society broke down, because of the influence of the *Horizon*, the federation is responsible," Kirk said. "We've got to try to straighten the mess out. Spock, if you could get to the sociological banks of the computer, could you come up with a solution?"

"Quite possibly, Captain."

Signaling Spock and McCoy to follow him unobtrusively, Kirk gradually drifted toward the card game. The players looked up at him warily, free hands on guns; but they relaxed again as he pulled over a chair and sat down. The game was a variety of stud poker.

After a few moments, Kirk said, "That's a kid's game."

"Think so?" Kalo said.

"I wouldn't waste my time."

"Who's asking you to?"

"On Beta Antares Four, they play a game for men. Of course, it's probably too involved for you. It takes intelligence."

Antares is not a double star; Kirk had taken the chance in order to warn the sometimes rather literal-minded that he was lying deliberately.

"Okay, I'll bite," Kalo said. "Take the cards, big man. Show us how it's played."

"The Antares cards are different, of course, but not too different," Kirk said, riffling through them. "The game's called Fizzbin. Each player gets six cards—except for the man on the dealer's right, who gets seven. The second card goes up—except on Tuesdays, of course . . . Ah, Kalo, that's good, you've got a nine. That's half a fizzbin already."

"I need another nine?"

Spock and McCoy drew nearer with quite natural curiosity, since neither of them had ever heard of the game. Neither had Kirk.

"Oh, no. That would be a sralk and you'd be disqualified. You need a King or a deuce, except at night, when a Queen or a four would . . . Two sixes! That's excellent—unless, of course, you get another six. Then you'd have to turn it in, unless it was black."

"But if it was black?" Kalo said, hopelessly confused.

"Obviously, the opposite would hold," Kirk said, deciding to throw in a touch of something systematic for further confusion. "Instead of turning your six in, you'd get another card. Now, what you are really hoping for is a royal fizzbin, but the odds against that are, well, astronomical, wouldn't you say, Spock?"

"I have never computed them, Captain."

"Take my word they're considerable. Now the last card around. We call it the cronk, but its home name is *klee-et*.* Ready? Here goes."

He dealt, making sure that Kalo's card went off the table.

"Oops, sorry,"

"I'll get it."

Kalo bent over. In the same instant, Kirk put his hands under the table and shoved. It went over on the other two. McCoy and Spock were ready; the action was hardly more than a flurry before the three guards were helpless. Kirk parceled out the guns.

"Spock, find the radio transmitting station. Uhura is monitoring

*A Vulcan word meaning, roughly, "prepare to engage."

their broadcasts. Cut in and have yourself and Bones beamed up to the ship."

"Surely you are coming, Captain?"

"Not without Bela Okmyx."

"Jim, you can't . . ."

"This mess is our responsibility, Bones. You have your orders. Let's go." Kirk at first felt a little uneasy walking a city street with a submachine gun under his arm, but no one passing seemed to find it unusual. On the contrary, it seemed to be a status symbol; people cleared the way for him.

But the walk ended abruptly with two handguns stuck into his ribs from behind. He had walked into an ambush. How had Bela gotten word so fast?

The answer to that was soon forthcoming. The two hoods who had mousetrapped him crowded him into a car—and the ride was a long one. At its end was another office, almost a duplicate of Bela's; but the man behind the desk was short, squat, bull-shaped and strange. He arose with a jovial smile.

"So you're the Fed. Well, well. I'm Krako—Jojo Krako, Boss of the South Territory. Hey, I'm glad to see you."

"Would you mind telling me how you knew about me?"

"I got all Bela's communications bugged. He can't make a date with a broad without I know about it. Now you're probably wondering why I brought you here."

"Don't tell me. You want to make a deal."

Krako was pleased. "I like that. Sharp. Sharp, huh, boys?"

"Sharp, Boss."

"Let me guess some more," Kirk said. "You want—uh—heaters, right? And troops to teach you how to use them. And you'll hit the other bosses and take over the whole planet. And then we'll sit down and talk, right?"

"Wrong," Krako said. "More than talk. I know Bela. He didn't offer you beans. Me, I'm a reasonable man. Gimme what I want, and I cut you in for, say, a third. Skimmed right off the top. How do you like that?"

"I've got a better idea. You know this planet has to be united. So let's sit down, you, me, and Bela, get in contact with the other bosses, and discuss the matter like rational men."

Krako seemed to be genuinely outraged. "That ain't by The Book, Kirk. We know how to handle things! You make hits! Somebody argues, you lean on him! You think we're stupid or something?"

"No, Mr. Krako," Kirk said, sighing. "You're not stupid. But you are peculiarly unreasonable."

"Pally, I got ways of getting what I want. You want to live, Kirk? Sure you do. But after I get done with you, you're liable to be sorry—unless you come across. Zabo, tell Cirl the Knife to sharpen up his blade. I might have a job for him." The smile came back. "Of course, you gimme the heaters and you keep your ears."

"No deal."

"Too bad. Put him on ice."

The two hoods led Kirk out.

On shipboard, Spock's fortunes were not running much better.

There turned out to be no specifics in the computer, not even a record of a planet-wide culture based on a moral inversion. Without more facts, reason and logic were alike helpless.

"Mr. Spock," Uhura said. "Mr. Okmyx from the surface is making contact. Audio only."

Spock moved quickly to the board. "Mr. Okmyx, this is Spock."

"How'd you get up there?" Bela's voice asked.

"Irrelevant, since we are here."

"Uh—yeah. But you'd better get back down. Krako's put the bag on your Captain."

Spock raised his eyebrows. "Why would he put a bag on the Captain?"

"Kidnapped him, dope. He'll scrag him, too."

"If I understand you correctly, that would seem to be a problem. Have you any suggestions?"

"Sure. You guys got something I want. I can help you get the Captain back. No reason we can't make a deal."

"I am afraid I find it difficult to trust you, sir."

"What's to trust? Business is business. We call a truce. You come down. My boys spring Kirk. Then we talk about you giving me a hand."

"Since we must have our Captain back," Spock said after a moment, "I accept. We shall arrive in your office within ten minutes. Spock out."

McCoy had been standing nearby, listening. "You're going to trust him?"

"If we are to save the Captain, without blatant and forceful interference on the planet, then we must have assistance from someone indigenous. At the moment, we are forced to trust Mr. Okmyx." He turned toward Scott. "Mr. Scott, although I hope to avoid their use, I think you should adjust one of the phaser banks to a strong stun position."

"Now," McCoy said, "you're starting to make sense."

Spock did not reply, since nothing in the situation made sense to him. Trusting Okmyx was nothing short of stupid, and the use of force was forbidden by General Order Number One. In such a case, the only course was to abide by the Captain's principle of letting the situation ripen.

Bela, of course, had a trap arranged. Spock had expected it, but there had been no way to avoid it. What he had not expected—nor had Bela—was the abrupt subsequent appearance of Kirk in the doorway, with a submachine gun under his arm.

"How did you get away?" Spock asked interestedly, after the gangsters had been disarmed—a long process which produced a sizable heap of lethal gadgets, some of them wholly unfamiliar.

"Krako made the mistake of leaving me a radio; that was all I needed for the old trip-wire trick. I thought I told you to get to the ship."

"We have been there, Captain. The situation required our return."

"It may be just as well. Find out anything from the computers?"

"Nothing useful, Captain. Logic and factual knowledge do not seem to apply here."

"You admit that?" McCoy said.

"With the greatest reluctance, Doctor."

"Then you won't mind if I play a hunch?" Kirk said.

"I am not sanguine about hunches, sir, but I have no practical alternative."

"What are you going to do, Jim?"

"Now that I've got Bela," Kirk said, "I'm going to put the bag on Krako."

"On Krako?" Bela said. "You ain't serious?"

"Why not?" Kirk turned to Bela and fingered his suit lapel. "That's nice material."

"It ought to be. It cost a bundle."

"Get out of it. You, too."

"Hey, now, wait a minute . . ."

"Take it off—Pally! This time nobody's going to bag me."

Seeing that he meant it, Kalo and Bela got out of their clothes; Kirk and Spock donned them. Scooping up the required submachine guns as passports, they went out, leaving McCoy in charge.

In front of the office sat the large black car that Bela used. Fishing in the pockets of his borrowed suit, Kirk found the keys. They got in.

"Any idea how to run this thing, Spock?"

"No, Captain. But it should not be too difficult."

"Let's see," Kirk said, studying the controls. "A keyhole. For the—ignition process, I think. Insert and turn. Right."

He felt around with his foot and touched a button. The car stuttered and the engine was running.

"Interesting," Spock said.

"As long as it runs. Now, let's see. I think—gears . . ."

He pulled the lever down, which produced nothing but an alarming grinding sound which he could feel in his hand as well as hear.

"As I recall," Spock said, "there was a device called the clutch. Perhaps one of those foot pedals . . ."

The right-hand pedal didn't seem to work, but the left-hand one allowed the gear lever to go down. Kirk let the pedal up cautiously, and the car started with a lurch.

Kirk remembered the way to Krako's offices well enough, but the trip was a wild one; there seemed to be some trick to working the clutch which Kirk hadn't mastered. Luckily, pedestrians gave the big black vehicle a wide berth. Spock just hung on. When it was over, he observed, "Captain, you are a splendid starship commander, but as a taxi driver you leave much to be desired."

"Haven't had time to practice. Leave these clumsy guns under the seat; we'll use phasers."

They made their way to Krako, leaving a trail of stunned guards behind. The Boss did not seem a bit taken aback when they burst in on him; he had four hoods behind him, guns aimed at the door.

"You don't shoot, we don't shoot," he said rapidly.

"This would appear to be an impasse," Spock said.

"Who's your friend with the ears?" Krako asked. "Never mind. Ain't this nice? I was wondering how I was going to get you back, and you delivered yourself! You don't think you'll get out of it this time, do you?"

"We didn't come here for games," Kirk said. "This is bigger than you or Okmyx or any of the others."

The phaser which Krako had previously taken from Kirk was on the desk, still on safety lock. Krako nudged it. "Don't talk fancy. All you gotta do is tell me how to work these things."

"Krako," Kirk said, "can you trust all your men?"

"Yeah, sure, I either trust 'em or they're dead."

"Maybe. But when it comes to weapons like these—well, one of them could make a man a pretty big boss around here."

Krako thought about it. At last he said, "Zabo and Karf, stay put. You other guys vanish . . . All right, these two is okay. Now that we got no busy little eyes around, how do you work this thing?"

Kirk moved in on Krako hard and fast, spitting his words out like bullets. "Knock it off, Krako. We don't have time to show you how to play with toys."

"Toys?"

"What do you think we're here for, Krako? To get a cut of your deal? Forget it. That's peanuts to an outfit like the Federation."

"It is?" Krako said, a little dazed by the sudden switch.

"Unquestionably," Spock said.

"We came here to take over, Krako. The whole ball of wax. Maybe, if you cooperate, we'll cut *you* in for a piece of the action."

"A minute piece," Spock added.

"How much is that?" Krako asked.

"We'll figure it out later."

"But—I thought you guys had some kind of law about no interference . . ."

"Who's interfering? We're just taking over."

Spock seemed slightly alarmed. "Uh—Captain . . ."

"Cool it, Spocko. Later."

"What's your deal?" Krako asked.

Kirk motioned him to his feet and, when the bewildered gangster stood, Kirk sat down in his chair and swung his feet up onto the desk. He appropriated one of Krako's cigars.

"The Federation wants this planet, but we don't want to have to come in and use our muscle. That ain't subtle. So what we do is help one guy take over. He pulls the planet's strings—and we pull his. Follow?"

"But what's your cut?"

Kirk eyed the unlit cigar judiciously. "What do you care, so long as you're in charge? Right, Spocko?"

"Right on the button, Boss," Spock said, falling into his role a little belatedly but with certain relish. "Of course, there's always Bela Okmyx . . ."

Krako thought only a moment. "You got a deal. Call your ship and bring down your boys and whatever you need."

Kirk got to his feet and snapped open his communicator. "Kirk to *Enterprise*."

"*Enterprise*. Scott here, sir."

"Scotty, we made the deal with Krako."

"Uh—we did, sir?"

"We're ready to make the hit. We're taking over the whole planet as soon as you can get ready."

"Is that wise, sir?"

"Sure, we can trust Krako—he doesn't have any choice. He's standing here right now, *about three feet to my left,* all ready to be our pal. I'd like to show him the ship, just so he's sure I'm giving him the straight dope. But you know how it is."

"Oh aye, sir," Scott said. "I know indeed."

"We'll be needing enough phasers to equip all of Krako's men, plus advisers—troops to back them up on the hit. You moving, Scotty?"

"Aye, Uhura's on to the Transporter Room and two of the boys are on their way. Ready when you say the word."

"Very well, Scotty, begin."

Krako looked curiously at Kirk. "You mean you're gonna start bringing all those guys down now?"

"No—not exactly." As he spoke, the hum of the Transporter effect filled the room, and Krako shimmered out of existence. Zabo and Karf stared, stunned—and a second later were stunned more thoroughly.

"Well played—Spocko."

Spock winced. "So we have—put the bag on Krako. What is our next maneuver, Captain?"

"Back to Bela's place."

"In the car, Captain?"

"It's faster than walking. Don't tell me you're afraid of cars, Spock."

"Not at all. It is your driving which alarms me."

Through the door of Bela's office, they heard McCoy saying worriedly, "Where *are* they?"

And then Bela's, "Knowing Krako, we'll be lucky if he sends 'em back on a blotter."

Kirk walked in. "Wrong again, Okmyx." He brushed past the relieved McCoy. "Outta my way, Sawbones. I want to talk to this guy. I'm getting tired of playing patty-cake with you penny ante operators."

"Who you calling penny ante?" Bela said, bristling.

"Nobody but you, baby. Now listen. The Federation's moving in here. We're taking over, and if you play ball, we'll leave a piece of the pie for you. If you don't, you're out. All the way out. Got that?" He shoved the phaser under Bela's nose to make the point.

"Yeah—yeah, sure, Kirk. Why didn't you say so in the first place? I mean—all you hadda do was explain."

The communicator came out. "Scotty, you got Krako on ice up there?"

"Aye, Captain."

"Keep him till I ask for him. We're going to be making some old-style phone calls from these coordinates. Lock on at the receiving end and transport the party here to us. Okay, Okmyx. Start calling the other bosses."

216

Shrugging, Bela went to the phone and dialed four times. "Hello, Tepo? Guess who? . . . Yeah, I got a lot of nerve. What're you going to do about it?"

With a hum, Tepo materialized, holding a non-existent phone in his hand. McCoy moved in to disarm him.

". . . coming over there with a couple of my boys, and . . . Brother!"

Bela grinned at Kirk. "Hey, this ain't bad."

"Keep dialing."

Half an hour later, the office was crowded with dazed gang leaders, Krako among them. Kirk climbed up on the desk, now cradling a local gun to add weight to his argument.

"All right, pipe down, everybody. I'll tell you what you're going to do. The Federation just took over around here, whether you like it or not. You guys have been running this planet like a piecework factory. From here on, it's all under one roof. You're going to form a syndicate and run this planet like a business. That means you make a profit."

"Yeah?" Tepo called. "And what's your percentage?"

"I'm cutting the Federation in for forty per cent." He leveled the gun. "You got objections?"

Tepo had obviously had guns pointed at him too many times to be cowed. "Yeah. I hear a lot of talk, but all I see here is you and a couple of your boys. I don't see no Federation."

"Listen, they got a ship," Krako said. "I know—I been there."

"Yeah, but Tepo's got a point," Bela said. "All we ever see is them."

"I only saw three other guys and a broad while I was in the ship," Krako said. "Maybe there ain't any more?"

"There are four hundred . . ."

Kirk was interrupted by an explosion outside, followed by a fusillade of shots. Krako, who was nearest the window, peered around the edge of it.

"It's my boys," he reported. "Must think I'm still in the ship. They're making a hit on this place."

"My boys'll put 'em down," Bela said.

"Wanna bet?"

Kirk's communicator was already out. "Scotty, put ship's phasers on stun and fire a burst in a one-block radius around these coordinates, excluding this building."

"Right away, sir."

Kirk looked at the confused gangsters. "Gentlemen, you are about to see the Federation at work."

The noise roared on a moment more, and then the window was lit up with the phaser effect. Dead silence fell promptly.

Krako smiled weakly and swallowed. "Some trick."

"They're not dead, just knocked out for a while," Kirk said. "We could just as easily have killed them."

"Okay," Bela said. "We get the message. You were saying something about a syndicate."

"No, he was saying something about a percentage," Tepo said. "You sure forty percent is enough?"

"I think it will be just fine. We'll send someone around to collect it every year—and give you advice if you need it."

"That's reasonable," Bela said. He glared at the others. "Ain't that reasonable?"

There was a murmur of assent. Kirk smiled cheerfully. "Well, in that case, pull out some of that drinking stuff of yours, Okmyx, and let's get down to the talking."

The bridge of the *Enterprise* was routinely busy. Kirk was in the command chair, feeling considerably better to be back in uniform.

"I must say," Spock said, "your solution to the problem on Iotia is unconventional, Captain. But it does seem to be the only workable one."

"What troubles you is that it isn't logical to leave a criminal organization in charge. Is that it?"

"I do have some reservations. And how do you propose to explain to Starfleet Command that a starship will be sent around each year to collect 'our cut,' as you put it?"

"'Our cut' will be put back into the planet's treasury—and the advisers and collectors can help steer the Iotians back into a more conventional moral and ethical system. In the meantime, the syndicate forms a central government that can effectively administer to the needs of the people. That's a step in the right direction. Our group of 'governors' is already learning to take on conventional responsibilities. Guiding them is—our piece of the action."

Spock pondered. "Yes, it seems to make sense. Tell me, Captain. Whatever gave you so outlandish an idea—and where did you pick up all that jargon so quickly?"

Kirk grinned. "Courtesy of Krako. A radio wasn't all he left in my cell. He also left me some reading matter."

"Ah, of course. The Book."

"Spocko, now you're talkin'."

★Probe Questions

If this chapter has any "hidden" meanings, it is to encourage the reader to experience other cultures, to leave the comfort of the expected, known, and understood, and to experience the shock of the unexpected, the unknown, and the mysterious. Without actually experiencing the "differences" described in this chapter, it is easy for one to fall into an attitude that one's home culture represents the "right" way to perceive and to think about the world, and that foreign cultures represent the "wrong" way.

Are there means of gaining this experience without actually traveling? Have you seriously sought out and known a foreign visitor? Foreign dress? Foreign foods? It is possible to live in another culture and still remain an American, isolated from non-American experiences.

Are there risks involved in learning that one's own culture does not represent the only way to view the world? Can a culture's leader or representative also be a world-wide leader? Should there be world-wide leaders, or a world-wide single culture? What would be the advantages? The disadvantages?

Summary

A culture is whatever one has to know or believe in order to fit into the society, and it is what distinguishes one social group from another. Cultural differences are learned through the process of socialization. Differences in perceiving result from what the culture has learned to name various stimuli and how it categorizes them. Differences in thinking may be classed according to inductive and deductive thought processes. American thinking is inductive, whereas Eastern thinking is deductive. Language differences arise according to the needs of the culture. The Sapir-Whorf hypothesis states that "language is culture and that culture is controlled by and controls language," thus , reality exists in terms of the language one knows. Communication habits, too, vary across cultures depending, to a large extent, on such cultural factors as technological development and whether or not the society is public-oriented or private-oriented. Cultural differences in values depend, in part, on the society's relationship with nature. If people see themselves as integrally connected to nature, then they are likely to have more respect for other life forms than do people who view themselves as separate from nature. These attitudes are reflected in the culture's architecture, among other things. Differences in self-concept can be seen in the Oriental concept of "face" and in the American concept of individuality. Different self-concepts determine the types of friendships that people form. In America, friendships tend to be compartmentalized, whereas in Russia, friendships are more total.

By studying cross-cultural differences, one can hopefully come to understand and respect these differences and, as a result, come to better understand oneself. When cultural differences remain unexplored, an attitude of egocentricism develops, which can result in a syndrome of domination/subjugation.

Footnotes

[1]Ward H. Goodenough, "Cultural Anthropology and Linguistics," in *Language in Culture and Society: A Reader in Linguistics and Anthropology*, Dell Hymes, ed., New York: Harper & Row Publishers, 1964, p. 36.

[2]Marshall R. Singer, "Culture: A Perceptual Approach," in *Readings in Intercultural Communication*, vol. I, David S. Hoopes, ed., Pittsburgh, Pennsylvania: Regional Council for International Education, (not dated), p. 12.

[3]Frank A. Geldard, *The Human Senses*, New York: John Wiley & Sons, Inc., 1953, p. 53.

[4]Marshall H. Segall, Donald T. Campbell, and Melville J. Herskovits, *The Influence of Culture on Visual Perception*, Indianapolis: The Bobbs-Merrill Company, Inc., 1966.

[5]Edward C. Stewart, *American Cultural Patterns: A Cross-Cultural Perspective* (Dimensions of International Education, Number Three), Pittsburgh, Pennsylvania: Regional Council for International Education, 1971, copyright by Edward C. Stewart, 1972.

[6]This description of Chinese thought is taken from Stewart and is based on Marcel Granet, *La Pensée Chinoise*, Editions Albin Michel, Paris: 1950, and Chang Tung-sun, "A Chinese Philosopher's Theory of Knowledge," *ETC., A Review of General Semantics*, 1962, 9(3), 203–226.

[7]Goodenough, "Cultural Anthropology and Linguistics," p. 37.

[8]Eugene A. Nida, *Learning a Foreign Language*, New York: Friendship Press, 1947.

[9]Peter Farb, *Man's Rise to Civilization as Shown by the Indians of North America from Primeval Times to the Coming of the Industrial State*, New York: E. P. Dutton & Co., Inc., 1968, pp. 235–239.

[10]K. S. Sitaram, "A Model of Intercultural Communication," in *Readings in InterCultural Communication*, vol. I, p. 3.

[11]Edward T. Hall, *The Silent Language*, New York: Doubleday, 1959, and Edward T. Hall and William Foote Whyte, "Intercultural Communication: A Guide to Men of Action," *Human Organization*, 1960, 19, 5–12.

[12]Marshall McLuhan, *Understanding Media: The Extensions of Man*, New York: McGraw-Hill, 1964.

[13]Stewart, pp. 58–59.

[14]Bob Maxwell, "Review: 'Wild Kingdom,'" *Media Ecology Review*, 1972, 2(4), 14.

[15]Stewart, p. 60.

[16]Farb, p. 238.

[17]Stewart, pp. 66–68.

[18]Hajime Nakamura, *Ways of Thinking of Eastern Peoples: India-China-Tibet-Japan*, Honolulu: East-West Center Press, 1964, pp. 409–417.

[19]Weston La Barre, "Some Observations on Character Structure in the Orient: The Japanese," in *Japanese Character and Culture*, Bernard S. Silberman, ed., Tucson: The University of Arizona Press, 1962, pp. 325–359.

[20]Alvin Toffler, *Future Shock*, New York: Random House, 1970.

[21]Stewart, pp. 45–58.

[22]Edmund S. Glenn, "Meaning and Behavior: Communication and Culture," *Journal of Communication*, 1966, 16, 248–272.

[23]Gary L. Althen and Josephine Jaime, "Assumptions and Values in Philippine, American and Other Cultures," in *Readings in InterCultural Communication*, vol. I, pp. 68–72.

[24]Andrea L. Rich and Dennis M. Ogawa, "Intercultural and Interracial Communication: An Analytical Approach," *Intercultural Communication: A Reader*, Larry A. Samovar and Richard E. Porter, eds., Belmont, California: Wadsworth Publishing Company, Inc., 1972, pp. 23–31.

Chapter

7

After reading this chapter, you should be able to:

❡ Discuss the concept of deviance as it relates to subcultures.

❡ Explain the relationship between "typing" and "self-fulfilling prophecy."

❡ Give examples of ways in which subcultures can be studied.

❡ Discuss the value of studying various subcultures.

SUBCULTURAL COMMUNICATION

¶ In the previous chapter we examined the special circumstances of cross-cultural communication with the objective of becoming more skilled in communicating with people from different cultural backgrounds. This chapter will examine the special circumstances of *subcultural* communication. Subcultural communication, as used here, refers to the process of interpersonal communication whereby one gains and maintains the ability to communicate effectively and meaningfully with members of a subculture. By understanding this process, I feel we can begin to improve our understanding and respect for different subcultures even if we have no desire to gain membership in them.

Our focus, then, is necessarily closely related to the sociological study of *deviance*—that is, the behaviors or attitudes for which people are regarded as abnormal and objectionable in their particular society or culture. People who are considered deviant include alcoholics, prostitutes, criminals, nudists, homosexuals, and even the mentally retarded or physically disabled. Deviance, like beauty, is in the eye of the beholder. This means that virtually anyone, including you and I, could be labeled deviant according to the norms of some culture or group. In other words, there is nothing *inherently* deviant in any human act; something is deviant only because some people label it so. We want to look at this labeling process, too, as a factor in interpersonal communication. An examination of deviance most compatible with the perspective on interpersonal communication taken in this text has been advanced by Earl Rubington and Martin S. Weinberg. Rubington and Weinberg devised "the deviance corridor," as shown in Figure 7.1, as a means of visualizing this process.[1]

Along this corridor are openings for both entrance and exit at the front, the rear, and along both sides. An individual symbolically passes through this corridor on his way to membership in a subculture. Area 1 represents the situation that any one of us may face living in a group in which our qualities and acts are viewed *by that group* as deviant. Area 2 represents the situation in which a person is believed by the group to exhibit deviance. Area 3 represents being typed and assigned deviant status. Area 4 represents the situation in which one's actions come to official (i.e. police) attention and in which one then becomes an official "case" for various agencies of social control. Area 5 represents becoming a part of organized deviant life (i.e. of a subculture apart from conventional society). Finally, Area 6 represents one redefining himself or changing his self-concept to assume the deviant role of becoming in the end what the group said he was at the outset. This final stage of self-redefinition is not unlike the function of consciousness-raising groups discussed in Chapter 5.

This model can also be reversed. When it is reversed, a person defines himself as a certain kind of person (Area 6), enters a deviant subculture to confirm that identity (Area 5), becomes an official case (Area 4), engages in more deviant behaviors (Area 3), and reinforces the system of social typing by his actions. A person may enter the deviance corridor and may move forward, backward, or out of the process at any one of its stages.

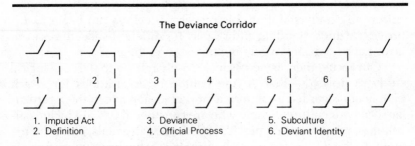

The Deviance Corridor

1. Imputed Act   3. Deviance   5. Subculture
2. Definition   4. Official Process   6. Deviant Identity

SOURCE: Earl Rubington and Martin S. Weinburg, eds., *Deviance: The Interactionist Perspective*, New York: Macmillan, 1968, p. 204.

FIGURE 7.1 The deviance corridor demonstrates the different stages of assuming a deviant identity.

Central to Rubington and Weinberg's explanation is the interpersonal communication between the individual and others. The critical factor is the social audience, since it is others who confer deviance upon the individual. Thus, deviance is a social concept, and as such, a person may change group membership and thereby change his self-definition.

The process of defining may be called a process of *typing*. It is an interactive process in which agents of a group or a society label, or redefine, a person according to specific norms of the defining group. This redefinition alters others' future interpersonal communication with the person and the individual's future interpersonal communication with others. Thus, successful typing occurs when the typer, witnesses to the typing, and the person being typed understand and reaffirm this definition in all future interactions. Because both the typer and the witnesses share a new understanding of the person, they act on the understanding in the individual's presence. The person being typed becomes aware of this new definition and takes this new understanding of self into account when communicating with others.

For example, a particular woman may be casual about her sexual contacts. Over a period of years, she engages in sexual contacts more or less promiscuously. If one day she should hint at receiving a gift for her sexual favors or if one of her sexual partners presents her with a gift or some money shortly after the sex act, her status has been redefined. Other people may begin to think of her as a prostitute and she may, reciprocally, come to think of herself in that manner. Remember that in Chapter 4 we discussed Rosenthal and Jacobson's study in which they identified students on a random basis to their teachers as having scored high on a test for intellectual abilities. In a related fashion they concluded that teachers often initiate a "self-fulfilling" prophecy when they label students; that is, teachers' expectations of a student's performance associated with labels such as "high achiever" or "trouble-maker" often help to determine that same performance.

Why Do Subcultures Exist?

What is the relationship between deviance and membership in a subculture? When persons defined as deviant associate with one another more frequently than they do with persons of nondeviant status, a subculture may develop. These subcultures, much like the cultures discussed in the previous chapter, create among their members a common understanding of the world as well as prescribed ways of thinking, feeling, and acting.

Involvement in a subculture facilitates access to others with similar constructs—the interpersonal attraction process described in Chapter 4. On the other hand, the subculture serves a protective function, shielding members from negative attitudes and pressures imposed by outsiders. Thus, the subculture is both facilitative and protective for the individual. And, as was discussed in Chapter 5 in the analysis of interpersonal conflict, conflict with outsiders serves to unify the subculture.

It should be emphasized that subcultures within the dominant culture are not restricted to deviant groups. Similar interpersonal communication processes apply as equally to professional football players, college professors, and accountants as to drug abusers, motorcycle gangs, and sex offenders. It's just that the latter groups are of greater interest to most of us because their differences are more striking.

A subculture, then, may come into being when a category of persons in contact with one another acknowledge a common life style. The subculture then develops a social organization, however weak, which serves to admit and socialize new members. This should remind you of Mead's theory of the social self, discussed in Chapter 4. In Adapted Reading No. 17 by Martin S. Weinberg, try to trace these communication processes in the "deviance" of nudists.

Observations of Subcultures

There are many reports of observations of subcultures that range in method from "insider reports" to "insider participant-observer reports." Insider reports can be most interesting and valuable; however, all too many seem to be written for self-justification or profit. Insider participant-observer reports are based on one's orderly and scientific study of a subculture (whose members are unaware that they are being studied) by actually becoming accepted as a member of that subculture. True, this does present an ethical problem, but the process of insider participant-observer reports illustrates a form of the interpersonal communication process by which one learns to become a member and is accepted by members of a subculture.

There are several fascinating reports of this kind available. Although it is interesting and useful to examine extreme cases, we should remember that there are many interpersonal communication problems that arise among members of different subcultures that are far less dramatic than the ones stressed in this chapter. One of the more interesting examples is given by Saul D. Alinsky who was a brilliant organizer of community-action groups. Alinsky was born in Chicago's South Side and worked his way through the University of Chicago. As a graduate student in criminology, Alinsky decided to do as his doctoral dissertation an inside study of the Al Capone mob. In an interview in *Playboy* magazine, given shortly before his death, Alinsky described how he finally gained membership after some unsuccessful attempts:

Nudism as a Subculture

This chapter has primarily dealt with the interpersonal communication process of typing—the process through which a person learns and accepts deviant status. In this adapted reading, trace this process. Why are men and women initially influenced by different communication sources? After a time, what function does nudism provide?

In order to better understand deviant life styles and the meanings they have for those engaged in them, it is often useful to conceptualize a lifestyle as a career, consisting of various stages. We can then study the interpersonal processes that draw and sustain people at each of these various stages. In this way, we can appreciate the motivations, perceptions, and experiences that characterize involvement in that way of life at various points in time—e.g., these may differ for novices, "veterans," etc.

Using such a career model, this [adapted reading] deals with the interpersonal processes and phases involved in nudist camp membership. Specifically, it deals with the processes by which people come to contemplate a visit to a nudist camp, attend for the first time, and then continue attending over a period of time. The data come from three sources—101 interviews with nudists in the Chicago area; two successive summers of participant observation in nudist camps; and 617 mailed questionnaires completed by nudists located throughout the United States and Canada.

Prenudist Attitudes Toward Nudism

Most people seldom give much thought to the subject of nudism. Responses in the interviews indicated that nudism is not a prominent object of thought even for many persons who will later become nudists. Thus when nudist members were asked what they had thought of nudism before visiting a camp, 50 percent stated that

Adapted from Martin S. Weinberg, "Becoming a Nudist," *Psychiatry: Journal for the Study of Interpersonal Processes, 1966, 29, 15–24. Reprinted by special permission of The William Alanson White Psychiatric Foundation, Inc. Copyright is held by the Foundation. Some tables and footnotes deleted and renumbered.*

they had never really given it any thought. Until their initial experience, the interviewees' conceptions of nudism had been vague stereotypes, much like those held by the general public. In the words of a now active nudist: I never gave it too much thought. I thought it was a cult—a nut-eating, berry-chewing bunch of vegetarians, doing calisthenics all day, a gymno-physical society. I thought they were carrying health to an extreme, being egomaniacs about their body.

Many of those who had thought about the subject conceived of nudists' camps as more exclusive, luxurious, and expensive than they actually are. Others had different conceptions: I'm afraid I had the prevailing notion that they were undignified, untidy places populated (a) by the very poor, and (b) by languishing bleached blonds, and (c) by greasy, leering bachelors.

Table 1 sums up the attitudes that nudists reported themselves to have taken before their affiliation.

The Initial Interest in Nudism

If prenudist attitudes are of the nature indicated by Table 1, how does one become interested enough to make a first visit to a nudist camp? As shown in Table 2, the highest percentage of men mentioned magazines as the source of their interest, and the next largest source was other persons (exclusive of parents or parents-in-law). For women, the pattern was different; the highest percentage were first informed about nudism by their husbands. In 78 percent of the families, the husband had been more interested in visiting a camp. In all other cases both spouses had equally wanted to go. There were no cases in which the wife had wanted to go more than the husband.

The fact that the overwhelming majority of women became interested in nudism through their relationships with other people, rather than through the mass media which played such an

TABLE 1. PRENUDIST ATTITUDES TOWARD NUDISM

Attitude	Percentage of Interviewees
Positive	35
Live and let live	16
Negative	19
Very negative	1
Does not know	29

TABLE 2. SOURCE OF INITIAL INTEREST IN NUDISM

Source	Male	Female
Magazines	47%	14%
Movies	6	6
Newspapers	6	0
Spouse	0	47
Parents or parents-in-law	2	8
Other person	31	23
Medical advice from physician	0	2
Other source	8	0

important part with men, was reflected in the finding that interpersonal trust had to be sustained in order to evoke the women's interest. This was indicated in the content of many interviews. The interviews also indicated that commonsense justifications and "derivations" were important in overcoming the women's anxieties.

The following quotation is from an interview with a woman who became interested in nudism after being informed about it by a male friend. Here she was describing what her feelings would have been prior to that time. (In this quotation, as in others in this adapted reading, Q is used to signify a neutral probe by the interviewer that follows the course of the last reply—such as "Could you tell me some more about that?" or "How's that?" or "What do you mean?" Other questions by the interviewer are given in full.)

. . . (Whether or not I would go to a nudist camp would) depend on who asked me. If a friend, I probably would have gone along with it. . . . (Q) If an acquaintance, I wouldn't have been interested. (Q) I don't know, I think it would depend on who was asking me to go. (Q) If it was someone you liked or had confidence in, you'd go along with it. If you didn't think they were morally upright you probably wouldn't have anything to do with it.

A man described how he had persuaded his wife to become interested in nudism: I expected difficulty with my wife. I presented it to her in a wholesome manner. (Q) I had to convince her it was a wholesome thing, and that the people there were sincere. . . . (Q) That they were sincere in efforts to sunbathe together and had only good purposes in mind when they did that. (Q) All the things that nudism stands for: a healthy body and a cleansed mind by killing sex curiosities. . . .

Even though they had enough confidence to make the decision to visit a camp, the respondents did not necessarily anticipate becoming nudists themselves. For many the first trip was merely a joke, a lark, or a new experience, and the main motivation was curiosity. They visited the camp as one might make a trip to the zoo, to see what it was like and what kind of characters would belong to such a group. There was also curiosity, on the part of many of the respondents, about seeing nude members of the opposite sex. The original thought was that we were going to see a bunch of nuts. It was a joke going out there. I thought they must be a little nutty. Eccentric. I didn't think there'd be so many normal people. . . . (Q) I felt that people that are nudists are a little bohemian or strange. (Q) I don't feel that way now. I thought we'd be the only sane people there. I thought it was kind of an adventure. . . . (Q) I like feeling I'm doing something unusual that no one knows about. It's a big secret. . . . (Q) The novelty, the excitement of driving up in the car; no one knew we were going. . . .

Table 3 presents the motivations given by interviewees for their first trip to a nudist camp.

The First Visit

The first trip to camp was frequently accompanied by extreme nervousness. Part of this might be attributed simply to the experience of entering a new group. The visitors did not know the

TABLE 3. MOTIVATIONS FOR THE FIRST VISIT TO A NUDIST CAMP

Motivation	Male	Female
Curiosity over what it was like	33%	25%
Sexual curiosity	16	2
To satisfy spouse or relative	2	38
Combination of curiosity and to satisfy spouse	0	13
For relaxation	2	4
For health	12	6
To sunbathe	8	2
To make friends	6	0
Other	21	10

patterns common to the group, and they were uncertain about their acceptance by group members. . . . But, in the instance of a first visit to a nudist camp, this anxiety of entering a new group was considerably heightened by the unknown nature of the experience that lay ahead. Mead, in his discussion of the "social psychology of the act," has described how people, in planning an action, imaginatively rehearse it and its anticipated consequences.[1] The nudist camp, however, presents a totally unfamiliar situation; the person planning a visit has no past of similar situations, and usually no one has effectively described the situation to him in advance. This gap in effective imagination produces apprehension, anxiety, and nervousness. . . .

In most instances the initial nervousness dissipated soon after the newcomer's arrival. Forty-six percent of the interviewees said that they were not nervous at all after arriving at camp. An additional 31 percent felt at ease in less than three hours. Thus most visitors adjusted rapidly to the nudist way of life. Seventy-one percent of those interviewed reported that *no* major adjustment was necessary. Sixteen percent of the residual group reported that undressing for the first time, or becoming used to being nude, was the only adjustment. Of these people who had to adjust, only 15 percent found the adjustment to be difficult. . . .

The Adoption of Nudism as a Way of Life

Coaching and Social Validation

The newcomers to camps received no formal indoctrination in the nudist perspective, but acquired it almost imperceptibly as the result of a subtle social process. . . .

The nudist way of life becomes a different reality, a new world: It seems like a different world from the world we live in every day. No washing, ironing, worries. You feel so free there. The people are friendly there, interested in each other. But not nosy. You can relax among them more easily than in the city.

And this new reality imposes a different meaning on the everyday life of the outside world: my daughter told us today the boys and girls don't sit together at school, but it makes no difference to her. Several times they're out playing and the boys get excited when they see their panties. My children don't understand that. They have a different state of mind toward different sexes.

[1]Anselm Strauss, editor, *The Social Psychology of George Herbert Mead*; Chicago, Univ. of Chicago Press, 1956; p. xiii.

Motives for Becoming a Nudist

Persons who became nudists—that is, became members of a camp and conceived of themselves as nudists—usually demonstrated an autonomy of motives, in the sense that their motives for doing so differed from their motives for first visiting a camp. That is to say, participation in different stages of the "nudist career" were usually characterized by different sets of motives. Hence the curiosity that had often been the overriding motive for initial visits was satisfied, and the incentive for affiliating with a nudist camp was based on the person's experiences at the camp, experiences which may not have been anticipated before visiting the camp. It should be noted, however, that the decision was sometimes prompted by the owner's insistence that visitors join if they wished to return. As Table 4 shows, there was a considerable change, after the first visit, in the pattern of male versus female desire to attend the camp. . . .

The interviewees were asked what they liked most about nudism, with the results shown in Table 5. . . .

Friendliness and sociability were the characteristics of the nudist experience mentioned most often by interviewees. In addition, nudists extended the concept of "family" to include fellow nudists; they cited a "togetherness" that is rare in the clothed society. . . .

A number of interviewees, supporting the nudist contention that social distinctions diminish in the nudist camp, believed that class distinctions would reappear if clothing were donned. . . .

TABLE 4. COMPARATIVE DESIRES OF MALE AND FEMALE MEMBERS OF COUPLES TO VISIT A NUDIST CAMP

	Male Wanted To Go More	Male and Female Wanted To Go Equally	Female Wanted To Go More
First visit	79%	21%	0%
Return visits	40	51	9

TABLE 5. WHAT INTERVIEWEES LIKE MOST ABOUT NUDISM

	Percent of Sample Mentioning the Item
Friendliness, sociability	60%
Relaxation, getting away from the city	47
Enjoyment of outdoors and sports	36
Freedom	31
Sunbathing	26
Physical health	26
Children becoming informed about the human body	11
Mental health	8
Economical vacation	4
Family recreation, keeping family together	4
Seeing people nude	1
Other aspects	15

Nudists extend the concept of "family" to include fellow nudists. Is this a characteristic of a subculture?

Although these statements may be somewhat idealized, the nudist camp does effectively break down patterns common to country clubs, resorts, and other settings in the outside society. Sex, class, and power lose much of their relevance in the nudist camp, and the suspension of the barriers they create effects a greater unity among the participants. This is not to say, however, that there is no social hierarchy. . . .

The "togetherness" of nudists is exaggerated. Personality clashes, cliques, and intergroup disagreements exist, and social stratification remains in evidence. . . .

Furthermore, it is doubtful that many people find a Utopia in nudism. The nudists interviewed were asked how seriously they felt that they would be affected if nudist camps were closed. As Table 6 shows, 30 percent of the interviewees considered that they would be relatively unaffected. When they were asked to identify their three best friends, almost half of the interviewees did not name another nudist. . . .

The fact that nudists were able to participate in a group which they viewed as stigmatized (and also the sense of belonging they claimed to have found in nudism) suggested that nudists might be isolated in the larger society. If they were isolated they could more easily participate in such a deviant group, being insulated from social controls.

TABLE 6. THE DEGREE TO WHICH THE CLOSING OF NUDIST CAMPS
WOULD AFFECT INTERVIEWEES

Closing Camps Would Affect Respondent	Percent of Respondents
Very much	43
Somewhat	26
Not too much	17
Not at all	13

A comparison of nudist interviewees with a sample of the general population did show the nudists to fall substantially below the general population in frequency of informal association. . . . Further, while members of the general population got together most often with relatives, nudists got together most often with friends. . . . The fact that 34 percent of the nudist sample got together with relatives less than once a month may reflect a considerable insulation from informal controls, since it is relatives who would probably provide the greatest pressure in inhibiting participation in such deviant groups.

The degree to which nudists were isolated in the clothed society was found to be related to the length of time they had been nudists. . . . The longer a person had been in nudism, the more likely he was to be isolated. This may be interpreted in different ways. For example, there may be a tendency to become more isolated with continued participation, perhaps to avoid sanctions. (Yet, in regard to formal organizations nudists did *not* drop out or become less active.) Or, in the past it is likely that nudism was considered even more deviant than it is today and therefore it may have appealed primarily to more isolated types of people.

Regardless of which interpretation is correct, as previously discussed, many nudists found a sense of belonging in nudism. People are lonely. It gives them a sense of belonging. Until I started going out . . . (to camp) I never felt like I was part of a crowd. But I do out there. I was surprised. (Q) Well, like I said, I was never part of a crowd . . . I had friends, but never outstanding. My wife and I were (camp) King and Queen.

However, while the nudist experience helps solve this life problem for some, it creates this same problem for others. For the latter group, nudism may only ease the problem that it creates—that is, the isolation that results from concealing one's affiliation with a deviant group.

. . . one night I was sitting in the restaurant [in the Lexington Hotel, which was the gang's headquarters] and at the next table was Big Ed Stash, a professional assassin who was the Capone mob's top executioner. He was drinking with a bunch of his pals and he was saying, "Hey, you guys, did I ever tell you about the time I picked up that redhead in Detroit?" and he was cut off by a chorus of moans. "My God," one guy said, "do we have to hear that one again?" I saw Big Ed's face fall; mobsters are very sensitive, you know, very thin-skinned. And I reached over and plucked his sleeve. "Mr. Stash," I said, "I'd love to hear that story." His face lit up. "You would, kid?" He slapped me on the shoulder. "Here, pull up a chair. Now, this broad, see . . . ." And that's how it started.[2]

Notice that the strategy used is no great secret: All people like to feel that others are interested in listening to them. Obviously, the strategy does not apply only to subculture access.

During a two-year honorary membership in the mob, Alinsky met Frank Nitti, Capone's number-two man in control at that time. Nitti took Alinsky under his wing, and as one of Nitti's "boys," Alinsky saw all the mob's operations, from gin mills and bookie joints to legitimate businesses. Alinsky summarized his honorary membership in the mob as follows:

I was a nonparticipating observer in their professional activities, although I joined their social life of food, drink and women. Boy, I sure participated in that side of things—it was heaven.

And let me tell you something, I learned a hell of a lot about the uses and abuses of power from the mob, lessons that stood me in good stead later on, when I was organizing.[3]

Another example of an inside observation is provided by Hunter S. Thompson. Hunter Thompson, a political reporter for *Rolling Stone* magazine, "ran" with the Hell's Angels motorcycle gang for a whole year, and he did establish considerable trust with many of this subculture's members.[4] In the mid 1960s, perhaps 500 to 1000 motocyclists belonged to such clubs as the Gypsy Jokers, Nightriders, Comancheros, Presidents, Satan's Slaves, and the outlaw elite, the Hell's Angels, which is part of that supposed 1 percent of motorcyclists that the American Motorcycle Association refuses to claim as members.

Why would some people be frightened when encountering this subculture? Why would they experience a communications gap?

Thompson's contact was Frenchy, a twenty-nine-year-old part owner of a transmission repair garage called the "Box Shop" in San Francisco. Thompson describes his encounter with Frenchy:

> Frenchy ignored me long enough to make things uncomfortable, then nodded a faint smile and rapped a shot toward one of the corner pockets. I bought a glass of beer and watched. . . .
>
> When the pool game ended, Frenchy sat down at the bar, and asked what I wanted to know. We talked for more than an hour, but his style of conversation made me nervous. He would pause now and then, letting a question hang, and fix me with a sad little smile . . . an allusion to some private joke that he was sure I understood. The atmosphere was heavy with hostility, like smoke in an airless room, and for a while I assumed it was all focused on me—which most of it was when I made my initial appearance but the focus dissolved very quickly. The sense of menace remained; it is part of the atmosphere the Hell's Angels breathe. . . . Their world is so rife with hostility that they don't even recognize it. They are deliberately hard on most strangers, but they get bad reactions even when they try to be friendly. I have seen them try to amuse an outsider by telling stories which they consider very funny—but which generate fear and queasiness in a listener whose sense of humor has a different kind of filter.
>
> Some of the outlaws understand this communications gap, but most are puzzled and insulted to hear that "normal people" consider them horrible.
>
> That was in early spring of 1965. By the middle of summer I had become so involved in the outlaw scene that I was no longer sure whether I was doing research on the Hell's Angels or being slowly absorbed by them. I found myself spending two or three days each week in Angel bars, in their homes, and on runs and parties. In the beginning I kept them out of my own world, but after several months my friends grew accustomed to finding Hell's Angels in my apartment at any hour of the day or night.[5]

After Thompson's favorable article on motorcycles appeared in *The Nation* magazine, the Angels became more accepting of him. Thompson, however, failed in adapting to all of this subculture's norms in two ways: first, Thompson bought a BSA bike—even though an Angel's bylaw requires that an Angel ride only a customized Harley 74; second, Thompson fouled up an Angel's "game" of kissing as "a guaranteed square-jolter":

> One night after I'd known the Angels for many months I walked into the Hyde Inn in San Francisco and joined a cluster at the bar. While I was reaching in my pocket for some beer money I was nearly knocked off my feet by a flying body that wrapped itself around me before I could see who it was. Everything went black, and my first thought was that they'd finally turned on me and it was all over: then I felt the hairy kiss and heard the laughter. Ronnie, the Oakland secretary, seemed offended that I hadn't caught him in mid-air, as he'd expected, and returned the kiss heartily. It was a serious social error. . . .[6]

Thompson believed the Angels to be like any other subculture. The "all for one" concept was taken so seriously by the "Frisco Angels" that it was written into the club charter as Bylaw Number 10: "When an Angel punches a non-Angel, all other Angels will participate." Thompson quotes Tiny as saying, "Why can't people let us alone, anyway? All we want to do is get together now and then and have some fun—just like the Masons, or any other group." Thompson saw a similarity even to the police themselves—"they are both playing the same game, and usually by the same rules."

Denounced in the U.S. Senate by George Murphy (whom Thompson describes as "the former tap dancer"), the Angels eventually "stomped" Thompson himself on Labor Day, 1966, when four or five Angels seemed to feel that he was taking advantage of them.

Other insider participant-observer studies have been reported by individuals who were at one time members of a particular subculture, later became more scientific observers, and then rejoined the subculture. One such individual is Ned Polsky, who made a study of poolhall hustlers. Motivated by some inaccurate comments made by people who had seen the movie *The Hustler* (1961, re-released 1964), Polsky was struck with the idea of doing a more accurate study. Polsky had frequented poolrooms for over twenty years before he began his study, playing in the major poolrooms in New York, Chicago, San Francisco, Cleveland, Baltimore, and Los Angeles. During his eight-month study, Polsky acted as a direct observer of hustlers as they hustled, conducted informal interviews with hustlers, and acted as a participant-observer as a hustler's opponent, a hustler's backer, and as an actual hustler.

Every poolroom in the country probably has at least one "No Gambling" sign posted, but even the casual player reading this text has probably played—gambled—"for the time," i.e. the loser pays the check.

The hustler frequently has a backer who puts up the hustler's stake money, pays his losses, and receives 50 percent of his winnings. Polsky describes the hustler's cardinal rule as *don't show your real speed*, i.e. (1) the hustler must not make many of the extremely difficult shots, (2) the hustler must play so that the games he does win are won by only a small margin, and (3) the hustler must let his opponent win an occasional game.[7]

I once found myself in the role of a hustler's backer—by accident of course. A friend of mine, who had learned to play pool as a child in Cleveland, and I found ourselves in a rural Ohio bar, again by accident. He was on crutches at the time from an accident he had had while working. After several beers, he was playing "for time." I was sitting at the bar somewhat bored, so I engaged the owner and the only other customer at the bar in conversation over whether certain shots in the game then being played could be made. These comments soon grew to dollar bets. And the dollar bets soon grew to five-dollar bets on the games. As my friend and I always worked well together, we soon began communicating with each other, in a manner unknown to our new friends, as to which shots should be made and which games should be won.

As any subculture, the homosexual subculture supports different communication behaviors, such as nonverbal communication.

The Homosexual Subculture

The term *homosexuality* refers to sexual relations between members of the same sex, and thus applies both to males and to females. However, it seems that homosexuality is more common among males than females and more studies have been conducted with male homosexuals. This discussion, therefore, centers on male homosexuals. According to Alfred C. Kinsey, 37 percent of the white male population in the United States have had at least one homosexual experience during adolescence or beyond. However, only 4 percent of Kinsey's sample of white males had been *exclusively* homosexual throughout their lives.[8]

At the Reproductive Biology Research Foundation in St. Louis where Masters and Johnson pioneered the scientific study of sexual behavior, it has been determined that men who are predominantly homosexual generally have lower levels of male hormones in their blood. But, it has not been determined which came first—the homosexuality or the lower levels of male hormone. Dr. Robert Kolodny, director of endocrinology at the Reproductive Biology Research Foundation, has stated that although homosexuality may result both from biological, or hormonal, factors and from learning certain behaviors, the learned behavior is the most significant.

Objective research on homosexuality conducted in the last twenty years has demonstrated that not even psychiatrists can tell a homosexual personality from a heterosexual one, thus contradicting the social stereotype. Most gay people are invisible by the social standard by which they have been labeled. Still, the social stereotype casts the homosexual as a deviant rather than a human being whose sexual and emotional needs differ from those of a heterosexual person.

In five states, the homosexual is subject to life imprisonment. All but two states have sodomy laws, which entail prison sentences up to twenty years. Homosexuals can be denied state certification in such professions as education, law, and medicine, and state and federal regulations prohibit hiring homosexuals for civil service positions. Studies made between 1966 and 1970 show that two-thirds of the general population regard homosexuality as "vulgar and obscene" and "harmful to American life." Many people still believe they can "spot" a homosexual on sight and prefer not to associate with them.

After the Kinsey Report, the first homophile organizations, such as the Mattachine Society and the Daughters of Bilitis were founded in the 1950s. They tried to counsel homosexuals with the aim of helping them survive in society as it is, and they worked toward decriminalizing homosexuality, arguing that it was a sickness rather than a crime.

In the late 1960s, new organizations such as the Society for Individual Rights (SIR) and the Gay Liberation Front were created. And from the Civil Rights movement came a theory known as the Societal Reaction Theory (SRT). It implied that if homosexuals are sick, it is not because homosexuality is sick, but because society has cast them into the "sick" category.

Perhaps the beginning of a slow change in society's attitudes is reflected by the action of the board of trustees of the American Psychiatric Association in December, 1973, which declassified homosexuality as a mental disorder. To the estimated eleven million homosexuals in the United States, the removal of the label "homosexual" may also change fair housing, employment, child custody, and immigration rights.

A recent important book by Martin Weinberg and Colin Williams reports the results of questionnaires distributed in gay bars and clubs and mailed to homosexuals on homophile organizations' mailing lists.[9] The authors were studying living situations and adjustments in the United States, Holland, and Denmark. Generally, they concluded that despite the negative societal reaction toward homosexuals, there is little difference in self-acceptance and psychosomatic symptoms reported by them and the general male population. Their findings demonstrated that deviant identities may not reflect personal disintegration as is often supposed.

To find the support which the peer group provides, gay people need ways of finding one another. Weinberg and Williams suggest that to obtain the beneficial effects of a supportive environment, the homosexual may want to utilize the organizations and publications of the homosexual subculture.

As long, though, as society is repressive, the homosexual will remain a subculture with certain "safe" places to be open about homosexual identity and with certain communication behaviors known only to members as a means of finding one another. Gay bars provide a safe place for some.

Research conducted by Gerald Goldhaber indicates that certain movements of the body (nonverbal communication) aid male homosexuals in their attempts to meet other gay males. His interviews of twenty-five gays in the San Francisco area identified three key body cues as "most helpful": lengthy (greater than 3-4 seconds) gazes into another male's eyes, extended mutual touching of the knee area, and tapping toes.[10]

The Aged and Dying as a Subculture

As young people we tend to think of our lives as stretched out before us waiting fulfillment. Generally we expect the future to be positive. Growing old has been said to be a negative process; the progressive, forward-looking phase of life has come to an end. With increasing age, the roles once occupied in the family and society change. Individuals can no longer provide for themselves or their families, and they become increasingly dependent on society. Old people discover that they are not employable, even if they are physically able to work. Too many elderly persons are not prepared for the accompanying change in self-concept and can become depressed, frustrated, and discouraged.[11]

One of my favorite news photographs is of Annie Lewis and Elizabeth Bisson celebrating their 100th birthday together in a Seattle retirement home. They agreed, "Getting old is hell."

The media have provided us with several poignant examples of the aging. One, a CBS News program titled "Don't Count the Candles," photographed by Lord Snowden, equates old age with unloveableness, i.e. loneliness. This sensitive film showed how we treat the few eminent old with awe, and how we treat the rest quite differently.

In our society, it is common to put the elderly into nursing homes. Erving Goffman, when discussing the characteristics of the "total institution," describes the process whereby individuals may find themselves to be living in an enclosed and administered life.[12] Although Goffman was primarily .writing about mental hospitals, he argued that similar cases could be made for other total institutions, such as prisons, the military, perhaps even colleges and

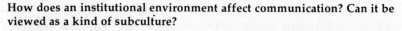

How does an institutional environment affect communication? Can it be viewed as a kind of subculture?

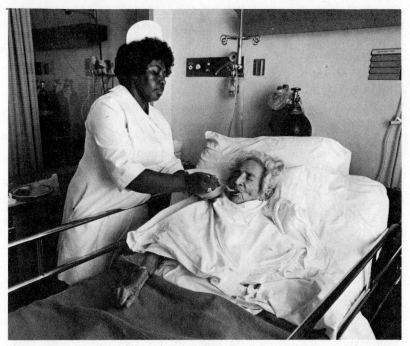

universities, because as Goffman writes, "every institution captures something of the time and interest of its members and provides something of a world for them; in brief every institution has encompassing tendencies."[13]

In such situations, an "inmate's" daily life consists entirely of his activities in and around the institution. Contact with the family is somewhat restricted, and the fact that the inmate does not live with his family makes normal family relations incompatible with total institutionalization. In addition, there may be a distinct split between the inmates and the staff, an arbitrary status distinction that is further reinforced by restricted communication between the two levels.

Goffman describes the process whereby the individual makes the transition from civilian to inmate, or person to patient, in two phases. In the first phase, the individual is a *prepatient*; that is, he has not yet been totally committed or hospitalized, and he still maintains all his rights and relationships in the outside world. It is only when the person has come in contact with what Goffman terms "the circuit of agents that participate fatefully in his passage from civilian to patient status" that the individual begins to realize feelings of abandonment, disloyalty, and embitterment. The circuit of agents may normally include some "next-of-relationship" who may cajole the individual into seeing a "mediator" and may also make the necessary arrangements. The mediator may be a doctor, lawyer, the police, a psychiatrist, or a member of the admitting staff. Primarily the "next-of-relationship" and the mediator cajole and comfort the prepatient in order to minimize the difficulty of incarceration. "If the prepatient heeds all of these implied requests and is reasonably decent about the whole thing, he can travel the whole circuit from home to hospital without forcing anyone to look directly at what is happening or to deal with the raw emotion that his situation might well cause him to express."[14]

Goffman's description of the reciprocal relationships of next-of-relationship and mediator provides some insight into the young's internment of the old. Quite obviously, the next-of-relationship—a son or daughter—may feel some guilt or anxiety about committing the prepatient to a total institution. In the second phase, *inpatients* may feel they are being unjustly deprived of their freedom, and by communicating this feeling to the next-of-relationship must be reassured of the fact that what is being done is for the good of the loved one. This is the function of the mediator. These relationships and the consequent reciprocation of roles all add to the ease with which the young couple may conveniently "provide for Mom and Dad in their twilight years."

An interesting experiment with communication between generations is ongoing with a group of young people in Rochester, New York, at Portable Channel. Partially funded by a grant from the New York State Council on the Arts, the group took their portable television equipment to several homes for the aged.[15] One objective of Portable Channel is to facilitate access to television production to people other than television professionals. In one production, Portable Channel went to Seneca Towers, an apartment building for senior citizens, to interact with Sadie, a seventy-six year old senior citizen, as she makes apple strudel. Later, she and her daughter are shown viewing a playback. In other segments, senior citizens are shown dancing to accordian music and making references to Geritol at a birthday celebration for two ninety-eight-year-old senior citizens, and a sixty-seven-year-old senior citizen is shown at a rehearsal for a variety show saying, "I'm living to live; I'm not ready to die." Another senior citizen sings, ". . . the sweet by and by . . . we'll never grow old. . . ."

Elisabeth Kübler-Ross has spent several years interviewing terminally ill patients at the University of Chicago's Billings Hospital. Dr. Ross conducted seminars for which she interviewed dying patients that her students could observe. Typically, the interviews began with general information and flowed to the very personal concerns of the patient. After the interviews, Dr. Ross and her students discussed the patient's responses in an attempt to understand

the patient's communication. Dr. Ross' work can help us to understand communication with the dying because typically most of us
have had no experience with communicating with a dying person,
or if we have, it has been so emotionally charged as to preclude
analyzing.[16]

Figure 7.2 represents the stages of dying that Dr. Ross has
identified, each representing different interpersonal communication
situations. Generally, she has identified five stages. During the first
stage after the awareness of a terminal illness, either by being told
outright or by arriving at this conclusion on their own, dying patients react with denial that death is imminent. At least partial denial is used by almost all patients not only during this first stage but
also later on from time to time. This initial denial may be regarded
as a healthy response to a painful situation allowing patients time to
collect themselves and mobilize other defenses. Typical behaviors
during this stage are denying the accuracy of the information, such
as seeking out other doctors who might invalidate the original diag-
nosis.

The second stage may be characterized by *anger*, anger that is at
times directed onto the environment almost at random—at doctors
who are "incompetent," at nurses who are "uncaring," at family
members who "don't visit." All too often the family and even the

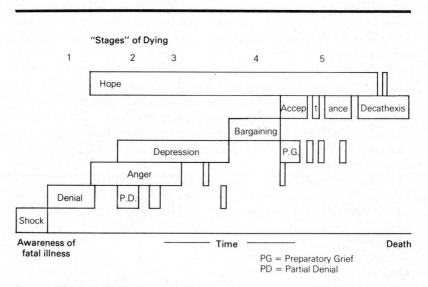

SOURCE: Elisabeth Kübler-Ross, *On Death and Dying*, New York: Macmillan, 1969,
p. 264.

FIGURE 7.2 Dr. Ross has identified several stages of dying, each representing different
interpersonal communication situations.

professional staff react personally to the patient's anger by responding in anger or by avoiding the patient.

The third stage, *depression*, frequently occurs following major surgery and is augmented by the financial burdens of treatment and hospitalization or by the loss of a job or the inability to function in family and social roles. Through interaction, an understanding person can elicit the cause of the depression and can help to relieve the patient of the guilt that may accompany the depression.

The fourth stage is characterized by *bargaining*—attempting to "buy" additional time with promises of a "good life" or a "life dedicated to one's God." Most such promises are made secretly with the patient's God and are only sometimes mentioned. Such promises may be associated with guilt and are all too often met with dismissal responses from the more "realistic" among the family and professional staff. Such promises may represent guilt feelings for *not* living a good life or for *not* living a life dedicated to one's God. Through communication, the patient may be relieved of these fears.

Preparatory grief, which overlaps with the bargaining stage, is a continuation of depression and is one that the terminally ill patient has to undergo in order to prepare himself for his death. This may be the depression of silence in which there is little need for words. It is the time for the interaction of touch or of silently being together.

If a patient has had enough time to work through the previous stages, he may reach a stage of *acceptance*—a stage almost void of feelings when the dying patient has found his peace and is able to accept death. In this stage, the patient wishes to be left alone; visitors are not desired as the patient is not in a communicative mood. Again, communication may be primarily nonverbal touching or silence. Frequently, it is at this stage that the patient's family and friends need more understanding and support than the patient himself.

Our discomfort in communicating with the dying has led to a new business. In Los Angeles, an organization called Threshold is being established to supply "death companions," who comfort lonely, dying clients at a cost of $7.50 an hour.

Communication Control

In this chapter we have focused on the interpersonal communication involved in the typing of deviance and in maintaining a subculture. The one additional relevant concept remaining here is the control of interpersonal communication by those who engage in activities deemed "bad" and "unacceptable" by others when communicating with individuals who are not kindred spirits and who consequently may pose some degree of threat.

Many situations that seem entirely innocuous to the ordinary person are sources of potential discovery for the deviant. Because the deviant must perform both in conventional and deviant roles, he tries to control all communications that might reveal his deviance to the nondeviant. A male homosexual, for example, probably will not comment on other males' attractiveness in the presence of his parents. Situations of potential discovery are those in which the deviant would prefer to hide his deviance from others and in which there is a possibility that his deviance may be "uncovered."

What about public denunciation of deviant activity? According to Jerry Simmons, the deviant can either:

1. Go along with the denunciation by contributing to it and, in effect, then ridiculing and condemning self;

2. Ignore the denunciation or attempt to redirect the discussion into other areas; or

3. Defend his or her deviance. This final alternative in the forms of defiant self-assertions and confession to significant others is referred to in the gay subculture as "coming out."[17]

★Probe Questions

A subculture is a group of people who have found commonality among themselves. Such commonality nurtures and sustains the members' self-concepts. You, as a person outside that subculture, are a deviant to the members within. From their mutually supported perspectives, you are seen as the valueless, strange one. Perhaps you will be viewed as naive, ignorant, arrogant, or stupid.

What are your feelings toward those who reject and condemn you? Deviants can become angry and alienated by public persecution.

Should deviants be trusted? Should they trust you?

What happens to your personal values if you begin to interact more and more with members of a subculture and less and less with members of the majority culture? How will members of the majority culture see you?

How is mingling and communicating with deviants seen by your associates? As an attitude of tolerance or as an antisocial attitude? Can you expect hostility from members of either the dominant culture or the subculture, perhaps from both?

Which is more costly to an individual's self-identity: socialization into a subculture or resocialization and a positive affirmation of one's membership in the dominant culture? Are deviants choosing the easy way out of a tough situation by organizing themselves and thereby advertising their mutual deviancies? Are they making a difficult situation even more difficult by their openly admitted denunciation of the dominant culture's norms and values?

Of course, it can be very uncomfortable to read and discuss many of the subjects presented in this chapter. But understanding the dying and other subcultural groups, with their own special characteristics of interpersonal communication, may help us to accept others in all states of existence.

Summary

Subcultural communication is the process of communication whereby one gains and maintains the ability to communicate effectively and meaningfully with members of a subculture. Subcultures may be said to be deviant in that they are composed of people who differ from the larger culture." Deviance is not necessarily "bad" or "harmful," rather it is simply a label given to people who are viewed as different from the labelers. Once an individual has been labeled "deviant," he may begin to behave even more in accordance with the label in order to justify its having been given him. Subcultures serve both a facilitative and a protective function—that is, they provide reinforcement and a sphere of acceptance while shielding their members from outside ridicule or pressure. The best way to observe a subculture is from a position within the subculture itself. This type of observation is called the "insider participant-observer" method. Two striking examples of this type of observation are Saul Alinsky's study of the Al Capone mob and Hunter Thompson's study of the Hell's Angels. A large subculture is that of homosexuals. Although long persecuted by the dominant culture, gay people are at last, through their own organizational efforts, beginning to find an acceptable place in society. Another large, and often forgotten, subculture is that composed of the aged and dying. Shuttered away in institutions, these elderly citizens often remain isolated and alienated from the rest of society. One researcher has identified five stages of the dying process: denial, anger, depression, bargaining, and acceptance. By paying attention to, and coming to understand dying persons, perhaps we can learn to better accept the inevitability of our own death.

Footnotes

[1]Earl Rubington and Martin S. Weinberg, eds., *Deviance: The Interactionist Perspective*, New York: Macmillan, 1968, pp. 1–12 and 203–208.

[2]"*Playboy* Interview: Saul Alinsky," *Playboy* 19(3), 1972, p. 66.

[3]*Playboy*, p. 66.

[4]Hunter S. Thompson, *Hell's Angels: A Strange and Terrible Saga*, New York: Ballantine Books, Inc., 1966.

[5]Thompson, pp. 64–66.

[6]Thompson, pp. 253–254.

[7]Ned Polsky, *Hustlers, Beats, and Others*, Chicago: Aldine Publishing Company, 1967, and "The Hustler," *Social Problems* 12, 1964, 3–15.

[8]Alfred C. Kinsey, Wardell B. Pomeroy, and Clyde E. Martin, *Sexual Behavior in the Human Male*, Philadelphia: W. B. Saunders Co., 1948.

[9]Martin S. Weinberg and Colin J. Williams, *Male Homosexuals: Their Problems and Adaptations*, New York: Oxford University Press, 1974.

[10]Cited by Gerald M. Goldhaber, *Organizational Communication*, Dubuque, Iowa: Wm. C. Brown Company Publishers, 1974, p. 137. Also see Wayne Sage, "Inside the Colossal Closet," *Human Behavior*, 1975, 4(8), 16–23.

[11]A. L. Vischer, *On Growing Old*, Boston: Houghton Mifflin, 1967.

[12]Erving Goffman, *Asylums: Essays on the Social Situation of Mental Patients and Other Inmates*, Chicago: Aldine Publishing Co., 1961.

[13]Goffman, p. 4.

[14]Goffman, p. 141.

[15]"Portable Channel Meets Senior Citizens" produced by Portable Channel, 8 Prince Street, Rochester, New York, November 1972.

[16]Elisabeth Kübler-Ross, *On Death and Dying*, New York: Macmillan, 1969.

[17]Jerry L. Simmons, *Deviants*, Santa Barbara, Calif.: University of California Press, 1969.

GLOSSARY INDEX

Bold face numbers indicate the page of the entry's definition.